Financial performance

Tutorial

Aubrey Penning

Janet Brammer

osborne
BOOKS

Published by Osborne Books Limited
Unit 1B Everoak Estate
Bromyard Road
Worcester WR2 5HP
Tel 01905 748071
Email books@osbornebooks.co.uk
Website www.osbornebooks.co.uk

Design by Laura Ingham
Cover and page design image © Istockphoto.com/Petrovich9

Printed and bound in Great Britain by MPG Books Group

British Library Cataloguing in Publication Data
A catalogue record for this book is available from the British Library

ISBN 978 1905777 372

Contents

Acknowledgements

The authors wish to thank the following for their help with the production of the book: Mike Gilbert, Claire McCarthy, Jon Moore and Cathy Turner. Thanks are also due to Lynn Watkins for her technical editing and to Laura Ingham for her designs for this new series.

The publisher is indebted to the Association of Accounting Technicians for its help and advice to our authors and editors during the preparation of this text.

Authors

Aubrey Penning has many years experience of teaching accountancy on a variety of courses in Worcester and Gwent. He is a Certified Accountant, and before his move into full-time teaching he worked for the health service, a housing association and a chemical supplier. Until recently he was the AAT course coordinator at Worcester College of Technology, specialising in the areas of management accounting and taxation.

Janet Brammer has over twelve years' experience lecturing on AAT and ACCA accountancy courses at Norwich City College. She is a Certified Accountant and worked in accountancy practice for a number of years. She has also tutored for the Open University and has written a workbook 'Management Information Framework' for the ACCA distance learning scheme.

Introduction

what this book covers

This book has been written specifically to cover the Learning Area 'Financial Performance' which covers two QCF Units in the AAT Level 4 Diploma in Accounting:

■ Principles of managing financial performance

■ Measuring financial performance

The book contains a clear text with worked examples and case studies, chapter summaries and key terms to help with revision. Each chapter has a wide range of student activities.

Osborne Workbooks

Osborne Workbooks contain practice material which helps students achieve success in their assessments. 'Financial Performance Workbook' contains a number of paper-based 'fill in' practice exams in the style of the computer-based assessment. Please telephone the Osborne Books Sales Office on 01905 748071 for details of mail ordering, or visit the 24-hour online shop at www.osbornebooks.co.uk

International Accounting Standards (IAS) terminology

In this book the terms set out below are quoted as follows when they first appear in a chapter (and elsewhere where it seems appropriate): IAS terminology (UK terminology), ie

receivables or trade receivables (debtors)

payables or trade payables (creditors)

inventory (stock)

non-current assets (fixed assets)

revenue or sales revenue (sales)

profit from operations (operating profit)

income statement (profit and loss account)

statement of financial position (balance sheet)

1 Management accounting techniques

this chapter covers...

This introductory chapter provides a summary of some of the main techniques that are applied later in the book. While some may be familiar from your earlier studies, others will be examined here for the first time. They are all important to your studies throughout this learning area.

We will start by reminding ourselves of the internal and external information sources available to managers, and then go on to examine the key differences between management accounting (which includes this area of study) and financial accounting.

Next we will examine the three main management accounting systems, absorption, marginal and activity based costing. We will learn about their impact on reported profits and how they have strengths and weaknesses that influence the situations where they are most useful. We will also remind ourselves about the principles of cost behaviour that are utilised in marginal costing, and learn how to analyse semi-variable costs using the 'high-low' method.

Finally, we will examine four specific techniques; sampling, time series analysis, index numbers and discounted cash flow. Each of these will be explained using practical examples.

FINANCIAL PERFORMANCE

In this book we are going to learn how to calculate and understand the financial performance of organisations, by using a range of techniques. This area of study is part of 'Management Accounting', and the techniques that we will be using build on those used in costing.

In this chapter we are going to examine a range of concepts and tools that we will then use for specific applications later in the book. Some of the ideas covered in this first chapter will be familiar to you from your earlier studies, but others will be introduced for the first time. Whether or not you have come across these topics previously, it is important that this chapter is studied carefully. A thorough understanding of the content of this chapter is vital for your success in this learning area.

Before we remind ourselves exactly what is meant by 'Management Accounting', we will put this into context by seeing what sources of information are available to managers, and what they can be used for.

SOURCES OF MANAGEMENT INFORMATION

The information needed by managers can be obtained from internal and external sources. The table below gives examples of specific sources, the kind of information that may be available, and what it could be used for. The list is not intended to be exhaustive, so you can probably think of further examples.

internal sources and uses of management information		
Source	**Information**	**Use**
Purchase Invoices	Quantity and Cost of Goods Purchased	Costing Output of Organisation
Wages Analysis	Time and Cost of Labour	Costing Output of Organisation
Work Study Reports	Labour Time to Undertake Activities	Standard Costs of Output
Unfulfilled Sales Orders	Type and Quantity of Output Demand	Planning Future Output
Suppliers' Accounts	Amounts Owed and When Due	Planning Future Payments
Inventory Records	Quantity of Goods in Inventory & Ordered	Planning Future Purchases
Production Schedules	Type and Quantity of Output Planned	Planning Resource Requirements
Quality Control Records	Number of Items Rejected	Monitoring Input and Output

external sources and uses of management information		
Source	**Information**	**Use**
Government Statistics	Forecast Inflation, Economic Growth, Social Trends	Planning Future Activities
Financial Press	Competitors' Performance	Comparison and Resulting Action
World Wide Web	Information and Commentary on Most Issues	Planning Future Activities
Trade Associations	Typical Performance in the Trade	Comparison and Resulting Action
Market Research	Views of Prospective Customers	Planning Future Activities

Some of the information generated can be used for more than one purpose. For example the information contained on a purchase invoice can become a part of the information for all of the purposes shown in the diagram below. Note also the references at the bottom of the diagram to financial accounting and management accounting; these concepts are explained in the text which follows.

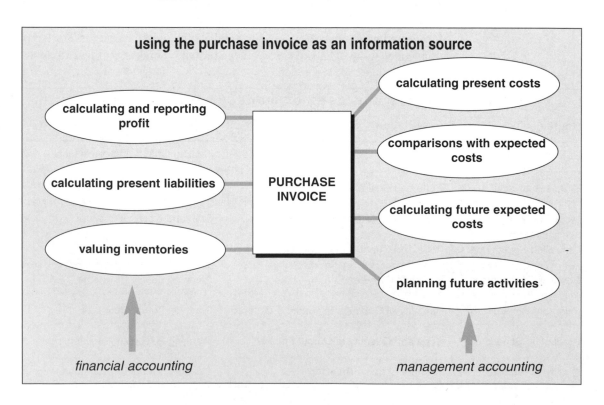

FINANCIAL ACCOUNTING AND MANAGEMENT ACCOUNTING

If you look at the diagram at the bottom of the previous page you will see that the activities on the left-hand side relate to 'Financial Accounting', while those on the right-hand side relate to 'Management Accounting'.

financial accounting

Financial accounting is concerned with recording accounting information so that accounts can be published and used by those outside the organisation. It is governed by legislation and accounting standards, and focuses on the needs of stakeholders from outside the organisation, like shareholders, suppliers, and prospective investors. Strict formats and timescales are imposed on organisations that determine exactly how and when the information is produced.

management accounting

Management accounting is the general term used for the production of accounting information for those inside an organisation. Because it is an internal system there are no external rules about how or when the information should be produced. Management accounting exists to help managers plan, monitor, control, and make decisions about the organisation. Its emphasis is on providing information that can help with the future of the organisation. The guiding principle for management accounting information is that it should be **useful** to its readers. If the information fails that simple test, then it has been a pointless waste of time producing it!

The study of 'Financial Performance' is part of the wider area of management accounting (despite the use of the word 'financial' in the title). The other main part of management accounting that will form part of your studies is 'Budgeting', and this is covered in the text of that name published by Osborne Books.

financial and management accounting compared

The table on the next page sets out a summary of the main differences between financial accounting and management accounting.

financial and management accounting compared		
	Financial Accounting	Management Accounting
Users	External Stakeholders	Internal
Format	Summarised	Specific
Governed by	Legislation & Standards	Usefulness
Frequency of Information	Annual (& possible six monthly)	As required
Time Focus	Past	Future

MANAGEMENT ACCOUNTING SYSTEMS

methods of costing

Management accounting is the branch of accounting that deals with providing internal information within an organisation. Providing costing information is an important area of management accounting, and you will be familiar with the principles of costing from your earlier studies. Just as management accounting has no external rules governing how it should be carried out, cost information can also be developed in various ways. Although costing systems should always be tailored to the needs of the organisation and its managers, there are three general approaches to costing which you will need to become familiar with. They all attempt to calculate a cost for the units that the organisation produces. These 'units of output' could be bicycle wheels made by a bicycle component manufacturer, or operations carried out in a hospital.

- **Absorption Costing**

  This is a system that attempts to determine a 'full' cost for each unit of output. It therefore includes both direct and indirect costs, and uses the mechanisms of allocation, apportionment and absorption to incorporate the indirect costs.

- **Marginal Costing**

  This costing system categorises costs according to their cost behaviour, and divides them simply into variable and fixed costs. This system uses a cost for each unit of output based purely on the variable (or 'marginal') costs. All fixed costs are regarded as time based and are therefore linked to accounting periods rather than units of output.

- **Activity Based Costing (ABC)**

  This is a development of absorption costing, and uses a more sophisticated system to deal mainly with the indirect costs. This involves examining the costs to determine what causes them, and using this information to charge the costs to the units of output in an appropriate manner.

You will need to understand the working and implications of these three systems, so we will now examine how each one works in more detail.

ABSORPTION COSTING

You will probably be familiar with the absorption costing process from your earlier studies, but the following will enable you to recall firstly the terminology and then the steps involved.

terminology:

- **Direct Costs**

    Costs that are directly attributable to the units of output. They can be divided into Direct Materials, Direct Labour, and Direct Expenses.

- **Indirect Costs**

    Costs that cannot be directly attributed to the units of production. They are also referred to as overheads. In a manufacturing environment only the indirect costs relating to production are usually absorbed into the product cost.

- **Cost Centres**

    Parts of the organisation where it is convenient to gather costs. It could be a department or section, or an area where a certain activity is carried out. 'Production' cost centres are where the unit of output has some activity carried out on it, whereas 'Service' cost centres provide a service to other cost centres rather than do anything directly to the units of output.

- **Absorption Bases**

    The methods available to absorb cost from the production cost centres into the units of output (or products). All absorption bases use expected (or budgeted) costs and activity levels to work out an absorption rate. Examples of absorption bases are Direct Labour Hours, Machine Hours, and Units of Output.

steps in absorption costing

1   Costs are divided into direct costs and indirect costs. The direct costs can immediately form part of the cost of the units of output known as 'prime cost', while the indirect costs (overheads) will need to be absorbed into the cost of the units via the next stages.

2   Indirect costs are either allocated to one cost centre (if the cost relates to only one cost centre), or apportioned to several cost centres by some fair

system (if the cost relates to several cost centres). For example rent costs might be apportioned using the area of the building used by each cost centre.

3   If costs have now accumulated into service cost centres, the total cost of each service cost centre is shared amongst the production cost centres that benefit from the service provided. This is carried out using secondary apportionment. For example the total cost of running the stores service cost centre could be shared out by using the numbers of requisitions from the various production cost centres as a basis for secondary apportionment.

4   The costs that have been gathered in the production cost centres can now be absorbed into the units of output by using a predetermined absorption rate based on the expected activity level. The indirect cost is absorbed from the cost centre into the units of output as they pass through the cost centre. A common basis for this absorption is direct labour hours, so that the longer a product is worked on in the production cost centre, the greater the amount of cost is absorbed.

Case Study

THE ABSORPTION COMPANY: ABSORPTION COSTING

The Absorption Company manufactures several products, one of which is the Sorp. Its factory is divided into two production cost centres (Assembly and Finishing) and one service cost centre (Maintenance). 80% of the activity in the Maintenance cost centre benefits Assembly, while the remainder benefits Finishing.

Before the financial period started the expected indirect costs for the forthcoming year were:

	£
Assembly	208,000
Finishing	72,000
Maintenance	40,000

Each unit of Sorp uses direct material that costs £42. It takes 5 direct labour hours in Assembly and 2 direct labour hours in Finishing to make one unit of Sorp. Indirect costs are absorbed from the production cost centres using a direct labour hour rate. The expected direct labour hours for the year were 120,000 in Assembly and 25,000 in Finishing. All direct labour hours are paid at £8.

required

Calculate the following:

1   The indirect cost absorption rate in each of the two production cost centres.

2   The absorbed cost of one unit of Sorp.

solution

1 the indirect absorption rate

	Assembly	Finishing	Maintenance
Expected Indirect Costs:	£	£	£
Allocated / Apportioned	208,000	72,000	40,000
Secondary Apportionment	32,000	8,000	(40,000)
Total	240,000	80,000	
Expected Direct Labour Hours	120,000	25,000	

Absorption Rates:
Assembly   £240,000 ÷ 120,000   = £2.00 per direct labour hour
Finishing   £80,000 ÷ 25,000   = £3.20 per direct labour hour

2 the absorbed cost of one unit of Sorp

		Cost of one unit of Sorp:
Direct Materials		£42.00
Direct Labour:		
Assembly 5 hours @ £8.00	£40.00	
Finishing 2 hours @ £8.00	£16.00	
		£56.00
Prime Cost		£98.00
Indirect Costs:		
Assembly 5 hours @ £2.00	£10.00	
Finishing 2 hours @ £3.20	£6.40	
		£16.40
Total Absorbed Cost		£114.40

MARGINAL COSTING

Marginal costing accepts that there is a fundamental difference between costs that are based, not on the origin of the costs, but purely on the behaviour of the costs when the activity level (or output level) changes. There are several main ways that the costs could behave within a range of activity levels:

Variable Costs   Costs where the total amount varies in proportion to the activity level when the activity level changes. Variable costs are also known as marginal costs when using marginal costing.

Fixed Costs   Costs that do not change when the level of activity changes (within certain parameters).

Semi-Variable Costs   Costs where a part of the cost acts as a variable cost, and a part acts as a fixed cost.

Stepped Fixed Costs	Costs which are fixed within an activity range, but change to another (higher) fixed level when the activity level increases outside that range (and so on).

All the costs (regardless of whether they might be viewed as direct or indirect) need to be divided into variable costs and fixed costs. Semi-variable costs are divided into their fixed and variable components. There are numerical techniques for dividing them into variable and fixed elements. One of these, the 'high-low' method is studied later in this chapter. Once the total variable and fixed costs have been determined, only the variable (or marginal) costs are linked to the units of output to provide a cost per unit. This enables a 'contribution' towards the fixed costs (and ultimately profit) to be calculated either per unit, or for a specified output level.

Unit Contribution	The difference between the selling price per unit and the variable costs per unit. It is the amount that each unit sold contributes towards the fixed costs of the organisation and profit.
Total Contribution	The difference between the sales income and the variable costs of the units sold in a period. This amount is the total contribution that the sales of all the units in the period make towards the fixed costs of the organisation and profit.

Fixed costs are taken straight to the profit statement, and are deducted from the total contribution for the period to arrive at the profit for the period. For this Learning Area you will need to be familiar with Marginal Costing, and recognise and use the formats and terminology that apply to this system.

Marginal costing has considerable advantages over absorption costing when it is used to help with making decisions. Uses of marginal costing are discussed later in this chapter.

Case Study

1.850

THE MARGINAL COMPANY: MARGINAL COSTING

The Marginal Company manufactures one product, the Marg. The following costs relate to a financial year, when 100,000 units of Marg are made:

Direct Materials	£350,000
Direct Labour	£230,000
Indirect Costs	£310,000

Investigations into the behaviour of the costs have revealed the following information:

- direct materials behave as variable costs.
- direct labour behaves as a variable cost.
- of the indirect costs, £270,000 behaves as a fixed cost, and the remainder as a variable cost.

required

1 Calculate the cost of one unit of Marg using Marginal Costing.

2 If each unit of Marg sells for £10, and all the production of 100,000 units is sold, draft a marginal costing statement for the financial year showing the contribution (per unit and in total), and the profit for the year.

solution

1 costing a unit of Marg

Using only the variable (marginal) costs to cost one unit of Marg:

Direct Materials (£350,000 ÷ 100,000)	£3.50
Direct Labour (£230,000 ÷ 100,000)	£2.30
Variable Overheads	
(£310,000 − £270,000 = £40,000) ÷ 100,000	£0.40
Total marginal cost per unit	£6.20

2 Marginal Costing Statement for the Financial Year.

	Per Unit £	For Year £
Sales	10.00	1,000,000
Less Variable Costs	6.20	620,000
Contribution	3.80	380,000
Less Fixed Overheads		270,000
Profit		£110,000

Note that the fixed costs are not calculated in per unit terms, but are simply deducted in total from the total contribution.

ACTIVITY BASED COSTING (ABC)

background to ABC

Activity based costing was developed in the 1970s and 1980s as an alternative to absorption costing. Since the time when absorption costing was initially developed (at the time of the Industrial Revolution), many aspects of manufacture had changed, and it was felt that absorption costing was not providing information of sufficient quality. The points that were made by advocates of ABC were:

Overheads (indirect costs) typically now account for the major part of product costs, and should therefore be accounted for in a less arbitrary way than they would under absorption costing. For example, simply absorbing overheads based on just one basis (e.g. direct labour hours) does not acknowledge the complexity of costs that can make up overheads.

Both production methods and batch sizes can have a major impact on product costs, yet these are largely ignored by absorption costing. For example the cost involved in setting up equipment will be far greater per unit of output for small production runs than for large ones.

Modern production methods do not lend themselves to the use of absorption rates such as direct labour hours or machine hours. Integrated production systems can often operate with minimal human intervention.

cost pools and cost drivers

ABC works by identifying the indirect activities, and grouping their costs into 'cost pools', one for each major activity. For each cost pool there must be a factor that drives the costs and causes those costs to change. This 'cost driver' is identified and its rate calculated. The rate is then used to charge the output with cost, based on the output's use of the activity.

For example in a stores department (which would typically form one service cost centre under absorption costing), the activities could be determined as:

1 Receiving goods inwards, and
2 Issuing goods to production.

The costs of running the stores department would be analysed into the costs for carrying out each of these activities – the 'cost pools'. The cost drivers might be agreed as:

1 Number of Deliveries Received (for receiving goods inward), and
2 Number of Requisitions (for issuing goods).

The rate per cost driver would then be calculated by dividing the cost pool by the cost driver for that pool.

Using this technique, a product that required many different components that were delivered separately and then issued frequently to production, would be charged with a high cost from the activities in the stores department. In comparison a product that was made from components delivered together and issued to production in bulk would incur fewer costs.

Using a suitable analysis of costs and their drivers an organisation can adapt the system to its own circumstances. Each different product will then be charged with a more accurate cost based on its use of the activities than if absorption costing had been used.

The diagram below shows how the system works. Study it and then read the two Case Studies that follow. They both illustrate the application of activity based costing, the first in a manufacturing company and the second to a college operating in the service sector.

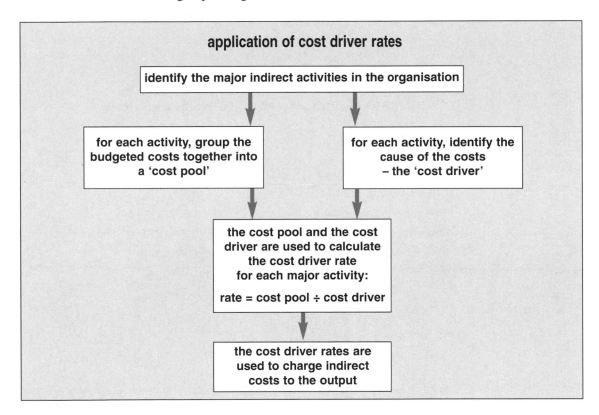

application of cost driver rates

identify the major indirect activities in the organisation

for each activity, group the budgeted costs together into a 'cost pool'

for each activity, identify the cause of the costs – the 'cost driver'

the cost pool and the cost driver are used to calculate the cost driver rate for each major activity:

rate = cost pool ÷ cost driver

the cost driver rates are used to charge indirect costs to the output

Case Study

1.850

ABC COMPANY:
ACTIVITY BASED COSTING

The ABC Company has introduced activity based costing to cost its output. It makes several products on mechanised production lines, including AB, and BC. AB is a product that is usually made in large batches of 1,000 units, since it sells in large quantities. BC is a specialised product selling to a niche market, and is therefore made in small batches of 20 units.

As a part of the introduction of ABC the company has identified one major activity as 'setting up the production equipment'. The cost associated with this activity in a

financial year is budgeted at £250,000, and therefore this amount forms the cost pool for setting up production equipment.

The company has identified the cost driver of this activity as 'number of set-ups performed', since if the number increases the cost will be proportionally greater. One batch of any product requires one set-up to be performed.

The budgeted figure of £250,000 was based on an estimated 500 set-ups in the financial year.

The unit costs for AB and BC have already been calculated excluding the set-up costs, as follows:

AB   £50.00 per unit
BC   £55.00 per unit

required

Calculate the total cost per unit of AB and BC, including set-up costs.

solution

The cost driver rate for set-ups = £250,000 ÷ 500 = £500 per set-up

Charging at this rate:

One unit of AB would incur set-up cost of £500 ÷ 1,000   = £0.50

One unit of BC would incur set-up cost of £500 ÷ 20 = £25.00

Incorporating this into the previous costs gives per unit costs of:

	AB £	BC £
Costs excluding set-ups	50.00	55.00
Cost of set-ups	0.50	25.00
Total Cost	50.50	80.00

In this case study set-ups account for approximately 1% of the total cost of a unit of AB, compared to 31% of the total cost of a unit of BC. These differences would not be identified using a traditional absorption costing system that treated set-ups as a part of general overheads.

Case Study

ABC COLLEGE:
ACTIVITY BASED COSTING IN THE SERVICE SECTOR

The ABC College is a small private college, providing a variety of part-time business related courses. The college has determined that there are four major activities that are undertaken, that have the following cost pools for the financial year and cost drivers.

Activity	Cost Pool	Cost Driver Information
Teaching	£500,000	Teaching Hours (25,000 in year)
Course Preparation	£300,000	New Courses (30 in year)
Lesson Preparation	£100,000	Teaching Hours (25,000 in year)
Student Administration	£100,000	Number of Students (1,000 in year)

The costs for two separate courses are to be calculated using ABC.

The first is the Advanced Marketing Course. This course will run for 250 teaching hours, and should attract 20 students. The course has been run previously.

The second is a new course in Taxation for Exporters to Scandinavia. The course will run for 100 teaching hours, and there are 5 prospective students.

required

Calculate the cost per course and cost per student for each of the two courses.

solution

First the cost driver rates need to be established:

Teaching	£500,000 ÷ 25,000	= £20 per teaching hour
Course Preparation	£300,000 ÷ 30	= £10,000 per new course
Lesson Preparation	£100,000 ÷ 25,000	= £4 per teaching hour
Student Administration	£100,000 ÷ 1,000	= £100 per student

Secondly these rates are applied to the courses according to their demand for the activities:

1 Advanced Marketing Course

Teaching	£20 x 250 =	£5,000
Course Preparation	(existing course)	-
Lesson Preparation	£4 x 250 =	£1,000
Student Administration	£100 x 20 =	£2,000
Cost for course		£8,000
Cost per student	£8,000 ÷ 20 =	£400

2 Taxation for Exporters to Scandinavia

Teaching	£20 x 100 =	£2,000
Course Preparation	£10,000 x 1 =	£10,000
Lesson Preparation	£4 x 100 =	£400
Student Administration	£100 x 5 =	£500
Cost for course		£12,900
Cost per student	£12,900 ÷ 5 =	£2,580

COSTING SYSTEMS AND RECORDED PROFIT

variations in inventory valuation

One of the reasons that organisations use a costing system is so that the value of the inventory (stock) of finished goods (and work in progress) can be calculated and incorporated into profit statements. Since the different approaches to costing that we have examined give different costs per unit, they will result in different valuations of inventory, this will in turn affect the profit calculation when inventory levels change. A marginal costing system will value inventory at just the variable costs, but a system that absorbs fixed costs into the inventory valuation can result in fixed costs being charged to a period other than the one in which they were incurred.

the effect of inventory valuation on profit

The costs incurred in producing goods in a period, together with the cost of the opening inventory must equal the cost of sales for the period, added to the cost of the closing inventory.

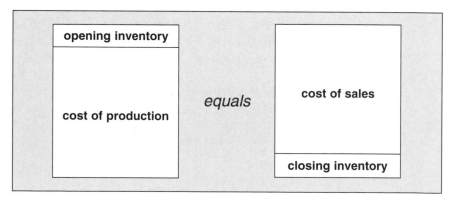

The valuation of the closing inventory will therefore affect the cost of sales and therefore recorded profit.

The following Case Study uses the same data under different costing systems to illustrate the situation.

Case
Study

1.850

THE ALTERNATIVE COMPANY: COSTING METHODS AND PROFIT

The Alternative Company manufactures a single product, and produces monthly management accounts.

In each of Month 1 and Month 2, 10,000 units were produced, and the following costs were incurred:

Direct Material	£100,000
Direct Labour	£150,000
Fixed Overheads	£250,000
Total Costs	£500,000

Both the costs and the volume of output were in line with the budget.

Units were sold for £70 each, and in Month 1 the whole production of 10,000 units were sold, whereas in month 2 only 8,000 units were sold. There was no inventory at the start of Month 1.

Direct Material and Direct Labour are both variable costs.

required

1 Calculate the cost per unit using
   (a) absorption costing using units as an absorption base
   (b) marginal costing

2 Draft management accounts for each month using
   (a) absorption costing
   (b) marginal costing

3 Comment on the reasons for any difference in profits.

solution

1 Calculation of cost per unit

(a) Absorption Costing (using all costs)

£500,000 ÷ 10,000 = £50 per unit

(b) Marginal Costing (using variable costs only)

£250,000 ÷ 10,000 = £25 per unit

2 Draft management accounts

(a) **Absorption Costing**

		Month 1		Month 2
Sales		700,000		560,000
Less cost of sales:				
opening inventory	–		–	
cost of production				
(10,000 x £50)	500,000		500,000	
less closing inventory	–			
(2,000 x £50)			100,000	
		500,000		400,000
Profit		200,000		160,000

(b)   **Marginal Costing**

	Month 1		Month 2	
Sales		700,000		560,000
Less variable cost of sales:				
opening inventory	–		–	
Variable cost of production				
(10,000 x £25)	250,000		250,000	
less closing inventory	–			
(2,000 x £25)			50,000	
		250,000		200,000
Contribution		450,000		360,000
Less fixed costs		250,000		250,000
Profit		200,000		110,000

3 Comments on the reasons for differences in profit

The profits are identical when there is no change in inventory level, as in Month 1, when both opening and closing inventories are zero. However when the inventory level changes between the start and end of the period (as in Month 2) the inventory valuation has an impact on profit.

The additional reported profit of £50,000 (£160,000 compared with £110,000) by using the absorption system is due to £50,000 of the fixed costs being absorbed into the closing inventory and effectively carried into the next period. If the inventory again fell to nil in Month 3 the profit difference would be reversed.

The differences in reported profits are only timing differences – the differences in profit are just reported in different periods.

conclusion

■   Where inventory levels increase, absorption costing will record a higher profit than marginal costing, as more of the cost incurred is pushed into the next period.

■   Where inventory levels decrease, absorption costing will record a lower profit than marginal costing as more of the costs from the previous period are set against income.

■   Where inventory levels are constant, then, providing there has been no change in unit costs, there will be no difference in recorded profit under either system.

You can therefore see that if an organisation uses absorption costing, significantly building up (or reducing) inventory levels can distort profits.

COMPARISON OF ABSORPTION AND MARGINAL COSTING

In the last section we learned how absorption and marginal costing systems can produce different results when used for reporting profits. We will now examine each of these costing systems so that we can establish their strengths and weaknesses. We can then understand why one approach may be better in some circumstances than another.

ABSORPTION COSTING

A clear benefit of using absorption costing is that the product cost developed is a 'full' cost – it includes an element of all the costs of production. The main problem is that the calculation of this full cost relies on two key issues:

- Arbitrary decisions that have been made regarding the apportionment and absorption of indirect costs (overheads). Although each decision may be logical (for example apportioning heating costs by using floor area), different costs would be arrived at if other decisions had been made (for example apportioning heating costs using building volume). There are many examples of such decisions in the calculation of absorption costs, including the choice of absorption base (for example direct labour hours or machine hours), all of which have an impact on the product cost.

- The expected volume of output (or activity level) will have been calculated in advance to arrive at an absorption rate. Any variation between the actual volume produced and this planned volume will mean that the product costs are inaccurate. This is also one of the main reasons that overheads can be either under absorbed or over absorbed. These terms relate to overheads that should (in an ideal world) be part of the product costs. Instead they are charged (debited) to the income statement if there is under absorption, or credited if there is over absorption. In both cases it results in inaccurate product costs.

The first issue can be addressed by the use of activity based costing, which can provide a more considered approach to the apportionment and absorption of overheads into product costs.

The problems in the use of absorption costing mean that it is most effective when

- the decisions made about apportionment and absorption are logical and consistent and do not distort the product cost unduly, and
- the volume (or activity level) can be predicted with a reasonable level of accuracy.

If we consider the main uses of management accounting of:

- planning
- monitoring and control, and
- decision making,

then we can see that absorption costing may be useful for planning, monitoring and control, provided the above issues are considered. This is because all costs are taken into account (which is important for planning), and monitoring and control can use a system that compares actual and expected figures on a like for like basis. One monitoring and control system is 'standard costing' that we will be examining in great detail later in this book, and often uses absorption costing.

Absorption costing is likely to be of very limited use in decision making, since expected volumes are often uncertain and many decisions need an awareness of cost behaviour which is not part of absorption costing.

In spite of the problems of sometimes distorting profit (as we saw in the last section), the valuation of inventory for financial accounting purposes needs to include an element of indirect costs to comply with accounting standards, and absorption costing fulfils this requirement. In particular, the standards dealing with inventory valuation (SSAP 9 and IAS 2) require a valuation that includes fixed and variable manufacturing overheads as part of the 'costs of conversion'.

One other use for calculating product costs is to provide a starting point for establishing a selling price. Provided the expected production and sales volume can be predicted fairly accurately, then the absorbed cost can be used to help with normal pricing by adding to it a suitable amount to cover non-factory overheads and profit. This is known as 'full cost plus pricing', and works by adding a profit mark-up to the full cost which has been arrived at through absorption costing. This is a popular method of pricing in many industries.

MARGINAL COSTING

Marginal costing, as we have already learned, uses knowledge of cost behaviour to analyse costs into variable costs and fixed costs. The product cost is then made up only of variable costs, and fixed costs are treated as relating to a period of time and charged directly to the Income Statement.

Marginal costing does not provide a 'full' product cost – since no fixed costs are included. A benefit of this approach is that the marginal product cost does not depend on volumes – the variable cost will be the same no matter how many are produced or sold. This leads to some important techniques that can only be used with marginal costing, which are particularly useful for decision making. You will be familiar with some of these techniques already, and the following provides a summary of the main ones.

- **Minimum price-setting**

The marginal cost of a product or service can be used as the absolute minimum that could be charged. While not applicable to normal price-setting, it can be useful to help calculate the price to be charged for additional orders if all the fixed costs have already been covered by normal sales. For example it can be used by hotels to set discounted prices that are used to fill otherwise empty rooms.

- **Break-even analysis**

This enables the calculation of the number of items (or sales value) that will result in zero profit. This provides a base line against which expected volumes can be compared, in the knowledge that higher volumes will result in higher profits.

- **Margin of safety**

This follows from break-even analysis and shows how far away (often in percentage terms) the planned volume level is from the break-even volume.

- **Contribution analysis**

The calculation of contribution per unit (by deducting variable costs from selling price) provides a mechanism for quickly calculating profit. This is carried out by deducting the fixed costs from the total contribution which is based on the expected volume.

- **'What-if' analysis**

Marginal costing is an important tool in testing the outcomes of various scenarios. In addition to break-even analysis and margin of safety noted above, these situations could include (for example):

  - make or buy decisions
  - limiting factor decision-making
  - closure of a business segment
  - mechanisation

Later in the book we will examine these situations in detail, and explain how to tackle them.

- **Long term decision making**

The use of discounted cash flow (DCF) techniques often relies on the concept of marginal costing. We will be outlining DCF techniques later in this chapter, and later in the book learning how to apply these techniques in various situations.

calculating fixed and variable costs – the high-low method

A useful technique that can provide the cost data for marginal costing is the 'high-low' method. This can be used where costs are behaving as semi-variable in total, and the amount of the fixed and variable elements are required.

The high-low method can be used where the total of a semi-variable cost is known for at least two different activity levels. If the total is known for more than two levels, then the highest and lowest are chosen for the calculation.

The Case Study that follows illustrates the high-low method.

Case Study

HILO PRODUCTS: THE HIGH-LOW METHOD

Hilo Products makes ladders. We are given the total of a semi-variable cost at four different levels of activity, as follows:

Level of activity (units)	400	650	800	900
Total cost (£)	6,200	6,950	7,400	7,700

First we identify the lowest and highest totals, which are:

£6,200 for 400 units and £7,700 for 900 units.

To calculate the variable cost per unit, we use the fact that the extra cost has been caused by the variable cost of the extra units. That is:

	Cost		Units	
High	£7,700		900	
Low	£6,200		400	
Difference	£1,500	÷	500	= £3 per unit

Using £3 per unit, we then calculate the variable part of the cost for 400 units:

£3 x 400 = £1,200

But the total cost for 400 units is £6,200

Therefore the fixed part (which is the same for any number of units)

= £6,200 – £1,200 = £5,000

We can now check the solution by calculating the total cost for 900 units, using our answers:

Total cost = Fixed cost + (variable cost per unit x number of units)

= £5,000 + (£3 x 900)

= £5,000 + £2,700

= £7,700 which agrees with the original data.

The following graph illustrates the behaviour of the total cost in this Case Study. The variable cost per unit determines the gradient (slope) of the line, and the fixed cost is shown where the line cuts the vertical axis. The total costs for 650 units and 800 units lie exactly on the line, but in some cases the points between the high and low may not fit exactly. The high-low method still gives useful information provided that the cost behaviour is approximately semi-variable – that is provided that all the points are approximately in a straight line.

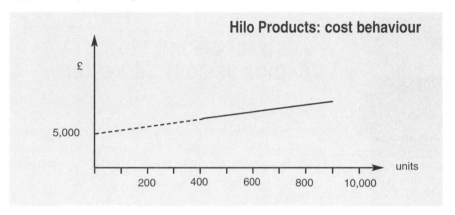

Now check your understanding of this subject by reading through the summary below:

---

high-low method summary

1   identify the highest and lowest cost totals and their levels of activity

2   calculate the difference between the two cost totals

3   calculate the difference in cost units between the two levels of activity

4   divide the difference in cost by the difference in units: this gives the variable cost per unit

5   use the variable cost per unit to calculate the variable part of one of the cost totals

6   deduct the variable part from the cost total to obtain the fixed part

7   check the answers by using them to calculate the other cost total, which should agree with the given data

---

practical limitations of cost behaviour

A problem that can arise when analysing costs based on their behaviour is that they may not always follow the (rather simplistic) categories of variable or fixed costs. For example, production costs which are often considered as fixed such as maintenance, cleaning, depreciation and insurance may in fact increase slightly as the activity level increases.

Unit costs which are normally categorised as variable (for example materials), may reduce due to bulk discounts or increase due to problems with availability as volumes increase. Costs which do not behave quite as variable costs are sometimes said to have 'non-linear behaviour' based on the way that the unit cost would appear on a graph when plotted against volume – i.e. not a straight line.

Case Study

ADD-VANTAGE LIMITED: CHOICE OF COSTING SYSTEM

situation

Add-vantage Limited is an accountancy training company. You have been asked to trial some learning material that is to be used to help the trainees understand the advantages and disadvantages of absorption and marginal costing.

required

Sort the following statements, based on whether they apply to absorption costing or marginal costing, and use the statements to complete the table.

Statements

1. This system relies on analysing costs based on their behaviour.
2. The unit cost produced under this system can be used to help establish normal selling price.
3. When inventory levels increase this system records a lower profit than the alternative system.
4. The accuracy of unit costs calculated under this system relies heavily on activity levels being as expected.
5. This system relies on some decisions about apportionment and absorption that may be arbitrary.
6. This system can be used to establish break-even levels and margins of safety.
7. Absolute minimum selling prices can be calculated with this system, and these can be used to help price 'extra' sales.
8. A practical problem with the analysis used for this system is how to deal with non-linear costs.
9. The unit costs calculated using this system can be used to value inventory for financial accounting purposes, since the method complies with accounting standards.
10. The high-low method can be used to help analyse costs so that they can be used in this costing system.

Absorption Costing	Marginal Costing
2	1
4	3
5	6
9	7
	8
	10

solution

Absorption Costing	Marginal Costing
The unit cost produced under this system can be used to help establish normal selling price.	This system relies on analysing costs based on their behaviour.
The accuracy of unit costs calculated under this system relies heavily on activity levels being as expected.	When inventory levels increase this system records a lower profit than the alternative system.
This system relies on some decisions about apportionment and absorption that may be arbitrary.	This system can be used to establish break-even levels and margins of safety.
The unit costs calculated using this system can be used to value inventory for financial accounting purposes, since the method complies with accounting standards.	Absolute minimum selling prices can be calculated with this system, and these can be used to help price 'extra' sales.
	A practical problem with the analysis used for this system is how to deal with non-linear costs.
	The high-low method can be used to help analyse costs so that they can be used in this costing system.

RESPONSIBILITY CENTRES

As already mentioned an important area of management accounting is the monitoring and control of costs. This is usually carried out by making certain managers responsible for each of the various aspects of the organisation and the costs that are incurred there. This concept is known as responsibility accounting. Standard costing, which will be examined in detail in the next few chapters usually makes good use of the idea of responsibility accounting.

Responsibility accounting often divides the organisation into 'responsibility centres' of three main types. We have already come across the first type of responsibility centres – the cost centre.

cost centres

These are responsibility centres where costs are charged and can be monitored and controlled. They are parts of the organisation that incur costs but do not have any direct income, and therefore the manager responsible for a cost centre could only be held accountable for the costs incurred there. We have already seen the role that cost centres can play in absorption costing where costs are allocated or apportioned to cost centres before being absorbed into product costs.

profit centres

Profit centres are parts of the organisation where costs are incurred, but income is generated as well. This means that profit can be calculated, and the manager responsible would be accountable for the amount of profit based on both the income and the expenditure in that responsibility centre. The profit would be measured in monetary amount, and also as a percentage of sales income.

investment centres

Investment centres are responsibility centres where the manager is responsible for income and expenditure (as in a profit centre), but also for the level of investment. The investment could be in the form of non-current (fixed) assets, and also could include elements of working capital such as inventory (stock), receivables (debtors), and payables (creditors) and maybe also cash. An investment centre is in effect a mini business within the main organisation. Monitoring would be carried out by comparing the profit with the investment, often by measures such as return on net assets or return on capital employed.

MANAGEMENT INFORMATION TECHNIQUES

In this chapter we will look at the techniques in outline form. The specific applications will be examined in later chapters. The following techniques involve the collection and the analysis of data to provide useful information.

primary and secondary data

Where data is collected specifically for analysis undertaken at that time by an organisation, then the data is known as 'primary data'. Where the data has been collected and provided by another organisation then it is known as 'secondary data'. For example, if a business analyses its sales figures, that is primary data; if it uses inflation figures provided by the Government's statistical services, that is secondary data.

census or sample?

If we want to collect data about a population (not just a population of people, but any large group of items or data) there are two approaches that we could use.

- A **census** could be used to collect data about every item in the population. One example of this technique is the Government's 10 yearly census of all the people in the UK. This provides information which can be used by the Government to plan services. A census provides a complete picture of the 'population', but is expensive, and will often be impractical.

- **Sampling** is a commonly used technique for collecting data from a small number within a 'population', to estimate information regarding the whole 'population'. Market research questionnaires are an example of sampling. Sampling is cheaper to carry out than a full census, but it must be carried out carefully if the results are to be used with confidence.

SAMPLING

The critical issue to consider when examining sampling techniques is that the sample must be as free from bias as is practical. If you wanted to estimate the faults in the whole production output of a factory it would not make sense to only sample the output of a machine manned by a trainee on his first day at work!

Some common uses of sampling are to estimate:
- customer satisfaction levels
- quality of production output
- the views of prospective customers of a new product or service

You could be asked to comment on the use of sampling for any of the above uses within this area of learning.

There are various approaches to sampling. The approach taken will depend on the type of population and the resources available. The approach will influence the reliability of the estimates produced.

random sampling

This is the approach that will provide the best estimate. It is based on the rule that every item in the population has an equal chance of being selected. In order for this to happen the exact size of the population must be known, and a 'sampling frame' created by numbering every item. From this frame the sample can be selected using random numbers. This approach could be used (for example) as a way of sampling sales invoices to estimate the likely number of errors in all the sales invoices within a period. This is because the whole population (the number of sales invoices) would be known from the outset. It could not be used to ascertain the views of bald men in Bradford because there is no way of accurately knowing how many there are and who they are.

quasi-random sampling

This approach contains a number of techniques that can provide a good approximation to random sampling. Although they are not quite as accurate as random sampling, they can produce similar outcomes, often using fewer resources. The techniques are:

- **Systematic Sampling**

  Choosing every 'n'th item after a random start. For example selecting sales invoices by starting at number 63, and then checking every 17th invoice from there.

- **Stratified Sampling**

  Dividing the population into groups ('strata' means 'layers'), and then choosing a sample from each of the strata based on its size. For example sales invoices could be grouped according to the location of the customer. If there were more invoices for customers in London than in Devon then the sample for London would be larger. Each group would be sampled independently in this way according to its size.

- **Multistage Sampling**

  Dividing the 'population' into groups, and then randomly selecting several groups as an initial sample. These selected groups are then sub-divided and sub groups randomly chosen (the procedure may be repeated several times). For example sales invoices could be divided into groups based on the location of the customers, and the groups of Yorkshire, Sussex and Cornwall randomly selected. Within each group towns could then be chosen at random (for example Halifax, Brighton and Truro), and the invoice sample selected from customers within these areas.

non-random sampling

This approach must be used when a sampling frame cannot be established (for example because the size of the population is not known). The results generated by this approach will typically be less reliable than random or quasi-random approaches, but are nevertheless useful. These techniques are often used for market research:

- **Quota Sampling**

  Restricting the sample to a fixed number per stratum. For example interviewing people in the street within certain categories (for example age groups, gender etc.) until a predetermined number have been interviewed.

- **Cluster Sampling**

  Selecting one subsection of the population as representative, and just sampling that. For example interviewing dog owners who live in Cardiff as being representative of dog owners throughout the UK.

TIME SERIES ANALYSIS

Time series analysis involves analysing numerical trends over a time period. It is often used to examine past and present trends so that future trends can be forecast. The term 'trend analysis' is used to describe the technique that we will now examine. At its simplest the concept is based on the assumption that data will continue to move in the same direction in the future as it has in the past.

Using the sales of a shoe shop as an example we will now look at a range of techniques for dealing with trends.

an identical annual change

A shoe shop 'Comfy Feet' has sold the following numbers of pairs of shoes annually over the last few years:

20-1	10,000
20-2	11,000
20-3	12,000
20-4	13,000
20-5	14,000
20-6	15,000
20-7	16,000

It does not require a great deal of arithmetic to calculate that if the trend continues at the previous rate – an increase of 1,000 pairs a year – then shoe sales could be forecast at 17,000 pairs in 20-8 and 18,000 pairs in 20-9. Of course this is a very simple example, and life is rarely this straightforward. For example, for how long can this rate of increase be sustained?

average annual change

A slightly more complex technique could have been used to arrive at the same answer for the shoe shop. If we compare the number of sales in 20-7 with the number in 20-1, we can see that it has risen by 6,000 pairs. By dividing that figure by the number of times the year changed in our data we can arrive at an average change per year. The number of times that the year changes is 6, which is the same as the number of 'spaces' between the years (or alternatively the total number of years minus 1).

Shown as an equation this becomes:

Average Annual Sales Change $=$

$$\frac{(Sales\ in\ Last\ Year - Sales\ in\ First\ Year)}{(Number\ of\ Years - 1)} = \frac{(16,000 - 10,000)}{(7 - 1)}$$

$=$ $+ 1,000$, which is what we would expect.

The + 1,000 would then be added to the sales data in 20-7 of 16,000 (the last actual data) to arrive at a forecast of 17,000.

This technique is useful when all the increases are not quite identical, yet we want to use the average increase to forecast the trend. A negative answer would show that the average change is a reduction, not an increase. We will use this technique when estimating the trend movement in more complicated situations.

This is not the only way that we can estimate the direction that data is moving over time, and it does depend on the data (including especially the first and last points) falling roughly into a straight line. We will note alternative methods that can be used later in this section.

constructing a graph

The same result can be produced graphically. Using the same shoe shop example we can extend the graph based on the actual data to form a forecast line.

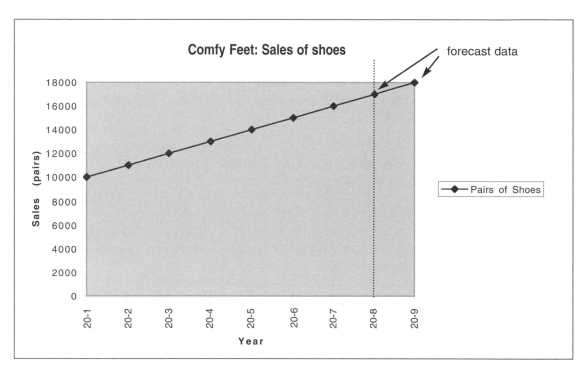

If in another situation the actual data does not produce exactly equal increases, the graph will produce the same answer as the average annual change provided the straight line runs through the first and last year's data points.

using a formula

The data in the example could have been expressed in the following formula:

$$y = mx + c$$

where

    y is the forecast amount

    m is 1,000 (the amount by which the data increases each year)

    x is the number of years since the start year (20-1)

    c is 10,000 (which is the sales figure in the start year of 20-1)

If we wanted a forecast for the year 20-9, we could calculate it as:

Forecast	=	(1,000 x number of years since 20-1) + 10,000
y (the forecast)	=	(1,000 x 8) + 10,000
	=	18,000, which is what we would expect.

This formula works because the formula is based on the equation of a straight line.

using a formula for more calculations

The formula of a straight line ($y = mx + c$) that we have just used to calculate a forecast for 'y' can also be used to work out other information. The formula always has the following components:

- a fixed value ('c' in the formula $y = mx + c$); this is the point where the straight line starts from

- a gradient value ('m' in the formula); this determines how steep the line is, and whether it is going up (when 'm' is positive) or going down (when 'm' is negative)

The formula can be used (for example) to predict prices, costs or demand. Sometimes the formula is shown in a slightly different style (for example $y = a + bx$), but the components are still the same.

The formula of a straight line ties in with the calculations that we carried out on pages 22 – 23 for the 'high-low' method of calculating cost behaviour. There the fixed value represented the fixed costs, and the gradient value was the variable cost per unit. You will notice that the calculation methods that we used for analysing costs can also be used for other situations.

We will now use the formula to demonstrate how different elements can be calculated.

practical example

For example, suppose we are told that the price of a component over time is believed to increase based on the formula $Y = a + bX$, where

- Y is the price in £, and
- X is the year number

We are told that in year number 4 the price was £68, and in year number 8 the price was £76.

We would like to calculate 'a' and 'b' in the formula, and then use this information to predict the price in year 11.

We can use a calculation similar to the 'high-low' method, to determine how much the price is moving by each year:

	Price		Year	
	£76		8	
	£68		4	
Differences	£8	divided by	4	= £2 per year

This is the 'gradient' amount 'b', and we can use it to calculate the amount 'a' by using price information from either of the years that we know. For example, using year 4 data and putting it into the formula gives:

£68 = a + (£2 x 4 [the year number])

£68 = a + £8   So a must be £60

Now we have the full formula that we can use for any year:

$Y = £60 + £2 \times X$

In year 11, this would give a price of:

$y = £60 + (£2 \times 11)$ $= £82$

Just like in the high-low method, if you are provided with more than two pairs of data, then using the highest and the lowest will probably give the most reliable answer.

We will now use an example to illustrate the use of the formula to predict demand.

Sales of a national daily newspaper have been declining steadily for several years. The demand level is believed to follow the formula $Y = a + bX$, where Y is the demand in numbers of newspapers, and X is the year number. Calculations have already been carried out to establish the values of 'a' and 'b', which are:

- a is 200,000

- b is -2,500

Note that 'b' is a negative figure, so each year the demand decreases.

You are asked to calculate the expected sales in year 14.

If we insert the known data into the formula, we can calculate the demand for year 14 as follows:

$Y = 200,000 - (2,500 \times 14)$ $Y = 165,000$

linear regression

In the last section on time series analysis we saw that when some historical data moves in a consistent and regular way over time we can use it to help estimate the future trend of that data. We also saw that in these circumstances the data can be represented by

- a straight line on a graph, and / or
- an equation of the line in the form $y = mx + c$

to help us develop the trend.

Linear regression is the term used for the techniques that can be used to determine the line that best replicates that given data. You should be aware of the techniques in general terms, and be able to appreciate their usefulness. You may be given historical data or the equation of a line and asked to use it to generate a forecast.

Where data exactly matches a straight line (as with the 'Comfy Feet' data) there is no need to use any special techniques. In other situations the following could be used:

- **Average annual change**. This method was described earlier, and is useful if we are confident that the first and last points (taken chronologically since we are looking at data over time) are both representative. It will smooth out any minor fluctuations of the data in between. We will see this method used in the 'Seasonal Company' case study later in this chapter.

- **Line of best fit**. Where the data falls only roughly into a straight line, but the first and last points do not appear to be very representative the average annual change method would give a distorted solution. Here a line of best fit can be drawn onto the data points on a graph that will form a better estimate of the movement of the data. The following graph illustrates a situation where the line of best fit would provide a better solution than the average annual change method.

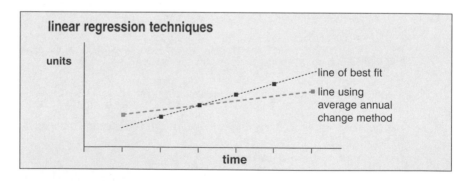

- **Least squares method**. This is a mathematical technique for developing the equation of the most appropriate line. It is more accurate than drawing a line of best fit onto a graph by eye, but the calculations involved are outside the scope of this book.

All linear regression techniques assume that a straight line is an appropriate representation of the data. When looking at time series this means that we are assuming that the changes in the data that we are considering (known as the dependent variable) are in proportion to the movement of time (the independent variable). This would mean that we are expecting (for example) the sales level to continually rise over time. When we use time series analysis later in the book we must remember that sometimes data does not travel forever in a straight line, even though they may do so for a short time. For example share prices on the stock market do not continue to go up (or down) steadily, but often move in a more erratic way.

The ideas behind regression analysis apply not only to time series analysis, but can be used in many other situations, for example:

- examining the behaviour of semi-variable costs at different activity levels. Earlier in this chapter we used the 'High-Low' method to split costs between their fixed and variable components. This method uses an identical principle to the 'average annual change' method described above.

- looking at the number of defects in goods produced to see if it varies with output volume. In Chapter 5 we will examine various issues connected with quality.

The data that is used for analysis in various situations, including these examples is often the result of using sampling techniques (as outlined earlier in this chapter). The reliance that can be placed on the outcomes of our analysis will then depend not only on the regression analysis, but also on the validity of the sampling techniques used.

TIME SERIES ANALYSIS AND SEASONAL VARIATIONS

There are four main factors that can influence data which is generated over a period of time:

- **The underlying trend**

   This is the way that the data is generally moving in the long term. For example the volume of traffic on our roads is generally increasing as time goes on.

- **Long term cycles**

   These are slow moving variations that may be caused by economic cycles or social trends. For example, when economic prosperity generally increases this may increase the volume of traffic as more people own cars and fewer use buses. In times of economic depression there may be a decrease in car use as people cannot afford to travel as much or may not have employment which requires them to travel.

• **Seasonal variations**

This term refers to regular, predictable cycles in the data. The cycles may or may not be seasonal in the normal use of the term (eg Spring, Summer etc). For example traffic volumes are always higher in the daytime, especially on weekdays, and lower at weekends and at night.

• **Random variations**

All data will be affected by influences that are unpredictable. For example flooding of some roads may reduce traffic volume along that route, but increase it on alternative routes. Similarly the traffic volume may be influenced by heavy snowfall.

The type of numerical problems that you are most likely to face will tend to ignore the effects of long-term cycles (which will effectively be considered as a part of the trend) and random variations (which are impossible to forecast). We are therefore left with analysing data into underlying trends and seasonal variations, in order to create forecasts.

The technique that we will use follows the process in this diagram:

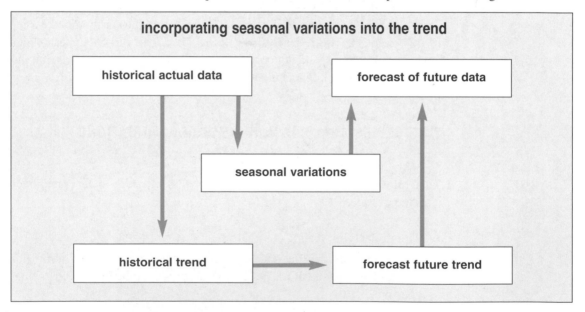

The process is as follows:

1 The historical actual data is analysed into the historical trend and the seasonal variations.

2 The historical trend is used to forecast the future trend, using the techniques examined in the last section.

3 The seasonal variations are incorporated with the forecast future trend to provide a forecast of where the actual data will be in the future.

analysing historical actual data

In a task the analysis may have been carried out already, or you may be asked to carry out the analysis by using 'moving averages'. If you are using moving averages it is important that:

- your workings are laid out accurately
- the number of pieces of data that are averaged corresponds with the number of 'seasons' in a cycle
- where there is an even number of 'seasons' in a cycle a further averaging of each pair of averages takes place.

how do moving averages work?

A moving average is the term used for a series of averages calculated from a stream of data so that:

- every average is based on the same number of pieces of data, (eg four pieces of data in a 'four point moving average'), and
- each subsequent average moves along that data stream by one piece of data so that compared to the previous average it
  - uses one new piece of data and
  - abandons one old piece of data.

This is easier to calculate than it sounds! For example, suppose we had a list of six pieces of data relating to the factory output over two days where a three-shift pattern was worked as follows:

Day 1	Morning Shift	14 units
	Afternoon Shift	20 units
	Night Shift	14 units
Day 2	Morning Shift	26 units
	Afternoon Shift	32 units
	Night Shift	26 units

If we thought that the shift being worked might influence the output, we could calculate a three-point moving average, the workings would be as follows:

First moving average:	$(14 + 20 + 14) \div 3$	$= 16$
Second moving average:	$(20 + 14 + 26) \div 3$	$= 20$
Third moving average:	$(14 + 26 + 32) \div 3$	$= 24$
Fourth moving average	$(26 + 32 + 26) \div 3$	$= 28$

Notice how we move along the list of data. In this simple example with six pieces of data we can't work out any more three-point averages since we have arrived at the end of the numbers after only four calculations.

Here we chose the number of pieces of data to average each time so that it corresponded with the number of points in a full cycle. By choosing a three-point moving average that corresponded with the number of shifts we always had **one** example of the output of **every** type of shift in our average. This means that any influence on the average by including a night shift (for example) is cancelled out by also including data from a morning shift and an afternoon shift.

We must be careful to always work out moving averages so that exactly one complete cycle is included in every average. The number of 'points' is chosen to suit the data.

When determining a trend line, each average relates to the data from its mid point, as the following layout of the figures just calculated demonstrates.

		Output	Trend (Moving Average)
Day 1	Morning Shift	14 units	
	Afternoon Shift	20 units	16 units
	Night Shift	14 units	20 units
Day 2	Morning Shift	26 units	24 units
	Afternoon Shift	32 units	28 units
	Night Shift	26 units	

This means that the first average that we calculated (16 units) can be used as the trend point of the afternoon shift on day 1, with the second point (20 units) forming the trend point of the night shift on day 1. The result is that we:

• know exactly where the trend line is for each period of time, and

• have a basis from which we can calculate 'seasonal variations'

Even using our limited data in this example we can see how seasonal variations can be calculated. *A seasonal variation is simply the difference between the actual data at a point and the trend at the same point.* This gives us the seasonal variations shown in the following table, using the figures already calculated.

		Output	Trend	Seasonal Variation
Day 1	Morning Shift	14 units		
	Afternoon Shift	20 units	16 units	+ 4 units
	Night Shift	14 units	20 units	- 6 units
Day 2	Morning Shift	26 units	24 units	+ 2 units
	Afternoon Shift	32 units	28 units	+ 4 units
	Night Shift	26 units		

The seasonal variation for the afternoon shift, calculated on day 1, is based on the actual output being 4 units greater than the trend at the same point (20 minus 16 units).

dealing with an even number of 'seasons'

In the last example the trend could be calculated just by using the three-point moving average. This was because using three points provides an average centred at its middle figure – the second point. If there are four 'seasons' we need to use a four-point moving average, but the problem is that then the average relates to the middle of the four pieces of data, and that means that it falls in between the two middle figures. The effect of this is that the four-point moving average cannot be used directly as a trend since its points are not located at actual periods of time.

This problem can be overcome by a further averaging of each pair of moving averages. This gives figures that can be used as a trend since they are based on an equal number of representatives of each season, and are naturally aligned with actual periods of time. This calculation of additional averages (called centred moving averages) needs to be performed whenever there is an even number of 'seasons' in each complete cycle (for example when using the four quarters of a year, or using data from a six working day week).

In the case study that follows, the full process (including further averaging) is used to determine the trend and seasonal variations, and these are then used to create a forecast.

Case Study

THE SEASONAL COMPANY: MOVING AVERAGES AND FORECAST TRENDS

The Seasonal Company sells various products, including Wellington Boots for use in wet weather. The quarterly management accounts for recent quarters have revealed that the following numbers of these boots were sold.

	Quarter 1	Quarter 2	Quarter 3	Quarter 4
20-0	4,000	1,600	2,200	4,800
20-1	4,400	2,000	2,500	5,200
20-2	4,800	2,400	3,100	5,600
20-3	5,200	2,800	3,400	6,000

required

1 Use moving averages to analyse the historical data into the trend and the seasonal variations.

2 Use the data from (1) to forecast the sales for each quarter of 20-4.

solution

1 Calculating the trend and seasonal variations

Step 1   The first thing to do is to rearrange the historical data into a single column with spaces in between each of the figures – this is to the right of the date column:

Year	Quarter	*Step 1* *Historical* *Sales Data*	*Step 2* *4-point Moving* *Average*	*Step 3* *Averaged* *Pairs (Trend)*	*Step 4* *Seasonal* *Variation*
20-0	1	4,000			
	2	1,600			
	3	2,200	3,150	3,200	–1,000
	4	4,800	3,250	3,300	+1,500
20-1	1	4,400	3,350	3,387.5	+1,012.5
	2	2,000	3,425	3,475	–1,475
	3	2,500	3,525	3,575	–1,075
	4	5,200	3,625	3,675	+1,525
20-2	1	4,800	3,725	3,800	+1,000
	2	2,400	3,875	3,925	–1,525
	3	3,100	3,975	4,025	–925
	4	5,600	4,075	4,125	+1,475
20-3	1	5,200	4,175	4,212.5	+987.5
	2	2,800	4,250	4,300	–1,500
	3	3,400	4,350		
	4	6,000			

Step 2   Calculate the 4-point moving averages. This is the average of each group of four figures, starting with 20-0 quarters 1 to 4, followed by 20-0 quarter 2 to 20-1 quarter 1, and so on. Place each moving average in the appropriate column, alongside the centre point of the figures from which it was calculated. We are using a 4-point average because there are 4 quarters in our data. This also means that the average will fall alongside gaps between our original data. Note that the shaded lines and arrows are drawn here for illustration only – to show where the figures come from.

Step 3   Calculate the average of each adjacent pair of moving averages. These are also known as 'centred moving averages'. This is carried out so that these figures can be placed alongside the centre of each pair, and will therefore fall in line with the original quarterly data (see shaded arrow). If there was an odd number of 'seasons' in a cycle (for example 13 four-weekly periods) then this stage would not be required. We have now calculated the trend figures. Notice that the first trend calculated is in quarter 3 of the first year, and the last one is in quarter 2 of the last year. This is inevitable when calculating a trend from quarterly data using moving averages.

Step 4 Calculate the seasonal variations, and insert them into the last column. These are the amounts by which the actual figures (left hand column) are greater or smaller than the trend figures. Be careful to use the correct + or − sign. The shaded arrows show the figures that are used.

2 forecast the sales for each quarter of 20-4

In order to use the data that we have calculated for a forecast we will need to work out some average figures. This is because in this case study you will notice that:

- the trend is not increasing by exactly the same amount every quarter
- the seasonal variations are similar, but not quite identical for each of the same quarters

We can use the technique for calculating the average increase in the trend that we looked at earlier:

$$Average\ Trend\ Change = \frac{(Last\ known\ trend - First\ known\ trend)}{(Number\ of\ Quarterly\ trends - 1)} = \frac{(4,300 - 3,200)}{11} = +100$$

We can also average the seasonal variations by grouping them together in quarters:

	Quarter 1	Quarter 2	Quarter 3	Quarter 4
20-0			− 1,000	+ 1,500
20-1	+ 1,012.5	− 1,475	− 1,075	+ 1,525
20-2	+ 1,000	− 1,525	− 925	+ 1,475
20-3	+ 987.5	− 1,500		
Totals	+ 3,000	− 4,500	− 3,000	+ 4,500
Averages	+ 1,000	− 1,500	− 1,000	+ 1,500

At this stage we should check that the average seasonal variations total zero. Here they do, but if they do not then minor adjustments will need to be made to the figures.

We can now use the average trend movements and the average seasonal variations to create a forecast. We start with the trend at the last point when it was calculated, and work out where it will be at future points by using the average movements. For example quarter 1 of 20-4 is 3 quarters past quarter 2 of 20-3, which is when we last knew the trend. We then incorporate the average seasonal variations to complete the forecast.

Forecast Workings:

		Forecast Trend		Seasonal Variations	Forecast
20-4	Qtr 1	4,300 + (3 x 100)	= 4,600	+ 1,000	5,600
	Qtr 2	4,300 + (4 x 100)	= 4,700	− 1,500	3,200
	Qtr 3	4,300 + (5 x 100)	= 4,800	− 1,000	3,800
	Qtr 4	4,300 + (6 x 100)	= 4,900	+ 1,500	6,400

All the data and the solution to this Case Study can be shown on a graph, as follows:

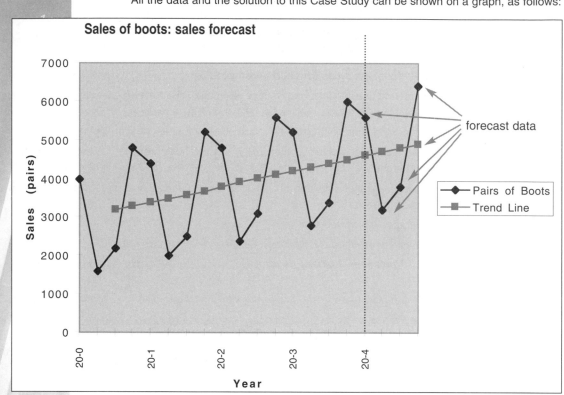

INDEX NUMBERS

Index numbers are used to assist in the comparison of numerical data over time. The most commonly used index is perhaps the Retail Price Index that gives an indication of inflation by comparing the cost of a group of expenses typically incurred by households in the UK from year-to-year. There are many other types of index numbers that have been created for specific purposes, for example:

• the average wage rate for a particular job, or for all employment

• the average house price either by region or throughout the UK

• the market price of shares (eg the FTSE 100 index)

• the quantities of specific items that are sold or used (eg litres of unleaded petrol)

• the quantities of a group of items that are sold or used (eg litres of all motor fuel)

• the manufactured cost of specific items or a range of items (sometimes called 'factory gate' prices).

Many government indices and other indicators are available at www.statistics.gov.uk. If you have the opportunity, have a look at the enormous range of data that can either be downloaded free, or can be purchased in government publications.

When using published statistics it is important to make sure that they are specific enough to be useful for your purpose. For example, data on the growth in the population of the West of England will be of limited use if you are trying to forecast the sales in a bookshop in Taunton. Of far more use would be details of proposed housing developments within the immediate area, including the numbers of new homes and the type of households that form the developers' target market.

leading and lagging indicators

Some indicators can be classified as 'leading' indicators, whilst others are known as 'lagging' indicators. This means that some indicators naturally give advance warning of changes that may take place later in other indicators. For example an index that monitors the prices of manufactured goods ('factory gate' prices) will react to changes before they have filtered through to retail price indices. The index of 'factory gate' prices can therefore be considered to be a 'leading' indicator of retail prices, and give early warning of implications to industrial situations.

In a similar way, an index recording the volume of manufactured output from factories will lag behind an index measuring the volume of purchases of raw materials made by industrial buying departments.

weightings of indices

Those indices that are based on information from more than one item will use some form of weighting to make the results meaningful.

For example while an index measuring the retail price of premium grade unleaded petrol is based on a single product and therefore needs no weighting, this would not be true for a price index for all vehicle fuel. In this case it will require a decision about how much weight (or importance) is to be placed on each component of the index. Here the relative quantities sold of types of fuel (for example unleaded petrol and diesel) would be a logical way to weight the index. This would ensure that if petrol sales were double those for diesel, any price changes in petrol would have twice the impact on the index than a price change in diesel.

As the purchasing habits of consumers change, then the weighting and composition of complicated indices like the Retail Price Index and the Consumer Price Index are often changed to reflect this. This will include changes to the weighting of certain items, for example due to the increase in the proportion of household expenditure on holidays. It can also involve the addition or deletion of certain items entirely (for example the inclusion of certain fast foods). You may have seen news items from time to time about the revision of items contained within the RPI or CPI as consumers' tastes change.

calculations using index numbers

Whatever type of index we need to use, the principle is the same. The index numbers represent a convenient way of comparing figures.

For example, the RPI was 82.61 in January 1983, and 218.0 in January 2010. This means that average household costs had much more than doubled in the 27 years between. We could also calculate that if something that cost £5.00 in January 1983 had risen exactly in line with inflation, it would have cost £13.19 in January 2010. This calculation is carried out by:

$$\textit{historical price} \quad \times \quad \frac{\textit{index of time converting to}}{\textit{index of time converting from}}$$

ie £5.00 x (218.0 ÷ 82.61) = £13.19

This is an increase of $\dfrac{(£13.19 - £5.00) \times 100}{£5.00} = 163.8\%$

You may be told that the 'base year' for a particular index is a certain point in time. This is when the particular index was 100. For example the current RPI index was 100 in January 1987. You do not need to know the base year to do the sort of calculations that are likely to be asked of you.

Index numbers referring to costs or prices are the most commonly used ones referred to in the units studied in this book. If we want to use cost index numbers to monitor past costs or forecast future ones, then it is best to use as specific an index as possible. This will then provide greater accuracy than a more general index.

For example, if we were operating in the food industry, and wanted to compare our coffee cost movements with the average that the industry had experienced, we should use an index that analyses coffee costs in the food industry. This would be much more accurate than the RPI, and also better than a general cost index for the food industry.

Case Study

1.850

1.600

MARY COX: PENSION CALCULATION

Mary Cox retired in January 2003, and her occupational pension at that point was £6,000 per year. By January 2011 the pension had risen to £7,200 per year. Assume that the index figures for the RPI and the Average Wage Index were as follows:

	RPI	Average Wage Index
January 2003	180.0	360.0
January 2011	220.0	460.0

required

1 Calculate what Mary's pension would have been in January 2011 if it had kept pace with

(a)   the RPI, and

(b)   the Average Wage Index since January 2003

2 Discuss the use of

- the Retail Price Index and
- the Average Wage Index

as a means of setting Pension levels.

solution

1 pension calculation

Converting Mary's 2003 pension in line with each index gives:

(a) Using the RPI   £6,000 x 220.0 ÷ 180.0 = £7,333 (rounded)

(b) Using Average Wage Index   £6,000 x 460.0 ÷ 360.0 = £7,667 (rounded)

2 discussion of the use of indices:

RPI

The justification for using the RPI to adjust pension levels is that the spending power of the pensioners remains constant as prices rise. The pensioners, it is argued, are equally as well off several years into their retirement as when it commenced. One drawback of using the RPI is that it is based on the average consumption of UK households. Pensioners do not have the same spending profile as typical households, and therefore their costs may move in a different way. For example fuel costs would take proportionally more of a pensioner's income, while other costs may take a lower proportion.

average wage index

If the average wage index was used for setting pensions, the pension would tend to rise slightly faster than general inflation, assuming previous trends continued. This would mean that pensioners slowly became slightly better off than they had been when they first retired, although their improvement would be at the same speed as that experienced by those in work. They would not find the gap between their spending power and that of those in work widening as it does when the RPI is used.

TECHNIQUES USING DISCOUNTED CASH FLOW (DCF)

You are probably familiar with the use of discounted cash flow techniques from your earlier studies. This section will act as revision of the main principles, which will then be applied later in this book.

DCF is used to help with long term decision making, by taking account of the 'time-value' of money when comparing cash flows. It works by using factors to multiply by the actual future cash flows to convert them into 'present value' cash flows. Once all future cash flows have been converted into their equivalent present values they can be added or subtracted from each other since they are all now comparable.

The logic of DCF is that future incoming cash flows have less value than current ones because we have to wait to receive the money. If we had received it immediately then it could have been invested to grow in value. For example, £751 invested now at 10% interest per year would grow to £1,000 after 3 years. This calculation is based on compound interest – check the figures yourself. In the language of DCF we would say that £1,000 in 3 years' time has a 'present value' of £751.

The further into the future the cash flow occurs (and the greater the assumed interest rate) the greater the difference between the actual future cash flow and its present value. We would be provided with 'discount factors' to convert the cash flows into present values. For example the discount factor for 3 years based on 10% is 0.751, and for 5 years at the same rate is 0.621. The interest rate used for discount factors is often the cost of capital to the organisation.

We use the term 'net present value' to describe the net result of comparing the present values of all the relevant future cash flows – deducting negative flows from positive ones. If the result is positive this shows that even after taking account of the 'time-value' of the cash flows, the incoming flows are greater than the outgoing flows. This usually means that the situation or project that the figures are based on is worthwhile.

The term 'internal rate of return' (IRR) is used to describe the interest rate that when applied to the cash flows from a project results in a net present value of zero. For example if a project shows a positive net present value based on 10%, but a negative net present value when using an interest rate of 20%, we would know that the internal rate of return must be somewhere in between these figures. We could calculate roughly what the IRR is by trial and error, and provided it is greater than the organisation's cost of capital then the project may be worthwhile.

Later in the book we will look at various applications of this technique, but for now we will use a fairly simple case study to remind us of how DCF works.

<table>
<tr><td>**Case Study**</td><td>

SOLAR SAVINGS:
CALCULATING NET PRESENT VALUE

situation

A company is considering installing solar panels on the roof of a block of flats that it is building to provide hot water for all the tenants. The solar panels will cost £30,000 to purchase and install, and have an expected useful life of 6 years. The total received from tenants would increase from the normal rental income of £45,000 per year to £52,400 per year if they were to be supplied with solar powered hot water. The company's cost of capital is 10%, and this rate is to be used for the DCF calculation.

required

Using the following discount factors, calculate whether the installation of solar panels is likely to be worthwhile.

</td></tr>
</table>

Year	Discount Factor
1	0.909
2	0.826
3	0.751
4	0.683
5	0.621
6	0.564

solution

Year	Detail	Cash Flow £	Discount Factor	Present Value £
0	Purchase and Installation	(30,000)	1.000	(30,000)
1	Increased	7,400	0.909	6,727
2	Receipts from	7,400	0.826	6,112
3	Tenants	7,400	0.751	5,557
4		7,400	0.683	5,054
5		7,400	0.621	4,595
6		7,400	0.564	4,174
Net Present Value				2,219

The net present value of £2,219 is positive, so the installation of solar panels appears worthwhile based on these figures.

Chapter Summary

- Information sources for managers are both internal and external. Much of the internal information is from the Management Accounting function of an organisation, and this book is based on many of the techniques used in this area. Management Accounting is guided by its usefulness to managers, and has no external rules or formats that must be followed.

- Management Accounts are based around the organisation's costing system, which can be derived from Absorption Costing, Marginal Costing, or Activity Based Costing. Each system uses different terminology and different ways of calculating the cost of an organisation's output or activities. The different ways that inventory can be valued in management accounts affects the amount of profit that is recorded in each period when inventory levels change.

- There are strengths and weaknesses of absorption and marginal costing, and each may be better in certain circumstances. Absorption costing can often be successfully used for planning, monitoring and control. Marginal costing is usually best for decision making.

- Responsibility accounting often uses cost centres, profit centres and investment centres to divide up an organisation into manageable and accountable sections.

- Management Information techniques that you need to be familiar with include methods of sampling, the techniques of time series analysis, and how index numbers can be used. Discounted cash flow techniques also need to be understood and applied.

Key Terms

financial accounting — the branch of accounting that is concerned with reporting performance to those outside the organisation

management accounting — the branch of accounting that is concerned with providing useful information to managers within the organisation. This book is concerned with some of the main aspects of Management Accounting

absorption costing — this is a system that attempts to determine a 'full' production cost for each unit of output. It therefore includes both direct and indirect costs, and uses the mechanisms of allocation, apportionment and absorption to incorporate the indirect production costs

marginal costing	this costing system categorises costs according to their cost behaviour, and divides them into variable and fixed costs. This system uses a cost for each unit of output based purely on the variable (or 'marginal') costs. All fixed costs are regarded as time based and are therefore linked to accounting periods rather than units of output
activity based costing	this is a development of absorption costing, and uses a more sophisticated system to deal with the indirect costs. This involves examining indirect costs to determine what causes them, and using this information to charge the costs to the units of output in an appropriate manner
high-low method	a method used to analyse semi-variable costs into their variable and fixed components so that costs can be predicted at various output levels
responsibility accounting	management accounting based on departments, activities or functions, each of which is the area of responsibility of an individual
sampling	sampling is a commonly used technique for using data about a small number of items within a population, to estimate information regarding the whole population
time series analysis	the examination of historical data that occurs over time, often with the intention of using the data to forecast future data
trend	the underlying movement in the data, once seasonal and random movements have been stripped away
seasonal variations	regular variations in data that occur in a repeating pattern
linear regression	using a mathematical formula to demonstrate the movement of data over time. This technique is sometimes used to help forecast the movement of the trend
index numbers	a sequence of numbers used to compare data, usually over a time period
discounted cash flow	a technique that takes account of the 'time-value' of money by discounting future cash flows to their present value

Activities

1.1   Suggest where (or from whom) each of the following sources of information might typically be obtained.

(a)   Monthly Management Accounts   *A/c nnanager*

(b)   Industry Average Performance Indicators

(c)   Retail Price Index

(d)   Historical Sales Data

(e)   Developments affecting Competitors

(f)   Regional Population Data

1.2   The Radical Company produces a variety of goods, according to customers' demands. Some items have been produced to the same specification for many years, while others are constantly updated to meet the needs of the consumers. Some products have long production runs, while others are produced in small batches for specific customers.

Explain whether you believe that Absorption Costing, Marginal Costing, or Activity Based Costing would appear to be most appropriate for this company.

1.3   The System Company manufactures one product, the Tem. Budgeted production is 4,000 Tems per week. During each of the first two weeks of this year it had costs as follows, exactly as budgeted.

Direct Materials   £5,000

Direct Labour   £9,000

Fixed Overheads   £6,000

The company had no finished goods in inventory at the start of week 1. In both weeks it produced 4,000 units. Sales in week 1 were 3,000 units, and in week 2 were 5,000 units, all at £8 per Tem.

Both Direct Materials and Direct Labour behave as Variable Costs.

(a)   Produce profit statements for each of the two weeks, using

(i)   Absorption costing, absorbing fixed overheads on a per unit basis.

(ii)   Marginal Costing

(b)   Explain briefly the reason for the difference between recorded profits under the alternative costing systems.

1.4   The Supashop that is open 5 days per week has the following cash sales over a period.

	Tues	Wed	Thurs	Fri	Sat
Week 1	£1,830	£1,920	£2,080	£2,160	£2,160
Week 2	£1,880	£1,970	£2,130	£2,210	£2,210
Week 3	£1,930	£2,020	£2,180	£2,260	£2,260

Required

(a)   Using moving averages, analyse this data into the trend and seasonal variations.

(b)   Use the data from (a) to forecast the cash sales for each day of week 4.

1.5 The following historical data relates to sales in units of the Enigma Company.

	Quarter 1	Quarter 2	Quarter 3	Quarter 4
Year 1	500	430	330	280
Year 2	460	390	290	240
Year 3	420	350	250	200
Year 4	380	310	210	160

Required

(a) Using moving averages, analyse this data into the trend and additive seasonal variations.

(b) Use the data from (a) to forecast the unit sales for each quarter of year 5.

1.6 The table below shows the last three months cost per kilo for product Beta:

Jan	Feb	March
Actual price was £6.80	Actual price was £6.40	Actual price was £7.00
Seasonal variation was +£0.40	Seasonal variation was -£0.10	Seasonal variation was +£0.40

Calculate the monthly movement in the price trend.

1.7 A company has provided the following information:

	Jan	Feb	March
Total cost	£20,000	£24,000	£25,000
Total quantity	2,000 kilos	2,200 kilos	2,140 kilos

10   10·91   11·68

The cost index (to nearest whole number) for March based upon January being the base period of 100 is:

(a) 107

(b) 117 ✓

(c) 125

(d) 108

1.8 The cost per unit of a product has increased from £72 in January to £80 in April. The cost per unit was £70 when the index was rebased to 100.

Select the one statement that is correct:

(a) The cost index in April was 114 and the increase from January to April is 11.11%. ✓

(b) The cost index in April was 111 and the increase from January to April is 11.11%.

(c) The cost index in April was 114 and the increase from January to April is 10.00%.

(d) The cost index in April was 111 and the increase from January to April is 10.00%.

2 Standard costing – direct costs

this chapter covers...

In this chapter we will start to examine one of the major topics of this learning area – standard costing. This chapter concentrates on using standard costing in conjunction with direct costs – we will examine overheads in Chapter 3.

The chapter commences with an overview of the background to standard costing and how it can be useful. It then goes on to see how standard costs are built up and what information is available to those in the organisation who set the standards.

A large part of the chapter is devoted to the calculation of variances relating to direct costs. These are the differences between standard and actual costs that are related to specific components of the cost. It is vital that you understand fully how the variances are derived so that you can carry out a variety of calculations if required.

The main variances covered in this chapter are:

- *total direct material variance*

- *direct material price variance*

- *direct material usage variance*

- *total direct labour variance*

- *direct labour rate variance*

- *direct labour efficiency variance*

We will also learn about the direct labour idle time variance where there is data available about idle time.

We will also discover how to use variances to reconcile standard and actual costs, and the chapter is rounded off with a summary of the main underlying causes of direct cost variances.

BACKGROUND TO STANDARD COSTING

Standard costing was developed primarily in the manufacturing industry as a formal method for calculating the expected costs of products. It differs from general budget setting (which is normally concerned with the costs of sections of the organisation), because it focuses on the cost of what the organisation produces (the 'cost units'). It is often used in conjunction with budgets, so that they work together consistently.

Standard costing establishes in detail the standard cost of each component of a product, so that a total cost can be calculated for that product.

Standard costing is ideal for situations where components are identical and manufacturing operations are repetitive.

advantages of standard costing

The main advantages of operating with a standard costing system in place are that the standard costs can be used:

- to help with **decision making**, for example as a basis for pricing decisions
- to assist in **planning**, for example to plan the quantity and cost of the resources needed for future production
- as a mechanism for **monitoring and controlling** costs: the standard costs for the actual production can be compared with the actual costs incurred, and the differences (called 'variances') calculated. This is so that appropriate action can be taken.

In addition there may be other benefits to setting up and using a standard costing system:

- The preliminary examination of current production techniques and resources may reveal hidden inefficiencies and unnecessary expenditure.
- The fact that costs are to be monitored may increase the cost consciousness of the workforce (and the management).
- The system lends itself to exception reporting. This is a technique where results are only reported when they are outside a predetermined range so that action can be taken. For example a company may decide that only when costs are more than 2% away from the standard should the variances be reported.

There are therefore a variety of arguments for developing and using a standard costing system. The main uses that a particular organisation intends to make of the system will determine how it goes about setting standards. In Chapter 4 we will examine the different ways that standards can be set and how this can affect the interpretation of any variances. At this point we will see what a 'standard cost' consists of, what information we will need to set the standards and where it can be obtained.

COMPOSITION OF STANDARD COSTS

elements of standard costs

The composition of standard costs – whether you are calculating the standard cost of a rubber washer, an aeroplane, or a hip replacement operation – can be analysed into common elements. These are the same elements of cost that you will be familiar with from your earlier studies:

Direct Costs	**Indirect Costs**
Direct Materials	Variable Overheads
Direct Labour	Fixed Overheads
Direct Expenses	

In this chapter we will concentrate on the standards and variances for direct materials and direct labour, and in the next chapter we will examine fixed overheads. You do not need to study either the direct expense variances nor the variable overhead variances for this unit.

absorption costing and marginal costing models

The breakdown of costs (shown above) into direct and indirect costs is based on the **absorption costing** model, where a suitable portion of all production costs (indirect as well as direct) is absorbed into the product's cost. A great many standard costing systems use this approach.

You should also be familiar with the **marginal costing** model. Here costs are analysed on the basis of the way they behave in relation to activity levels, and split into variable costs and fixed costs. This then gives the following alternative production cost breakdown:

ABSORPTION COSTING	**MARGINAL COSTING**
direct costs direct materials direct labour direct expenses	**variable costs** variable direct materials variable direct labour variable direct expenses variable overheads
indirect costs variable overheads fixed overheads	**fixed costs** fixed direct costs fixed overheads

Any category of direct or indirect costs could behave as either variable or fixed costs, but once the cost behaviour is established, standard marginal costing is very straightforward to use. The standard costs for direct materials and labour under absorption costing are developed in the same way as variable direct materials and labour under marginal costing.

standard direct material costs

You can assume when developing a standard direct material cost (and calculating variances) that this cost behaves as a variable cost. For example, it is reasonable to expect that the material cost for 2,000 items will be twice the cost of 1,000 of the same item. This assumption allows us to work out the standard cost for individual units, so that we can then multiply it by the quantity produced. It also explains why the absorption and marginal versions of these standards are effectively the same.

The standard direct material cost for a product comprises two elements:

• the amount of the material, and

• the cost of the material.

For example, a batch of 1,000 rubber washers may require 3 kilos of rubber, which costs £1.00 per kilo. If this data were accepted as the standard figures, then the standard direct material cost for each batch of washers would clearly be 3 kilos x £1.00 = £3.00.

The fact that the data needed to calculate a standard direct material cost is based on two elements determines:

• where the information will come from, and

• how the variances can be calculated.

standard direct labour costs

The composition of the standard direct labour cost for a cost unit is very similar to the material cost. It is also based on the implied assumption that this type of cost is variable, and so twice as many products will cost about twice as much. The standard direct labour cost for a product also consists of two elements:

• the amount of labour time to be used, and

• the labour cost per unit of time (the labour rate).

Using our example of a batch of rubber washers, if the standard direct labour time needed to manufacture them was 2 hours, and the standard labour cost was £9 per hour, then the standard direct labour cost would obviously be £18 per batch. Assuming there were no other direct costs, the total standard direct cost would be:

	£
Materials	3.00
Labour	18.00
	21.00 for one batch of washers

You will be familiar with this idea, and probably find the concept quite elementary, but it is a vital foundation for further understanding.

fixed overheads

We will look in detail at how fixed overheads can be dealt with in the next chapter. At this point we will show how fixed overheads could be incorporated into standard costs quite simply, by dividing the total fixed overheads by the expected number of units to be produced. The following case study shows how a 'standard cost card' could be completed using data for direct materials, direct labour and fixed overheads to arrive at the total standard cost for one unit of output.

Case Study

STANDARD LIMITED:
COMPLETING A STANDARD COST CARD

The following information has been calculated for the production of one unit of a product called 'Alpha'.

- Each unit will require 8 kilograms of direct material at a cost of £6.80 per kilogram.

- Each unit will require 3 hours of direct labour at a total cost of £33.

- Fixed overheads total £225,000, and the estimated output will be 7,500 units of Alpha.

required

Complete the standard cost card shown below. Note that the column headed 'cost per unit' refers to units of input (e.g. for materials it refers to cost per kilogram).

1 Unit of Alpha	Quantity	Cost per unit (£)	Total Cost (£)
Direct material	8	6·80	54.40
Direct labour	3	11·0	33·0
Fixed overheads	1	30	30
Total			117·40

solution

1 Unit of Alpha	Quantity	Cost per unit (£)	Total Cost (£)
Direct material	8	6.80	54.40
Direct labour	3	11.00	33.00
Fixed overheads	1	30.00	30.00
Total			117.40

Note that:

- The hourly rate for direct labour is calculated by dividing the total labour cost by the number of hours.
- The fixed overhead per unit of Alpha is calculated by dividing the total overheads by the estimated output in units of Alpha.

SOURCES OF INFORMATION FOR STANDARD SETTING

Now we are familiar with the elements that make up a direct cost standard, we can go on to look at the information sources for each of those elements. The way an organisation chooses to set standards will have an impact on how reliable and accurate they are, and for how long they can remain useful. There will be a range of values that could be used for each figure, and the organisation should have a policy that will guide managers in setting standards, and this will also determine how any variances are ultimately interpreted. This idea is considered further in Chapter 4.

The following examples of sources of information should not be learnt as lists. You are advised to think about each one so that you can see how it could be useful. In this way you can then suggest suitable information sources for a situation in a given case study.

the amount of material

The main information sources could be:

- product specifications (the 'recipe' for the product being made)
- technical data from the material supplier (eg recommended usage)
- historical data on quantities used in the past
- observation of manufacture

Standard setting may also need to take into account:

- estimates of wastage

- quality of material

- production equipment and machinery available, and its performance

the cost of material

The information sources could include:

- data from suppliers

- records of previous prices paid

- anticipated cost inflation (measured by general or specific price indices)

- anticipated demand for scarce supplies

- production schedules and bulk buying policy (in conjunction with availability of bulk discounts)

- seasonality of prices

- anticipated currency exchange rates

the amount of labour time

Here information sources could include:

- data on previous output and efficiency levels

- results of formal observations (work study, or 'time & motion' study)

- anticipated changes in working practices or productivity levels

- the level of training of employees to be used

the labour cost per unit of labour time

Possible sources of data include:

- current pay rates

- anticipated pay rises

- the expected effects of bonus schemes

To establish an appropriate rate it may also be necessary to take into account:

- equivalent pay rates of other employers in the locality

- changes in legislation (eg minimum wage rates)

- general or industry-specific wage cost indices

- grade of labour (or sub contractors) to be used

THE CALCULATION OF DIRECT COST VARIANCES

One of the most important uses of standard costing is the calculation and interpretation of the differences between the standard costs of the actual production and the actual costs incurred. These differences are called 'variances', and are described as adverse (abbreviated to 'A') when the actual position is worse than expected, or favourable (abbreviated to 'F') when the actual position is better than expected.

There are four direct cost sub-variances that we need to be able to calculate; two relating to materials and two to labour, as well as a total material variance and a total labour variance.

We will examine the direct cost variances in this chapter, and the fixed overhead variances in Chapter 3.

DIRECT MATERIAL VARIANCES

Direct material variances consist of a total direct material variance that can be divided into two sub-variances.

total direct material variance

The total direct material variance =

the standard cost of materials for the actual production level	*minus*	the actual cost of materials for the actual production level

So it is simply measuring the difference between what the materials were expected to cost for the actual production level and what the materials did cost. Notice that we are using the **actual production level** in both cases; this is quite logical and also means that we are making a valid comparison by comparing 'like with like'.

The two sub-variances that relate to the cost of materials are:

- the direct material **price** variance
- the direct material **usage** variance

The **price** variance measures how much of the difference between the expected and actual cost of materials is due to paying a **price** for materials that is different to the standard.

The direct material **usage** variance measures how much of the difference between the expected and actual cost of materials is due to **using a different quantity** of materials.

Together these two variances will account for the whole difference between the expected and actual cost of the materials.

direct material price variance

The direct material price variance =

the standard cost of the actual quantity of material used	*minus*	the actual cost of the actual quantity of material used

We are making a comparison between two values – the standard cost of the actual materials and the actual cost. Notice that both figures relate to the **actual materials used**, so that we are comparing two costs that both relate to the same actual quantity.

If the actual cost is less than the standard then the variance will be favourable; if it is more, the variance will be adverse.

If you carry out the calculation as outlined above, then a positive answer will be favourable and a negative one adverse.

direct material usage variance

The direct material usage variance =

the standard quantity of material for actual production at standard price	*minus*	the actual quantity of material used at standard price

With this usage variance we are also making a comparison between two values. This time the comparison is based on two quantities – the standard quantity for the actual production and the actual quantity used. These quantities are turned into values by costing them both at **standard price.**

remembering how to calculate direct variances

The key to calculating the variances accurately is remembering the basis of the formulas. One method that may help is the mnemonic 'PAUS', based on:

Price variances are based on
Actual quantities, but
Usage variances are based on
Standard prices.

One explanation why the variances are calculated in this way is that purchases are sometimes converted to standard price (and a price variance calculated) when the materials are bought. This price variance would relate to the actual materials bought. The materials in inventory (stock) would then be valued at standard price, and the usage variance would be calculated based on the amounts issued to production at standard price.

The two material sub-variances that we have looked at will account for the whole of any difference between the standard cost of the material used for the actual production level and the actual cost - the total direct material variance that was explained earlier. This provides a useful check that our calculations appear to be correct.

We will now demonstrate in a Case Study how the variances that we have looked at so far can be calculated in practice.

Case
Study

THE PINE DOOR COMPANY:
DIRECT MATERIAL VARIANCES

The Pine Door Company makes cottage doors from reclaimed pine. The company uses standard costing to plan and control its costs. The standard direct material cost for a door is as follows:

2.5 square metres of pine at £10.00 per square metre = £25 per door.

During the month of August, the company made 35 doors. The actual costs incurred were:

86 square metres of pine, costing £950 in total.

required

• Calculate the standard material cost of the August production of 35 doors.

• Calculate:
  - the total direct material variance
  - the direct material price variance
  - the direct material usage variance

- Check that, between them, the two sub-variances account for the total direct material variance.

- Explain what each of the variances tells us.

solution

The standard material cost of the 35 doors made in August is:

£25 per door x 35 doors = £875.

Notice that this amount is less than the actual cost of material.

The total direct material variance =

the standard cost of materials for the actual production level	*minus*	the actual cost of materials for the actual production level

£875 (calculated above) - £950 (from the data provided)

= £75 Adverse

This represents the difference between the standard cost of materials for 35 doors and the actual cost. It is adverse because the actual cost was greater (which is 'bad news').

The two sub-variances which will now be calculated should show how much is due to **prices** and how much is due to the **quantity** used.

The direct material price variance =

the standard cost of the actual quantity of material used	*minus*	the actual cost of the actual quantity of material used

86 square metres of pine were actually used, so the standard and the actual costs of this quantity of material can be compared as follows:

(86 sq metres x £10 per sq metre) - £950

£860 - £950 = £90 Adverse

The variance is adverse because the actual cost was more than the expected (standard) cost. This is confirmed by a negative numerical answer.

The direct material usage variance =

the standard quantity of material for actual production at standard price	*minus*	the actual quantity of material used at standard price

It was expected that 2.5 square metres of pine would be used for each of the 35 doors that were made. This gives a standard quantity of 87.5 sq metres for production. This standard quantity of 87.5 sq metres and the actual quantity of 86 square metres at the standard price of £10 per square metre are compared to calculate the variance.

(87.5 sq metres x £10) – (86 sq metres x £10)

£875 - £860 = £15 Favourable

Here the variance is favourable because less material was used than the standard quantity. This is confirmed by the fact that the numerical answer works out to a positive figure.

The calculation above could also be shown as:

£10 x (87.5 sq metres – 86 sq metres)

checking the overall position

Material price variance	£90 Adverse
Material usage variance	£15 Favourable
Total material cost variance	£75 Adverse

This is a useful check – although it is not a guarantee that the calculations are correct.

what the variances tell us

The material price variance shows that a higher price than standard was paid for the pine that was used, and this cost £90 more than expected. Against that cost can be set the fact that slightly less pine was used than allowed for, and this saved £15. Overall, the material for the 35 doors that we made cost £75 more than planned.

DIRECT LABOUR VARIANCES

The approach for calculating direct labour variances is very similar to direct material variances.

Direct labour variances consist of a total direct labour variance that can be divided into sub-variances.

total direct labour variance

The total direct labour variance =

the standard cost of labour for the actual production level	*minus*	the actual cost of labour for the actual production level

It is measuring the difference between what labour was expected to cost for the actual production level and what labour actually cost. Notice that again we are using the **actual production level** in both cases.

The two most important sub-variances that relate to the cost of labour are:

- the **direct labour rate variance**
- the **direct labour efficiency variance**

The direct labour rate variance measures the labour cost difference due to the rate paid, and the direct labour efficiency variance measures the cost difference due to the amount of labour time used. The concept of labour 'rate' is similar to material 'price', and labour 'efficiency' is similar to material 'usage', as explained below. This makes remembering the calculation method and interpreting the variances much easier.

direct labour rate variance

The direct labour rate variance =

the standard cost of the actual labour hours used	*minus*	the actual cost of the actual labour hours used

We are again making a comparison between two values – the standard cost of the actual labour hours and the actual cost. Just like the material price variance, the labour rate variance is comparing two figures that both relate to an actual quantity – here the actual quantity is the **actual number of labour hours**.

direct labour efficiency variance

The direct labour efficiency variance =

standard labour hours for actual production at standard rate	*minus*	actual labour hours used at standard rate

This also has a strong resemblance to the material usage variance; we are simply considering the quantity of labour hours instead of the quantity of material.

Just like the material usage variance, we are using a standard figure to value these two quantities – this time it is the standard labour rate that is used. Although this variance is all about comparison of two amounts of time, we must remember to convert the answer into an amount of money by valuing the hours at the standard rate.

Provided we can remember the similarity of the labour variances to the material ones, there is probably no need to use any other memory aid. The direct labour variances must add up to the total difference in labour cost between standard and actual – the total direct labour variance.

Case Study

THE PINE DOOR COMPANY: DIRECT LABOUR VARIANCES

The Pine Door Company (see page 61) makes cottage doors from reclaimed pine. The company uses standard costing to plan and control its costs. The standard direct labour cost for a door is as follows:

> 6 hours direct labour at £7.00 per hour = £42 per door.

During the month of August, the company made 35 doors. The actual costs incurred were:

> 200 hours direct labour costing £1,430 in total.

required

- Calculate the standard labour cost for the August production of 35 doors.

- Calculate

    - the total direct labour variance

    - the direct labour rate variance

    - the direct labour efficiency variance

- Check that, between them, the two sub-variances account for the total direct labour variance.

- Explain what each of the variances tells us.

solution

The standard labour cost of the 35 doors made in August is:

> £42 per door x 35 doors = £1,470

Notice that this amount is more than the actual cost of labour given as £1,430.

total direct labour variance =

| the standard cost of labour for the actual production level | *minus* | the actual cost of labour for the actual production level |

£1,470 (calculated above) − £1,430 (from the data provided)

= £40 Favourable

The two sub-variances which will now be calculated should show how much is due to **rate** and how much is due to the **amount of time** used.

direct labour rate variance =

| the standard cost of the actual labour hours used | *minus* | the actual cost of the actual labour hours used |

200 direct labour hours were actually used in August, so this is the basis of our comparison of costs for this variance.

(200 direct labour hours x £7) − £1,430 =

£1,400 − £1,430 = £30 Adverse

The numerical answer is negative because the actual cost of the direct labour hours used is greater than the standard cost of the same number of hours. This means that the hourly rate paid is greater than the standard hourly rate. This variance is therefore adverse.

direct labour efficiency variance =

| standard labour hours for actual production at standard rate | *minus* | the actual labour hours used at standard rate |

The standard labour time to make each of the 35 doors is 6 hours. This gives standard labour time of 210 hours for production.

We will value both the standard hours and the actual 200 hours used at the standard rate of £7 per hour to calculate the variance.

(210 hours x £7) − (200 hours x £7)

£1,470 - £1,400 = £70 Favourable

Here the variance is favourable because we actually spent less time making the doors than the standard time – the labour force have been efficient. This is confirmed by the fact that the numerical answer works out to a positive figure.

The calculation above could also be shown as:

£7 x (210 hours – 200 hours)

checking the overall position

Labour rate variance	£30 Adverse
Labour efficiency variance	£70 Favourable
Total labour variance	£40 Favourable

what each variance tells us

The labour rate variance shows that (on average) a little more was spent than the standard labour rate, and this cost an extra £30. However £70 was saved because the work was carried out more quickly than the standard time. Overall the labour cost for the 35 doors that were made was £40 less than planned.

idle time variance

We have seen that the total direct labour variance can be divided into two sub-variances – the direct labour rate variance and the direct labour efficiency variance. The direct labour efficiency variance values (at standard rate) the difference in time taken for the production between standard and actual.

In some circumstances this measurement of 'efficiency' may be considered misleading if it includes time where the labour force was 'idle' – being paid but not actually working on production. This could arise for a variety of reasons, for example a machine breakdown, and may not be within the control of the employees.

If this is the situation, and the amount of idle time is known, the direct labour efficiency variance can be divided into two further sub-variances. These are the variance related to the idle time, and the remainder of the direct labour efficiency variance.

The direct labour variance relating to idle time is (not surprisingly) known as the **direct labour idle time variance**.

The direct labour idle time variance =

actual **productive** labour hours used at standard rate	*minus*	**total** actual labour hours used at standard rate

The difference between 'productive' labour hours and total labour hours is equal to idle time, so a simpler way of expressing the idle time variance is:

> actual idle time
> at standard rate

This variance will always be adverse (or zero), since the total actual hours will never be less than the productive hours. If the productive hours are the same as the total actual hours then there is no idle time and the idle time variance will be zero.

Let us now return to the earlier Case Study to demonstrate how this variance can be calculated.

Case Study

THE PINE DOOR COMPANY: IDLE TIME VARIANCE

The Pine Door Company (see pages 61 and 65) makes cottage doors from reclaimed pine. The company uses standard costing to plan and control its costs. The standard labour cost for a door is as follows:

> 6 hours direct labour at £7.00 per hour = £42 per door.

During the month of August the company made 35 doors. The actual labour costs incurred were:

> 200 hours direct labour costing £1,430 in total.

The direct labour efficiency variance has already been calculated as £70 favourable.

Information just obtained reveals that in August there were 8 labour hours when the labour force were idle waiting for more material, leaving 192 productive hours.

required

- Calculate the direct labour idle time variance.

solution

- Calculation of variances

direct labour idle time variance =

actual **productive** labour hours used at standard rate	*minus*	**total** actual labour hours used at standard rate

(192 hours x £7.00) – (200 hours x £7.00) =

£1,344 - £1,400 = £56 Adverse

This is the same as:

actual idle time at standard rate

8 hours x £7.00 = £56 Adverse

Now that we have seen how to calculate and explain the direct cost variances, we can look at an alternative type of treatment where the data is provided in a slightly different form. In the Case Study on the page after next we will also work out both the direct material and the direct labour variances and sub-variances. First, however, we will look at the reconciliation of actual and standard cost in a reconciliation statement.

USING VARIANCES TO RECONCILE ACTUAL WITH STANDARD COSTS

reconciliation statements

It is important that we can show how variances account for all the cost differences between the standard cost of the production and the actual cost. We can do this by using a reconciliation statement. This is sometimes known as an 'operating statement'. Note that we must compare like with like and use the data for the standard cost of the actual production to compare with the actual cost. The actual cost will of course also relate to the actual production. The reconciliation statement can start with either the standard or the actual cost, and will arrive, via the variances at the other figure. We are accounting for the differences, in the same way that a bank reconciliation statement accounts for the differences between the cash book balance and the bank account balance.

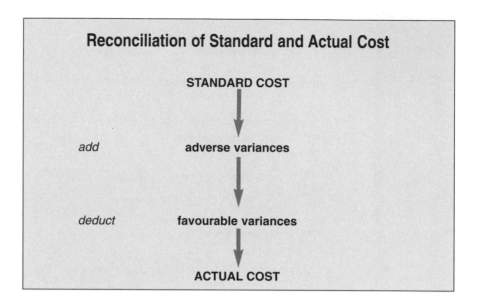

If we start the statement with the standard cost of the production, then each adverse variance will be added to this amount, since the actual cost we are working towards will be higher. Any favourable variances will be deducted since this accounts for a lower actual amount. Since a reconciliation only takes a short time to prepare, it is often worth producing since it will show if any variances are inaccurate.

Where summary variances and sub-variances have been calculated (for example total direct material variance and direct material price and usage variances), do not add the summary variance as well as the others into the statement. If you did you would be counting its value twice. The same applies to the labour efficiency variance when an idle time variance has also been calculated.

Remember that, like agreement of a trial balance, a satisfactory variance reconciliation is not a guarantee that the variances are correct!

In this chapter we are only examining direct cost variances, so our reconciliation will be just based on that part of the cost. We will see later how indirect costs can be incorporated into a full reconciliation.

The following case study demonstrates how to prepare a statement that reconciles the standard direct cost of production with the actual cost. It also illustrates how standard cost information (for one unit of output) can be derived from budget information based on a specific output level. This is a useful technique which is frequently tested.

Case Study

1,850

1,600

DIRECT VARIANCES:
ORME PRODUCTION COMPANY

The Orme Production Company has the following direct cost results for its production of the Orme for the month of September:

	Budget	Actual
Production Level (Ormes)	1,500	1,800
Material Quantity (kilos)	6,000	7,100
Material Cost	£45,000	£54,770
Direct Labour Hours	2,250	2,850
Labour Cost	£15,750	£19,400

required

Calculate the two direct material sub-variances and the two main direct labour sub-variances for the September production of 1,800 Ormes. Produce a statement reconciling the standard direct cost of production with the actual direct cost of production.

solution

1. Direct Material Variances

The first stage is to work out the standards for one Orme. We will do this by using the budget data, since the budget would originally have been built up using standard data.

Standard Material Quantity per Orme 6,000 kilos ÷ 1,500 Ormes   =   4 kilos

Standard Price of Material per Kilo   £45,000 ÷ 6,000 kilos   =   £7.50

We can then work out the standards for the actual production level. Note that we do not use the budgeted production level for calculating direct variances - they are always calculated using the actual production level.

We will first work out some standard data that we will find useful later on:

Standard Material Quantity
for actual production level   4 kilos x 1,800 Ormes   = 7,200 kilos

Standard Material Cost
for actual production level   7,200 kilos x £7.50   = £54,000

The variances can now be calculated:

direct material price variance =

the standard cost of the actual quantity of material used	minus	the actual cost of the actual quantity of material used

(7,100 kilos x £7.50) – £54,770

£53,250 – £54,770 = £1,520 Adverse

direct material usage variance =

The standard quantity of material for actual production at standard price	minus	the actual quantity of material used at standard price

(7,200 kilos x £7.50 per kilo) – (7,100 kilos x £7.50 per kilo)

£54,000 - £53,250 = £750 Favourable

Notice that the two material variances that we have calculated – the material price variance of £1,520 (adverse) and the material usage variance of £750 (favourable) equal £770 adverse. This accounts for the difference between the standard material cost of £54,000 and the actual cost of £54,770 (the total direct material variance).

2. Direct Labour Variances

The approach here will be almost identical to the calculation of the material variances as carried out earlier. The following calculations are therefore shown with little comment. Make sure that you can see the similarity to the earlier workings, and check that you can see where the figures come from and why they are used.

Standard Labour Hours per Orme	2,250 hours ÷ 1,500 Ormes	= 1.5 hours
Standard Labour Rate per hour	£15,750 ÷ 2,250 hours	= £7.00
Standard Labour Hours for Actual Production Level	1.5 hours x 1,800 Ormes	= 2,700 hours
Standard Labour Cost for Actual Production Level	2,700 hours x £7.00	= £18,900

direct labour rate variance =

the standard cost of the actual labour hours used	minus	the actual cost of the actual labour hours used

(2,850 hours @ £7.00) – £19,400

£19,950 – £19,400 = £550 Favourable

direct labour efficiency variance =

standard labour hours for actual production at standard rate	minus	the actual labour hours used at standard rate

(2,700 hours x £7) – (2,850 hours x £7)

£18,900 - £19,950   = £1,050 Adverse

Again we can see that the two labour variances that we have calculated (£550 favourable and £1,050 adverse) account for the difference between the standard labour cost of £18,900 and the actual cost of £19,400 (the total direct labour variance).

The full reconciliation of the direct costs can now be prepared.

Direct Cost Reconciliation Statement for September: Production of 1,800 Ormes	
	£
Standard Direct Cost of Production (£54,000 + £18,900)	72,900
Add adverse direct material price variance	1,520
Less favourable direct material usage variance	(750)
Less favourable direct labour rate variance	(550)
Add adverse direct labour efficiency variance	1,050
Actual Cost of Production (£54,770 + £19,400)	74,170

MATERIAL PRICE VARIANCES USING BOUGHT QUANTITIES

In our studies so far we have calculated the material price variance based on the actual quantity of material used to make the units. This is quite logical, and means that the cost reconciliation that we have just demonstrated will always agree.

An alternative approach is to calculate a material price variance as soon as the materials are purchased – when they are brought into the stores. Using this method the material price variance would be calculated using the quantity of materials bought. This may not be the same quantity that is subsequently used.

The calculation of the material price variance using this approach is no more difficult than the calculation that was learnt earlier. Instead of the quantity of materials used, we insert the quantity of materials bought.

The direct material price variance becomes:

the standard cost of the actual quantity of materials **bought**	*minus*	the actual cost of the actual quantity of materials **bought**

If this approach is used it means that materials can be converted to standard price when they are purchased (and the variance calculated at that point). The materials will then be held in inventory and issued to production at standard price. This means that the only material variance that is based on the production level is the direct material usage variance. Some businesses prefer to organise their systems in this way.

This approach does, however, have some important implications (unless the quantities purchased and used were identical):

- a total direct material variance would not normally be calculated since the actual cost of materials used would not be available, and
- a full cost reconciliation would not normally be produced

Any task should make it clear which approach is to be taken. However if the quantities purchased are the same as those used then either approach will, of course, produce the same result.

Case Study

THE PINE DOOR COMPANY: ALTERNATIVE MATERIAL PRICE VARIANCE

The Pine Door Company (see earlier pages) uses standard costing. The manager is interested to see how changing to a system where the material price variance was calculated based on the materials bought would impact on the material price variance calculation.

The standard direct material cost for one door is as follows:

    2.5 square metres of pine at £10 per square metre = £25 per door

During the month of August, the company made 35 doors.

There was no pine held in inventory at the start of August. The company then purchased 110 square metres of pine, costing £1,200 in total, and used 86 square metres of this to manufacture the 35 doors.

required

- calculate the direct material price variance, based on the pine that was purchased

- explain how the pine that was issued to production would be valued under this system, and how the pine that remains in inventory at the end of August would be valued

solution

The direct material price variance (based on purchases) =

the standard cost of the actual quantity of materials **bought**	minus	the actual cost of the actual quantity of materials **bought**

110 square metres x £10   - £1,200

£1,100 - £1,200   = £100 Adverse

Note that this is a different calculation to the one carried out earlier in the chapter.

The pine issued to the production area would be valued at the standard cost of £10 per square metre. This would value the 86 square metres used in manufacture at £860. This value would then be used to calculate the direct material usage (as it was in the earlier case study).

The pine remaining in inventory at the end of August would also be valued at the standard cost of £10 per square metre. The pine inventory of 110 – 86 = 24 square metres would be valued at 24 x £10 = £240.

THE MAIN CAUSES OF VARIANCES

It is important that we can not only calculate variances accurately, but also understand what has caused the individual variances.

This interpretation of variances is carried out by:

* identifying the possible range of causes for each variance, and then

* investigating the situation to establish the cause in the particular circumstances.

We will now look at the possible causes of the variances that we have studied so far.

In Chapter 4 we will examine the interpretation of variances in more detail.

If you are familiar with the sources of data for creating variances, and what each variance means, it should not be necessary to learn lists of possible causes of variances. Instead it should be possible to logically think your way through each situation to see its impact on variances. You may be given a scenario and asked to suggest the possible causes of variances. It is far better to use the facts given to you about the situation to develop a reasoned commentary, than to remember an 'all purpose' list of causes and simply regurgitate it.

Some situations may give rise to more than one variance. For example purchasing cheaper material of lower quality could cause a favourable price variance but an adverse usage variance if there was higher wastage. This is often referred to as the interdependence of variances. It can result in unfair praise or blame if different managers are responsible for each variance.

Unfair comparisons may also arise from the use of an unrealistic or out of date standard.

The table below gives examples of possible causes of variances. Read it carefully, and ensure that you can appreciate the logic of including each item, and its effect.

There may be situations where you can envisage the cause creating further variances, since the table is not intended to be exhaustive.

'A' or 'F' refers to whether adverse or favourable variances may result.

DIRECT VARIANCE: Possible Cause	Material Price	Material Usage	Labour Rate	Labour Efficiency	Labour Idle Time
Poorly set standard	A or F	A or F	A or F	A or F	A
Different material supplier	A or F				
Different material quality	A or F	A or F		A or F	
Different currency exchange rate	A or F				
Poor training		A		A	
Higher grade staff		F	A	F	
Unexpected pay increase			A		
High general inflation	A		A		
Improved production machinery		F		F	
Unexpected bulk discounts	F				
Low bonus payments			F	A	
Machine breakdowns		A		A	A

- Standard costing was developed in the manufacturing industry as a method of predicting the cost of products. When comparing actual costs with the expected (standard) costs, it enables variances to be calculated that help explain differences in the costs. There are various other benefits from setting up and using a standard costing system.

- Standard costs can be used based on a traditional absorption costing system, or on a marginal costing system. The main difference arises in the treatment of fixed overhead variances: direct cost variances are calculated in the same way under both types of costing. The direct cost variances for materials and labour can be divided into variances based on the cost per unit of the resource (Price or Rate variances) and the quantity of resource used (Usage and Efficiency variances). If the workforce are paid but not actually working on production, then an idle time variance can also be calculated.

- Information for setting standards can be derived from inside and outside the organisation. This information includes formal and informal historical data and technical specifications, and can be general or specific.

- Direct cost variances are calculated according to rules that help ensure uniformity. The variances can be used to reconcile the standard cost for the production with the actual costs.

- There can be many causes of variances, some influencing just one variance, while others affect several. The accurate calculation of a variance does not provide information on the cause itself, but the causes can often be deduced by examining the factors surrounding the situation.

standard costing	a formal method for predetermining the cost of cost units or products
variance analysis	the comparison of actual costs with standard costs and the calculation of variances which account for differences in the costs
marginal costing	a technique that values cost units based on variable costs only. Fixed costs are considered to relate only to the reporting period of time

absorption costing	a technique that values cost units based on a suitable part of all the costs of production, whether fixed or variable in behaviour
total direct material variance	the difference between the standard material cost for the actual production and the actual material cost
direct material price variance	the part of the total direct material variance due to differing material prices. It is based on the difference between standard and actual prices for the actual quantity of material used (or bought)
direct material usage variance	the part of the total direct material variance due to differing quantities of material used. It is based on the difference between the standard quantity of material for the actual production, and the actual quantity of material used, valued at standard price
total direct labour variance	the difference between the standard labour cost for the actual production and the actual labour cost
direct labour rate variance	the part of the total direct labour variance due to differing labour rates. It is based on the difference between the actual labour hours at standard rate and the actual labour cost
direct labour efficiency variance	the part of the total direct labour variance due to differing time being spent. It is based on the difference between the standard labour time for the actual production, and the actual labour time used, valued at standard rate
direct labour idle time variance	the part of the direct labour efficiency variance that is caused by idle time. It is calculated as idle time valued at standard rate
cost reconciliation statement	a statement reconciling the standard cost of the actual production with the actual cost by using relevant variances. This is also known as an operating statement

Activities

2.1   The glazing department of the Complete Window Company uses standard costs to monitor and control its output. The standard data for glazing one window are:

- 2 square metres glass at £25 per square metre
- 0.5 hours labour at £8.00 per hour

During one week in May, the department glazed 300 windows, with actual costs as follows:

- 610 square metres of glass, costing £15,400
- 145 labour hours, costing £1,220

Required

Calculate the following variances for the glazing department:

(a)   Direct material price variance

(b)   Direct material usage variance

(c)   Direct labour rate variance

(d)   Direct labour efficiency variance

2.2   A company purchases 5,000 kilograms of material at a cost of £53,000. The standard cost of material per kilogram is £10.

The material price variance is:

(a)   £0.60 A

(b)   £3,000 F

(c)   £3,000 A

(d)   £6.00 A

2.3   A company used 6,000 kilograms of material to produce 10,000 units. The budgeted production was 12,000 units, and the standard material for this output level was 6,600 kilograms at £2 per kilogram.

The material usage variance is:

(a)   500 kilograms

(b)   £1,200

(c)   600 kilograms

(d)   £1,000

State whether the variance is adverse or favourable.

2.4   A company plans to produce 20,000 units, using 15,000 direct labour hours. The actual production is 18,000 units. The standard cost of labour is £11.00 per hour.

The standard cost of labour for the actual production is:

(a)   £148,500

(b)   £165,000

(c)   £264,000

(d)   £183,333

2.5 The standard labour time to make one unit is 45 minutes. The standard labour rate is £10 per hour. Production was 5,000 units. Total labour time was 4,000 hours, of which 150 hours was idle time.

Required

Calculate the
- Labour efficiency variance
- Labour idle time variance

2.6 Your colleague has accurately produced the following direct cost variances for Week 23.

Direct Material Price Variance	£ 1,585 A
Direct Material Usage Variance	£993 F
Direct Labour Rate Variance	£ 2,460 F
Direct Labour Efficiency Variance	£ 1,051 F

The standard cost of one unit is £95.40, and the company produced 1,060 units in week 23.

Required

Calculate the total actual direct costs for the company for week 23.

2.7 Grimley Limited has the following budgeted and actual direct cost and production data for the month of August.

	Budget	Budget	Actual	Actual
Production Units		20,000		19,000
		£		£
Direct Materials	40,000 kg	300,000	37,000 kg	278,000
Direct Labour	10,000 hrs	60,000	9,800 hrs	58,600
Total Costs		360,000		336,600

Required

- Calculate the data for a standard cost card based on one unit.
- Calculate the relevant direct cost variances and use them to reconcile the standard cost for the actual production level with the actual costs.

2.8 The following comments were made by an inexperienced trainee accounting technician:

Required

State which of the comments are valid, and which are false.

(a) The likelihood of obtaining bulk discounts cannot be relevant when setting direct material price standards.

(b) Work study is often used to assist in setting times for direct labour standards.

(c) The interdependence of variances should be considered when examining the causes for variances.

(d) Material price standards must always be amended when a different supplier is used.

(e) Future production schedules can be used to assist in setting material price standards by helping to gauge the availability of quantity discounts.

(f) Two of the main reasons for using standard costing are to improve planning and control.

(g) Standard costing can be used in conjunction with responsibility accounting. Using this technique each manager would be expected to control the variances occurring in his/her area of responsibility.

(h) Interpretation of variances can help point to the reasons that costs are not in line with the plans.

(i) The inclusion of overtime premium rates when setting direct labour rate standards would depend on the company policy, since many organisations consider that such costs are indirect.

(j) Proposed bonus schemes should be taken into account when setting labour rate standards.

(k) Reconciling standard cost with actual cost is difficult because when variances are a mixture of adverse and favourable the statement may not agree.

(l) If a reconciliation of standard cost for the actual production level with the actual cost agrees this guarantees that all the variances are correct.

2.9 Marge Products Ltd uses marginal costing and has the following budgeted and actual variable cost and production data for the month of August.

	Budget	Budget	Actual	Actual
Production Units		30,000		32,000
		£		£
Variable Materials	3,000 kg	75,000	3,100 kg	81,000
Variable Labour	15,000 hrs	75,000	15,900 hrs	77,900
Total Variable Costs		150,000		158,900

Required

- Calculate the standard cost data for one unit of production.

- Calculate the relevant variable cost variances and use them to reconcile the standard marginal cost for the actual production level with the actual marginal costs.

2.10 Quango Limited has set its direct standard costs for one unit of its product, the quango as follows:

Direct Materials: 96 kg @ £9.45 per kilo.

Direct Labour: 5 hours 6 minutes @ £6.30 per hour.

During week 13 the company produced 700 units of quango, and incurred direct costs as follows:

Direct Materials: 71.5 tonnes were used, costing a total of £678,700

Direct Labour: 3,850 hours were worked, costing a total of £24,220

Note: there are 1,000 kilos in a tonne.

Required

Calculate the relevant direct cost variances and use them to reconcile the standard cost for the actual production level with the actual costs.

3 Standard costing – fixed overheads

this chapter covers...

In this chapter we will continue with our examination of standard costing, and look in detail at fixed overheads.

We will start by outlining why fixed overheads and their variances need a different approach to direct costs. The approach that is taken also depends on whether we are going to use marginal costing (and treat fixed costs as relating to a period of time), or use absorption costing (and treat fixed overheads as part of the product cost).

We will then learn how to calculate fixed overhead variances and to understand how they are derived. The fixed overhead variances that we will examine are:

- expenditure variance
- volume variance
- capacity variance
- efficiency variance

We will also make sure that we can deal with situations where overheads need to be apportioned before variances can be calculated.

Next we will see how we can interpret the variances that we have calculated and examine possible causes.

We will complete the chapter by learning how our knowledge can be applied to the service sector and also by reminding ourselves about the significance of selecting an appropriate absorption base.

FIXED OVERHEADS

the difference between variable and fixed costs

In the last chapter we examined the direct costs of materials and labour. We looked at how standard costing could be used to predict this part of a product's cost and how variances could be calculated to help analyse any differences between the standard cost and the actual cost. Since direct costs will often rise in proportion to the output of products there is logic in calculating a standard for the direct cost for one unit of production, and expecting it to remain the same when multiplied by the number of items produced. For example, it would seem fair to expect that the direct material for 2,000 widgets would cost about 2,000 times more than that for one widget.

You can assume that direct costs will behave in the same way as variable costs, ie they will change in line with the level of activity (the number of products produced). They are therefore different from fixed costs:

Variable Costs Costs where the total amount varies in proportion to the activity level when the activity level changes.

Fixed Costs Costs that do not normally change when the level of activity changes.

fixed costs: absorption or marginal costing?

When fixed costs are involved in costing products there are two traditional schools of thought about how they should be dealt with.

Absorption costing attempts to incorporate fixed costs into the cost of the product by absorbing a suitable part of the expected fixed cost into each unit produced.

Marginal costing views fixed costs as time-based rather than product based, and therefore does not attempt to incorporate these costs into each unit produced. Instead it costs each unit based on only the variable costs, and deals with the fixed costs in the income statement (profit and loss account) for the appropriate reporting period.

using absorption costing for fixed costs

One advantage that standard absorption costing can claim is that the standard cost for a product will be a 'full' cost, and incorporate a portion of all the costs of production. Therefore, provided the actual production level is close to the projected level, and all cost estimates are reasonably accurate, the standard cost of the product will be close to the actual full cost. However, the standard will give an inaccurate forecast of product cost:

- if the costs are not as expected, and/or
- if the production volume is not in line with expectations

For this reason the fixed overhead variances produced under standard absorption costing need to take account of:

- overhead costs
- production volumes

using marginal costing for fixed costs

With marginal costing, by contrast, the volume of production will not affect the standard marginal cost of a product, because the only costs contained in the standard are variable costs – fixed costs are excluded. As fixed costs are dealt with by comparing the expected fixed cost for the period with the actual fixed cost, the only fixed overhead variance that needs to be calculated under marginal standard costing is simply the difference between these two figures.

We will now look in detail at the treatment of fixed overhead variances using marginal costing.

FIXED OVERHEAD VARIANCES – MARGINAL COSTING

fixed overhead expenditure variance

Under standard marginal costing the only fixed overhead variance is usually called the **fixed overhead expenditure variance**. It is very simple to calculate, as follows:

Budgeted Fixed Overhead for period	*minus*	Actual Fixed Overhead for period

The variance would therefore be calculated for the week, month, quarter or other reporting period, and the number of items produced would not form part of the calculation.

If the actual cost was **lower** than the budgeted amount the variance would be **favourable**, and if it was **higher**, it would be considered **adverse**. The variance could be used as part of a reconciliation between actual and standard costs for the production in a period of time.

Note – throughout this and later case studies in this chapter, 'A' and 'F' have been used to denote **A**dverse and **F**avourable variances respectively.

Case Study

WENSHAM WHEELBARROWS:
FIXED OVERHEAD VARIANCES – MARGINAL COSTING

Wensham Wheelbarrows manufactures a single product – the 'Wensham' wheelbarrow. The company had the following results for their third quarter. The company used standard marginal costing. Both direct materials and direct labour are considered to behave as variable costs.

	Budgeted	Actual
Number of Units	10,000	12,000
Direct Materials	£ 50,000	£ 65,000
Direct Labour	£ 80,000	£ 94,000
Fixed Overheads	£ 75,000	£ 81,000
Total Costs	£205,000	£240,000

The direct variances have already been calculated (based on information not shown) as follows:

Direct material price variance	£6,000 A
Direct material usage variance	£1,000 F
Direct labour rate variance	£4,000 F
Direct labour efficiency variance	£2,000 A

required

1 Calculate the fixed overhead expenditure variance.
2 Calculate the standard cost of the actual production.
3 Reconcile the standard cost of the actual production with the actual cost of the production.

solution

Step 1
Fixed overhead expenditure variance

= Budgeted Fixed Overhead for period – Actual Fixed Overhead for period

= £75,000 – £81,000

= £6,000 A

This variance can logically be confirmed as adverse since the fixed overheads actually cost more than the amount that was budgeted.

Step 2

At first glance the direct variances that have been given in the Case Study do not seem to fit in with the rest of the data. This is because the budgeted production level is different to the actual level. To see how the direct variances would reconcile we must acknowledge that the standard cost must be based on the actual production level, as follows:

Standard Cost of Actual Production:

Direct Materials (£50,000 ÷ 10,000) x 12,000	£ 60,000
Direct Labour (£80,000 ÷ 10,000) x 12,000	£ 96,000
Fixed Overheads	£ 75,000
Total	£231,000

Step 3
We can then reconcile the figures as follows:

Standard cost of Actual Production			£231,000
Direct material price variance	£6,000	A	
Direct material usage variance	(£1,000)	F	
Direct labour rate variance	(£4,000)	F	
Direct labour efficiency variance	£2,000	A	
Fixed overhead expenditure variance	£6,000	A	
			£ 9,000
Actual cost of Production			£240,000

FIXED OVERHEAD VARIANCES – ABSORPTION COSTING

The fixed overhead variances under standard absorption costing are more complicated than under marginal costing. As mentioned earlier they attempt to take account of:

- differences arising due to cost
- differences resulting from the volume of production.

The variances analyse the differences between the amount of fixed overhead absorbed by a standard absorption costing system, and the actual cost of the fixed overheads.

total fixed overhead variances and expenditure and volume variances

The absorption rate is agreed before the period starts, and is arranged so that the planned level of output will cause enough overhead absorption to exactly match the expected overheads. If the absorption base is units, then the output will be measured in units, but if the absorption base is labour hours or machine hours, then we must also measure the output in standard labour or machine hours.

If everything goes to plan there will be no under-absorption or over-absorption, and no fixed overhead variances! The plan could be illustrated as follows:

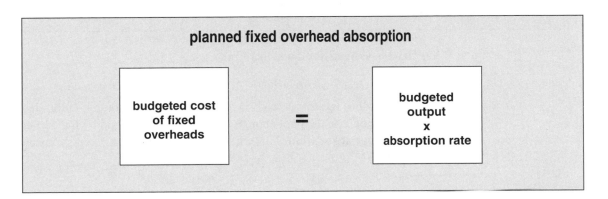

This diagram is based on the planned figures and so they will always agree. It would not make sense to plan for any other situation!

will the plan work? – possible imbalances

When actual figures are used there may be an imbalance – ie they may not always agree. This could be due to either:

- the fixed overheads not costing what was expected, or
- the output not turning out to be as planned, or (as usually happens)
- a combination of the two.

Since the absorption rate is worked out in advance and used throughout, the rate itself will not be a source of any imbalance.

Once the results for the period are known, then the **planned** figures on the diagram shown above can be replaced by the **actual** figures in the diagram shown on the next page.

The following diagram represents the actual figures. The total of the two boxes may not agree because of the possible differences explained on the previous page. The difference between the amounts in the two boxes will form the **total fixed overhead variance** – the amount by which the fixed overheads are either under-absorbed or over-absorbed.

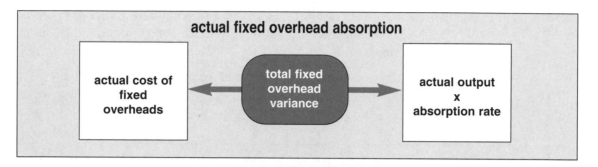

Total **fixed overhead variance** therefore equals:

Fixed Overhead Absorbed – Actual Cost of Fixed Overhead

If the actual cost of fixed overheads is more than the actual output multiplied by the absorption rate then not enough cost has been absorbed by the output – we have **under absorption**. This will give an **adverse** total fixed overhead variance.

fixed overhead double-entry account

The two boxes in the diagram represent the figures that would appear in a fixed overhead account when using double-entry accounting.

- the actual cost of fixed overheads would appear as a debit (generated by the posting of overhead invoices)

- the actual output multiplied by the absorption rate would appear as a credit entry (created by posting the overheads absorbed to the debit side of the 'work in progress account')

- the fixed overhead account balance (created by the difference between these two amounts) must ultimately be posted to the income statement – this posting will be a debit (or cost) in the income statement if the total fixed overhead variance is adverse

Now that we have an understanding of the total fixed overhead variance, we will see how it can be split into the two main fixed overhead variances.

fixed overhead expenditure and volume variances

The difference shown in the above diagram measures the **total fixed overhead variance** – this is due to the difference between the plan and what actually happens. There are two reasons why the actual results could be different from the plan, and these two reasons combine together to result in the total fixed overhead variance. They are:

1 The actual amount **spent** on fixed overheads may not be the same as the planned (or budgeted) fixed overheads. In the diagram, the left-hand box – the actual cost – will be different from the planned figure. This difference is measured by the **fixed overhead expenditure variance**.

2 The actual **volume of output** may not be the same as the planned level of output. This will cause a different amount of fixed overhead to be absorbed than was expected. In the diagrams the figures in the right-hand box will differ. This difference is measured by the **fixed overhead volume variance**.

The actual figures to be used in the diagram on the opposite page are likely to be different from the plan (see the diagram on page 73) because of changes in expenditure and output volume levels. It is the **combination** of these two differences/variances which will result in an overall **total fixed overhead variance**.

The main variances can be summarised when we bring the two diagrams together like this:

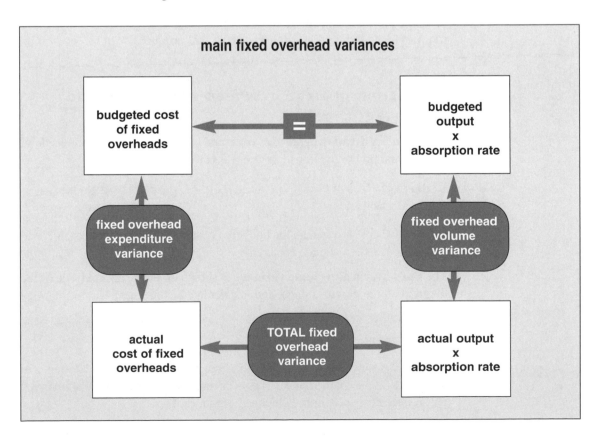

the absorption base

Remember that the amount of fixed overhead absorbed will be based on the actual output multiplied by the absorption rate. The way that the output is measured here will depend on the way that absorption is to take place (the absorption base). If the absorption base is production units, then the output needs to be measured in that form.

If the absorption base is direct labour hours, then the output must be measured in standard labour hours (ie the standard direct labour hours for the actual output). This is often a source of confusion. Remember that what we are measuring is the output; the standard hours for that output is sometimes a convenient way of expressing it.

The same principle will apply if the absorption base is machine hours. The actual output would then need to be expressed in standard machine hours.

Where standard hours are used as an absorption base it is vital to appreciate that absorption will normally take place based on the standard hours for the actual production level, not the actual time taken.

This is so that every identical item produced will absorb the same amount of fixed overhead – even if it took a bit more or less time to make. This will give us a uniform standard amount of overhead that will be absorbed for each identical product, that can be added to the standard material and labour costs to provide the standard absorption cost of that product.

calculation of fixed overhead expenditure and volume variances

The **fixed overhead expenditure variance** is shown on the left-hand side of the diagram on the previous page, and is calculated as follows:

Budgeted Cost of Fixed Overheads	*minus*	Actual Cost of Fixed Overheads

If the actual cost is less than the budgeted cost the variance is favourable, and if it is greater the variance is adverse.

The **fixed overhead volume variance** is shown on the right-hand side of the diagram on the previous page, and is calculated as follows:

Actual Output x Absorption Rate	*minus*	Budgeted Output x Absorption Rate

If the actual output is greater than the budgeted output, the calculation will result in a favourable variance. This is because producing more than planned will reduce costs per unit – which is a good thing.

As mentioned above in relation to the total fixed overhead variance, the form in which the output needs to be expressed will depend on the form of the absorption rate. If the absorption rate is expressed in an amount per unit, then the output should also be in units. If the absorption base is some form of standard hours, then the output must be expressed in standard hours, and the volume variance can be written as:

Standard Hours for Actual Output x Absorption Rate	*minus*	Standard Hours for Budgeted Output x Absorption Rate

The volume variance is therefore a straight comparison of the overheads that would be absorbed by the two output levels (actual and planned).

Some form of standard hours is often used to help measure output because:

- it can be used to convert different kinds of output into a common form – eg a carpenter who produces both tables and chairs, and . . .
- it enables further analysis of costs – eg by dividing the fixed overhead volume variance, as discussed later

If an organisation makes a single product then the fixed overhead variances discussed so far will be identical whichever absorption base is used, as illustrated in the Case study that follows.

Case Study

NODGE LIMITED:
FIXED OVERHEAD VARIANCES

Nodge Limited manufactures a single product – the 'nodge'. The company had the following budgeted and actual data for the first year of production. Each unit was budgeted to take four direct labour hours to produce, two of which would be using manned machines.

	Budget	Actual
Production Units	20,000	23,000
Standard Direct Labour Hours	80,000	
Standard Machine Hours	40,000	
Fixed Overheads	£ 200,000	£ 195,000

required

Calculate the total fixed overhead variance, and the breakdown into expenditure and volume, assuming the overhead absorption base is:

1   Units
2   Standard direct labour hours
3   Standard machine hours

solution

1 Absorption base of Units

The absorption rate would be £200,000 ÷ 20,000 units = £10 per unit

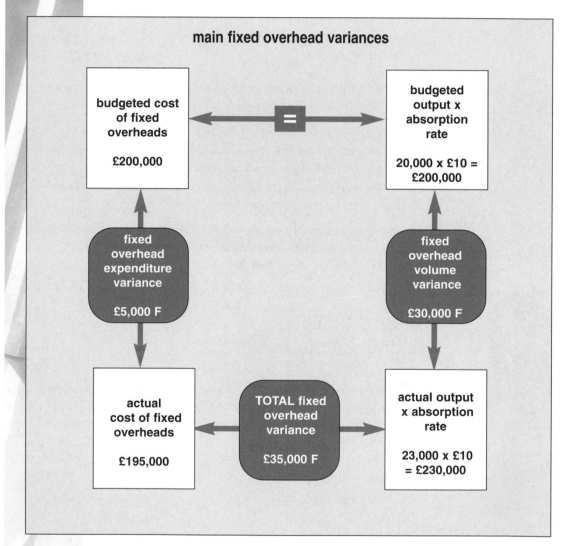

Here the combination of the higher volume achieved and lower actual cost of overheads has resulted in over-absorption and a favourable total fixed overhead variance.

2   Absorption base of Standard Direct Labour Hours

The absorption rate would be £200,000 ÷ 80,000 = £2.50

The standard direct labour hours for the actual production would be:

23,000 units x 4 hours = 92,000.

The total fixed overhead variance equals:

Fixed Overhead Absorbed – Actual Cost of Fixed Overhead

(£2.50 x 92,000) – £195,000 = £35,000 F

The volume variance equals:

Absorption Rate x (Actual Output – Budgeted Output)

Since we are measuring outputs in standard direct labour hours, we will insert the following figures:

Actual Output (in standard direct labour hours) is 92,000 (as calculated above)

Budgeted Output (in standard direct labour hours) is 80,000 (the figure given in the Case Study)

The volume variance therefore equals:

£2.50 x (92,000 – 80,000) = £30,000 F

This is the same result that is achieved when we use units as an absorption base.

The expenditure variance is also unchanged at £5,000 F.

3   Absorption base of Standard Machine Hours

The absorption rate would be £200,000 ÷ 40,000 = £5.00

The standard machine hours for the actual production would be:

23,000 units x 2 hours = 46,000

The total fixed overhead variance equals:

Fixed Overhead Absorbed – Actual Cost of Fixed Overhead

(£5.00 x 46,000) – £195,000 = £35,000 F

The volume variance equals:

Absorption Rate x (Actual Output – Budgeted Output)

Since we are measuring outputs in standard machine hours, we will insert the following figures:

Actual Output (in standard machine hours) is 46,000 (as calculated above)

Budgeted Output (in standard machine hours) is 40,000 (the figure given in the Case Study)

The volume variance therefore equals

$$£5.00 \times (46,000 - 40,000) \quad = £30,000 \text{ F}$$

This is again the same result that is achieved when we use units as an absorption base.

The expenditure variance is again unchanged at £5,000 F.

FIXED OVERHEAD VOLUME SUB-VARIANCES

The full breakdown of the total fixed overhead variance is shown in the following variance tree:

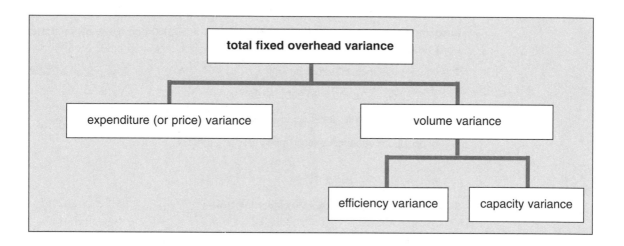

As we saw earlier in the chapter, the Total Fixed Overhead Variance is subdivided between the Expenditure Variance and the Volume Variance.

The Volume Variance can in turn be subdivided into the **Efficiency Variance** and the **Capacity Variance**. These two variances attempt to explain whether any difference in the volume of output can be accounted for through:

- efficient (or inefficient) working or
- by using more or less resources (often labour) than planned

These variances can only be calculated if we are using an absorption base that lends itself to this sort of analysis. If the absorption base is units of production then these variances could not normally be calculated.

We will now look at the two variances in turn.

fixed overhead efficiency variance

The Fixed Overhead Efficiency Variance compares the time the actual production should have taken with the time that it actually took, and multiplies the result by the absorption rate. When standard hours are used it equals:

Standard Hours for Actual Output x Absorption Rate	*minus*	Actual Hours Taken x Absorption Rate

The notion of efficiency here is identical to that used for direct variances, and if direct labour is the absorption base, then the calculation will use the same hours as the direct labour efficiency variance, but multiplied by the absorption rate.

The logic of whether the variance is adverse or favourable will also be identical; taking less time than standard for the output level achieved is considered efficient and therefore favourable; taking more time is inefficient and the variance is adverse. In conclusion, we are providing a variance that demonstrates how much more (or less) fixed overhead has been absorbed due to the difference in output caused by efficiency.

A Fixed Overhead Efficiency Variance can also be calculated where absorption is carried out through the use of machine hours or some other measure, which is usually time based. The 'efficiency' that is being measured will, of course, depend on the source of the data.

fixed overhead capacity variance

The Fixed Overhead Capacity Variance compares the time that the budgeted production should have taken with the actual hours worked, and multiplies the result by the absorption rate. When standard hours are used it equals:

Actual Hours Taken x Absorption Rate	*minus*	Standard Hours for Budgeted Output x Absorption Rate

The idea of capacity can be thought of as whether the workplace is filled to capacity with the intended resources. If we are using labour hours then we are examining how we are using the resource of people, by measuring their working hours. If people worked for longer than was originally planned then this produces a favourable variance since we are getting more use out of our factory than we had hoped for. A similar logic applies to the use of machine hours; the longer the machines are used then the better we are utilising that resource.

Since fixed overheads do not vary with output (by definition) the use of the volume variance and its analysis can be a useful reminder to managers that the greater the output the lower the cost per unit because the fixed overhead is spread over more units.

fixed overhead variances – a summary

All the fixed overhead variances can be incorporated into the diagram below, which is based on the format of the diagram on page 89, with the addition of the efficiency and capacity sub-variances.

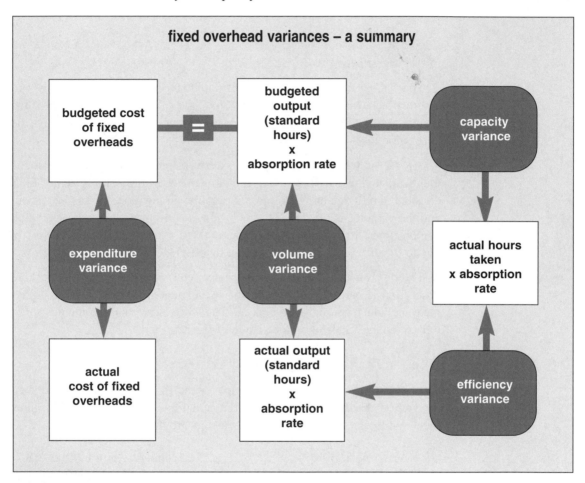

WALMER LIMITED: OVERHEAD VARIANCES AND SUB–VARIANCES

The Finance Department of Walmer Limited has recorded the following data:

- The budgeted production level is 5,000 standard hours. This will enable the absorption rate of £3.00 per hour to absorb the budgeted fixed overheads of £15,000
- Actual fixed overheads amount to £13,000
- Actual output is 5,800 standard hours.
- Actual time taken to achieve output is 5,500 hours.

required

Calculate the Total Fixed Overhead Variance, and analyse it into the sub-variances.

solution

We can either use the diagram to help with the calculation, or use the formulae.

using the diagram

Using the diagram on page 96, and inserting first the known figures – and then the variances as differences – gives this result:

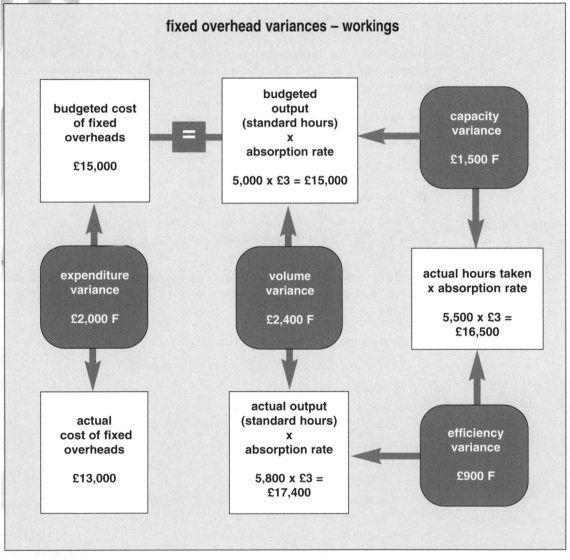

fixed overhead variances – workings

budgeted cost of fixed overheads £15,000	**budgeted output (standard hours) x absorption rate** 5,000 x £3 = £15,000	**capacity variance** £1,500 F
expenditure variance £2,000 F	**volume variance** £2,400 F	**actual hours taken x absorption rate** 5,500 x £3 = £16,500
actual cost of fixed overheads £13,000	**actual output (standard hours) x absorption rate** 5,800 x £3 = £17,400	**efficiency variance** £900 F

Using the formulas

Using the formulas we can confirm the results shown in the diagram.

The Expenditure Variance equals:

Budgeted Cost of Fixed Overheads – Actual Cost of Fixed Overheads.

£15,000 – £13,000 = £2,000 F

The Volume Variance equals:

Absorption Rate x (Standard Hours for Actual Output – Standard Hours for Budgeted Output)

£3 x (5,800 – 5,000) = £2,400 F

Since we have the data on the actual hours taken, we can analyse the volume variance into the fixed overhead efficiency variance, and the fixed overhead capacity variance.

The Fixed Overhead Efficiency Variance equals:

Absorption Rate x (Standard Hours for Actual Output – Actual Hours Taken)

£3 x (5,800 – 5,500) = £900 F

The Fixed Overhead Capacity Variance equals:

Absorption Rate x (Actual Hours Taken – Standard Hours for Budgeted Output)

£3 x (5,500 – 5,000) = £1,500 F

Note that the efficiency and capacity variances must add up to the volume variance, and that the volume and expenditure variances must add up to the total fixed overhead variance.

The Total Fixed Overhead Variance equals:

Fixed Overhead Absorbed – Actual Cost of Fixed Overhead

(£3 x 5,800) – £13,000 = £4,400 F

A full summary of the overhead variances reads:

Fixed Overhead Expenditure Variance		£2000 F
Fixed Overhead Efficiency Variance	£ 900 F	
Fixed Overhead Capacity Variance	£1500 F	
Fixed Overhead Volume Variance		£2400 F
Total Fixed Overhead Variance		£4400 F

INTERPRETATION OF FIXED OVERHEAD VARIANCES

Once we understand what the fixed overhead variances are trying to measure, their interpretation becomes quite straightforward. There may be a variety of different underlying causes for these variances in the same way that there are for direct variances, but the individual variances are always trying to measure the same kind of differences.

fixed overhead expenditure variance

The **fixed overhead expenditure variance** shows whether actual spending on fixed overheads was more or less than the budgeted amount.

The fixed overhead expenditure variance is measuring the difference between the budgeted cost of the fixed overheads and the actual cost. An adverse variance indicates that the actual cost is more than was expected, and a favourable variance that the actual cost is less. The reasons for the variances could include poor budgeting, or the fact that actual costs are different due to unforeseen price changes. The cost of these overheads are not expected to change because of differing output levels since they are defined as 'fixed' costs so any difference in output is irrelevant in the interpretation of this variance.

fixed overhead volume variance

The **fixed overhead volume variance** shows the difference between the overheads that would be absorbed by the planned volume of output and the amount absorbed by the actual volume of output.

The fixed overhead volume variance is measuring how much more or less fixed overheads have been absorbed compared to the planned amount of absorption. As the variance name indicates, this is entirely concerned with how the actual volume of output compares with the planned volume. The reason for this is because the system attempts to cost a set amount of overhead onto each unit of output. When the actual output is different to that which was planned, a volume variance will arise.

The effect of lower actual output than was planned would be an amount of overhead that has been left over and not accounted for as part of the output cost. This would mean that ideally (if adjustments could have been made in time) a larger amount of overhead should have been added to each unit. As this is not possible after the event there is an amount of unabsorbed overhead, which needs to be written off in the accounts. This is why low output causes an adverse variance that results in a further cost to be written off (debited) in the accounts.

output volume differs from budgeted volume?

If the actual output is greater than expected, the volume variance will be favourable, representing an amount which can be credited to the accounts to compensate for more overhead being absorbed than was planned.

The reasons behind a volume variance will be concerned with either:

- the setting of the budgeted level of output (eg unrealistically high output or output set at too conservative a level), or

- something which caused the actual output to differ from the budget, (eg a shortage or additional levels of some resource, or machine breakdown)

using efficiency and capacity variances to explain the volume variance

The breakdown of the volume variance into efficiency and capacity is an attempt to explain why there had been higher or lower output than the budget forecast.

The **fixed overhead efficiency variance** shows how the efficient use of resources affects the volume of output.

A favourable efficiency variance indicates that output has been created using less resources than had been expected. If the absorption base is standard labour hours then the efficiency relates to labour efficiency. If the absorption base is standard machine hours then any efficiency variance is based on how efficiently the output had passed through the machines.

The **fixed overhead capacity variance** shows how the amount of resources used (compared with the budget) affects the volume of output.

The capacity variance explains how the output has been achieved through the use of more or less resources. When using labour hours as a base a favourable capacity variance indicates that additional output was created through the use of additional labour hours. Since any additional volume of output is beneficial, the fact that this variance is favourable is quite logical; it is just an indication of how the higher output was achieved. It also means that we are using the infrastructure more intensely than was planned, and this must be seen as a beneficial move to spread the fixed overhead costs more widely.

Case
Study

WALMER LIMITED (continued):
INTERPRETATION OF FIXED OVERHEAD VARIANCES

solution

Using the data in the Case Study on page 96 the following interpretation could be put on the numerical results.

• The fixed overheads actually cost less than the budgeted amount by £2,000. This was demonstrated in the expenditure variance. We do not have any evidence as to whether this was caused by poor estimation of costs, or by changes in the overhead cost structure that occurred after the budget was prepared.

• The actual volume of output achieved was greater than was budgeted, and this caused £2,400 more fixed overhead to be absorbed than was planned. This additional volume was generated through a combination of higher efficiency than the budgeted level (accounting for absorption of an extra £900 of overhead), and the use of more labour hours than was anticipated (accounting for the other £1,500 of additional overhead absorption).

• In all, through the combination of lower cost and greater output a total of £4,400 more fixed overhead was absorbed than the fixed overheads actually cost. This over-absorption is represented by the total favourable variance, which will be credited to the accounts.

APPORTIONMENT OF FIXED OVERHEADS

In the discussion and case studies so far we have assumed a simple manufacturing system with just one product being made in a factory that is not divided into separate cost centres. While assessment tasks are often based on this type of scenario, they are also sometimes based on a slightly more complicated situation. The main situations that you may come across are as follows:

• Using cost centres to collect costs and apply them to the products made. We saw in Chapter 1 (pages 8-10) how several cost centres could be used to absorb overheads onto a product in stages. Fixed overheads would be allocated or apportioned to each cost centre, and absorbed into the products as they pass through. Standard costing and the calculation of variances can be used in conjunction with this mechanism.

• Where several products are made in a factory, but it is not divided into cost centres, the factory fixed overheads can be apportioned to the production of each type of product according to some relatively arbitrary mechanism. Examples of this are budgeted labour hours or machine hours for the expected output. We will examine this method below.

- Activity based costing can be used to apportion overheads as accurately as possible between products. We looked at how this system worked in Chapter 1.

Whatever system is used to apportion overheads, this will take place *before* we calculate fixed overhead variances under standard costing. The apportionment will be used to determine the budgeted and actual fixed overheads from which variances can be calculated.

The following case study uses the second apportionment mechanism outlined above. The key to being able to undertake such case studies is to read and follow the instructions very carefully. It is easy to confuse the apportionment method to be used by misreading the scenario.

Case Study

RANGE LIMITED: APPORTIONMENT OF FIXED OVERHEADS

Range Limited manufactures four products – the Standard, the Super, the Deluxe, and the Grand-Luxe. The policy of Range Limited is for both the budgeted and the actual fixed overheads to be apportioned to each product range. Both these apportionments are based on the budgeted labour hours for that product during the year as a proportion of total budgeted labour hours for the whole factory. Fixed overheads are absorbed on a standard direct labour hour basis.

The following data relates to Range Limited:

	Standard	Super	Deluxe	Grand-Luxe
Standard Direct Labour Hours per Unit	4	6	7	10
Budgeted Production Level (Units)	500	800	400	440
Actual Production Level (Units)	480	850	430	450

Budgeted fixed overheads for the year are £140,000. Actual fixed overheads for the year are £154,000.

Actual time taken for Super production was 5,000 direct labour hours.

required

Calculate the following:

1 The budgeted overhead apportioned to Super production.

2 The overhead absorption rate per direct labour hour.

3 The actual overhead apportioned to Super production.

4 The standard hours for the actual Super production.

5 The following fixed overhead variances *relating to the production of Supers*:

- total fixed overhead variance
- fixed overhead expenditure variance
- fixed overhead volume variance
- fixed overhead capacity variance
- fixed overhead efficiency variance

solution

1 The budgeted overhead apportioned to Super production is calculated as follows:

The budgeted direct labour hours are first calculated:

Standard	4 hours x 500 units =	2,000 hours
Super	6 hours x 800 units =	4,800 hours
Deluxe	7 hours x 400 units =	2,800 hours
Grand-Luxe	10 hours x 440 units =	4,400 hours
Total		14,000 hours

This gives an apportionment of the budgeted overheads of

£140,000 x (4,800 ÷ 14,000) = £48,000

2 The overhead absorption rate per direct labour hour is always based on the budgeted figures (since it is calculated before the period starts).
i.e Budgeted fixed overheads ÷ budgeted direct labour hours

Using the figures for the whole factory gives

£140,000 ÷ 14,000 hours = £10 per hour

(The figures for the Super only would have given the same result
£48,000 ÷ 4,800 hours = £10)

3 The actual overhead apportioned to Super production uses the same basis as the budgeted overheads:

£154,000 x (4,800 ÷ 14,000) = £52,800

Note that we are following the policy outlined in the case study, and using budgeted information to apportion the actual expenditure.

4 The standard hours for the actual Super production can be calculated as 850 units x 6 hours per unit = 5,100 standard hours. This will be used in the calculation of the variances, since it determines how much overhead is absorbed.

5 The fixed overhead variances *for the Super production* can now be calculated using the diagram previously explained, as follows:

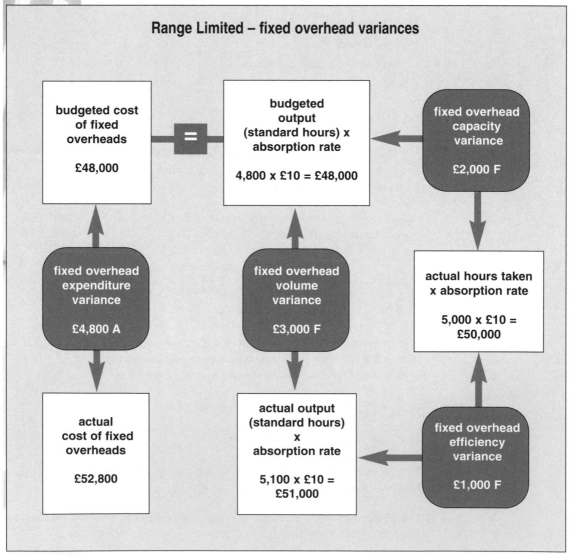

From the diagram the fixed overhead variances can be summarised as:

fixed overhead expenditure variance		£4,800 A
fixed overhead capacity variance	£ 2,000 F	
fixed overhead efficiency variance	£ 1,000 F	
fixed overhead volume variance		£ 3,000 F
total fixed overhead variance		£ 1,800 A

THE APPLICATION OF FIXED OVERHEAD VARIANCES TO THE SERVICE SECTOR

Standard costing and variance analysis have their origins in the manufacturing industry, but the concepts can often be applied to other sectors of industry, the service sector, for example. The problems which must be dealt with in applying fixed overhead variances to service organisations tend to concern the measurement of output and choice of absorption base. Sometimes the more general term of 'activity level' can be used in these situations instead of 'output', but they both relate to an attempt to measure what the organisations produce, eg holidays arranged or hospital operations carried out.

the use of standard hours

Where some form of standard hours can be used as an absorption base and to measure output, then the techniques already studied can be used without any modification. The interpretation will need to be consistent with the organisation, but the calculation of the variances should follow the usual pattern.

Case Study

BELLEVIEW HOSPITAL: FIXED OVERHEAD VARIANCES IN THE SERVICE SECTOR

situation

A private hospital carries out various surgical procedures in its operating theatre, using a standard team of five staff at all times. Each type of operation has a standard theatre time, and this is used to measure the output (or activity level) of the theatre in a universal manner. All the team record the time that they spend working in the theatre, and this information is also used to help calculate variances.

The fixed overheads of the operating theatre are budgeted at £2,000 per week, during which operations with a standard theatre time of 50 hours are planned to take place. During week 9 the fixed overheads amount to £2,350, and operations with a standard theatre time of 64 hours were completed. The total time logged by the staff on the theatre team that week was 295 hours.

required

Calculate the Total Fixed Overhead Variance, and analyse it into the sub-variances.

solution

The only point to be careful about in this Case Study is that the staff hours relate to the total hours worked by five people, whereas the theatre time relates to the time that the team is using the theatre. It would therefore make sense to work out the time that the theatre was in use before progressing. This can be calculated by dividing the total staff hours (295) by the 5 staff in the team (= 59 actual theatre hours).

The absorption rate is £2,000 ÷ 50 = £40 per theatre hour.

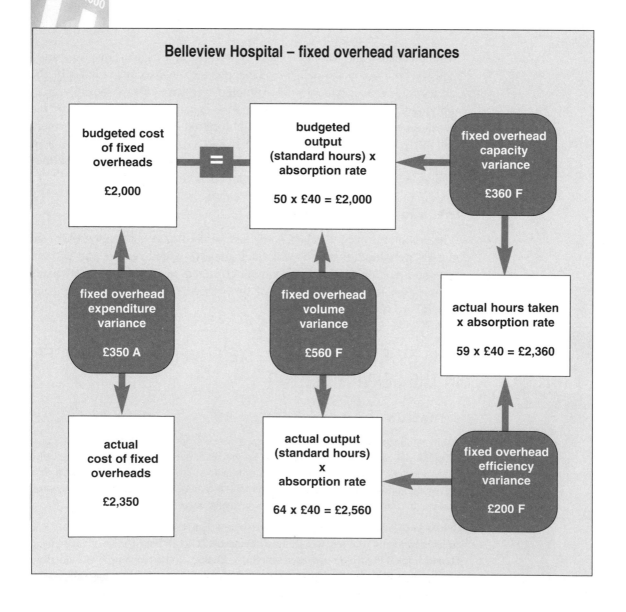

Although the overheads amounted to £350 more than planned, the theatre completed more operations than was budgeted, causing additional overhead absorption of £560. This was achieved through a combination of efficient working (carrying out operations with a standard time of 64 hours in only 59 hours) and more intensive use of the theatre than had been expected (using it for 59 hours instead of the planned 50 hours). The net result was over absorption of £210.

USING AN APPROPRIATE RESOURCE

It is important to remember that the fixed overhead capacity and efficiency variances are calculated to assist in the understanding of how actual output volume differs from that budgeted, and to what extent overhead has been absorbed. In order that this process is effective, the resource which is used to measure the output (for example standard direct labour hours or standard machine hours) must be **appropriate** in the particular circumstances.

To have an appropriate link between resource and fixed overhead, the chosen resource must be fundamental to the creation of the output. Only then will there be firm links between output and fixed overheads, via the chosen resource.

which resource should be used?

The two most common resources used in standard costing to absorb overheads are:

- standard labour hours
- standard machine hours

Standard labour hours are appropriate if the production is labour intensive – if labour is the key resource being used to achieve the organisation's output.

Standard machine hours are appropriate if the production is machine intensive, and the machine time being utilised is much more important than the labour time. This would be particularly relevant if the machinery and other equipment was very expensive, since a large part of the overheads may then relate to using the machinery. Using standard machine hours then makes perfect sense as there is a strong link between the reason for the overhead cost and the way that the output is achieved.

Chapter Summary

- Fixed overhead variances differ from direct variances due to the way that fixed costs behave and the way the chosen costing system deals with them.

- When marginal costing is used, fixed costs are considered time-based, and are not absorbed by the output. The fixed overhead variance under this system is a simple measurement of more or less expenditure than planned and is passed through the accounts.

- When absorption costing is used, fixed overheads are absorbed into the output based on a predetermined rate. The total fixed overhead variance is the amount by which the amount of overhead absorbed differs from the overhead actually incurred. This can be due to the expenditure on overhead being different to what was planned, or the volume of output being different, or both.

- Where the volume of output can be usefully measured in terms of the use of some fundamental resource (eg standard labour or machine hours), then the volume variance can be broken down into the efficiency variance (measuring the change in volume, and hence absorption, due to the efficiency with which that resource is used), and the capacity variance (measuring the effect of the amount of resource used compared to planned).

- Where several products are made and / or several cost centres are used in a manufacturing environment, some form of apportionment of fixed overheads will be necessary. Whatever the policy on apportionment, this will be carried out before the fixed overhead variances are calculated, so that the variances relate only to the appropriate part of the factory costs.

- The majority of fixed overhead variance techniques can be applied to the service sector as well as manufacturing, with little modification.

Key Terms

fixed overheads	indirect costs which do not vary in proportion to the volume of production or other output
marginal costing	a technique that values cost units based on variable costs only. Fixed costs are considered to relate only to the reporting period of time
fixed overhead expenditure variance (marginal costing)	the only fixed overhead variance generated using marginal costing. It measures the difference between the budgeted expenditure and the actual expenditure on fixed overheads in a reporting period
absorption costing	a technique that values cost units based on a suitable part of all the costs of production, whether fixed or variable in behaviour

absorption base	the mechanism by which absorption costing absorbs indirect costs into cost units. It may be simply per cost unit, or (for example) per standard labour or machine hour
total fixed overhead variance (absorption costing)	the difference between the actual expenditure on fixed overheads, and the amount of fixed overhead absorbed by the actual output. The expenditure and volume variances will combine in this total variance
fixed overhead expenditure variance (absorption costing)	the difference between the budgeted expenditure and the actual expenditure on fixed overheads in a reporting period
fixed overhead volume variance (absorption costing)	the difference between the fixed overhead which would have been absorbed by the budgeted output and the fixed overhead which was absorbed by the actual output. The efficiency and capacity variance will combine in this variance
fixed overhead efficiency variance (absorption costing)	the part of the volume variance attributable to the efficient or inefficient use of the resource used to measure the output. Where this resource is some form of standard hours the variance is based on the amount of overhead that would be absorbed by the difference between the standard hours for the actual output and the actual time taken
fixed overhead capacity variance (absorption costing)	the part of the volume variance attributable to the amount used of the resource chosen to measure the output. Where this resource is some form of standard hours the variance is based on the amount of overhead that would be absorbed by the difference between the actual time taken and the standard hours for the budgeted output
apportionment of fixed overheads	the division of fixed overheads into parts relating to different products or cost centres. This can be carried out in a variety of ways ranging from the application of activity based costing to more arbitrary approaches (eg budgeted labour hours)

Activities

3.1   You have been provided with the following information:

- Budgeted overheads are £500,000
- Budgeted output is 25,000 units
- Actual output is 30,000 units
- Actual overheads are £480,000

Required

Calculate:

(a)   the fixed overhead volume variance.

(b)   the fixed overhead expenditure variance.

3.2   You have been provided with the following information:

- Budgeted overheads are £60,000
- Budgeted output is 5,000 units and 500 labour hours
- Actual output is 3,500 units and 430 labour hours
- Actual overheads are £58,000

Required

Calculate:

(a)   the fixed overhead efficiency variance.

(b)   the fixed overhead capacity variance.

3.3   Sofa-so-Good Limited manufactures sofas and sells them to furniture shops. The company uses standard absorption costing, with an absorption rate of £200 per sofa for fixed overheads.

The budget for the year was to manufacture 2,200 sofas and incur £440,000 of fixed overheads.

The actual production for the year was 2,150 sofas, and the actual overheads incurred amounted to £428,000.

Required

(a)   Calculate the following variances:

  •   Fixed overhead expenditure variance

  •   Fixed overhead volume variance

(b)   Explain one disadvantage that Sofa-so-Good Limited may experience by absorbing overheads on a per-sofa basis.

3.4   Zorbant Ltd absorbs fixed overheads based on the budgeted fixed overheads of £94,600, and the budgeted number of standard direct labour hours to be worked of 2,200.

The actual output for the period turned out to be 2,500 standard hours, although this took the direct labour workforce 2,600 hours. The actual fixed overheads for the period were £99,000.

Required

(a)   Calculate the fixed overhead absorption rate.

(b)   Calculate all relevant overhead variances.

(c)   State which of the following comments are valid, based on the above data:

  1   The expenditure variance is adverse due to the increased volume of output which has been produced.

  2   The expenditure variance is favourable since the actual fixed overheads are less than were budgeted for.

  3   The expenditure variance is adverse since the actual fixed overheads are more than were budgeted for.

  4   The favourable volume variance reflects the fact that more output was achieved than was budgeted for.

  5   The favourable volume variance is due to the overheads being less than anticipated.

6   The adverse volume variance is due to more output being achieved than was budgeted for.

7   The capacity variance is adverse since the overheads cost more than expected.

8   The favourable capacity variance is due to more labour hours being worked than was budgeted for.

9   The adverse efficiency variance is due to more labour hours being worked than was originally budgeted for.

10   The adverse efficiency variance is due to the actual output taking more labour hours than standard.

11   The favourable efficiency variance is due to the actual output taking more hours than standard.

12   The adverse efficiency variance is due to the fact that the overheads cost more than was originally budgeted for.

3.5   G Loop Manufacturing Limited makes a single product, the Gloop, and absorbs fixed overheads on the basis of standard labour hours.

For the year it had budgeted to make 2,000 Gloops, and take 14,000 standard labour hours to do so. It budgeted that its fixed overheads would amount to £448,000.

During the year the company actually made 1,800 Gloops, taking a total of 12,000 actual labour hours.

The fixed overheads for the year actually amounted to £455,000.

Required

(a)   Calculate the budgeted absorption rate per standard hour.

(b)   Calculate the standard hours to make one Gloop.

(c)   Calculate the standard hours to make the actual output of 1,800 Gloops.

(d)   Calculate:

The fixed overhead expenditure (or price) variance, and

The fixed overhead volume variance, and subdivide it into:

•   The fixed overhead efficiency variance and

•   The fixed overhead capacity variance.

(e)   Reconcile the overhead absorbed by the standard hours for the actual production of 1,800 Gloops, with the actual fixed overheads using the above variances.

3.6   The Maxima Office Furniture Company manufactures a range of desks and chairs and sells them to furniture shops.

The company uses standard absorption costing, using standard direct labour hours as an absorption base.

Each desk takes 5 standard hours to produce, and each chair takes 2 standard hours.

The budget for the year was to utilise 40,000 direct labour hours by making 5,000 desks and 7,500 chairs.

The budget for fixed overheads for the year was £600,000.

The actual production for the year was 5,100 desks and 7,000 chairs. The actual number of direct labour hours worked was 38,700 hours. The actual overheads incurred amounted to £603,500.

Required

(a)   Calculate the standard direct labour hours for the actual production.

(b)   Calculate the fixed overhead absorption rate per standard direct labour hour.

(c)   Calculate the following variances:

- Fixed overhead expenditure variance

- Fixed overhead volume variance

- Fixed overhead efficiency variance

- Fixed overhead capacity variance

- Total fixed overhead variance

4 Standard costing – further analysis

this chapter covers...

In this chapter we complete our study of standard costing by examining several important topics.

We start by identifying the main types of standards that can be set. These are:

- *ideal standard – a 'perfect world' standard that can be aspired to but rarely achieved; this will result in many adverse variances*

- *attainable standard – where the standard is set at a level where in current conditions it could be achieved; this is how most standards are set*

- *basic standard – where the standard is set at an original unchanged level; this is only useful for long term comparisons*

We will then discuss the important implications that standard setting has for variance interpretation, as well as motivation and behaviour.

Next we will examine the decisions about when to take action as a result of variances, and what sort of action is appropriate in different circumstances.

We will then examine how variances can be divided up to account for problems like inflation. This is so we can isolate controllable variances from those that are outside our control, and take appropriate action.

Finally we will learn how standard costing bookkeeping works, and how journals can be used to post variances. We will then use a comprehensive case study to consolidate understanding in several key areas.

A SUMMARY OF VARIANCES

Before we examine some additional aspects of variances, it will be useful to review the variances that we have studied so far. We have seen that some variances depend on whether we are using absorption costing or marginal costing. The two charts shown below summarise these variances.

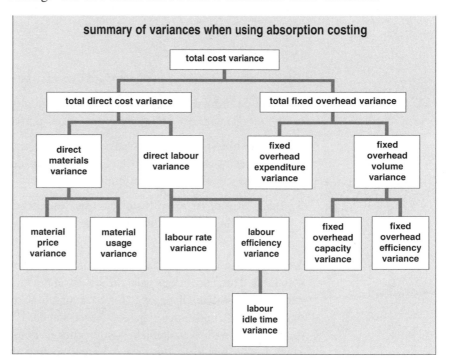

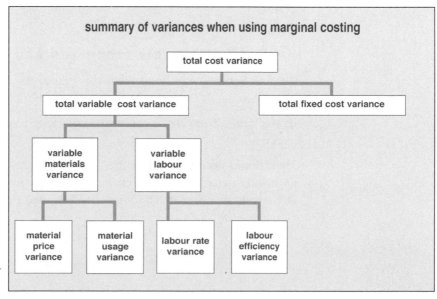

SETTING STANDARDS

In the previous chapters we have looked at how standard costing can be used to determine the expected level of costs, and to compare the actual costs incurred with these standard costs by calculating variances. We will now examine in more detail how standards may be set, and how this can have an impact on our interpretation of variances.

types of standard

There are three main types of standard that may be set:

1 **Ideal Standard** makes no allowances for inefficiency or wastage of labour or materials, and therefore assumes perfect conditions.

2 **Attainable Standard** allows for a small amount of normal wastage and inefficiency, but is set at a level that is considered to be a challenging target based on current operating conditions.

3 **Basic Standard** is an historical (and therefore effectively out-of-date) standard that allows comparisons to be carried out over long periods of time.

You may also come across the terms 'normal' and 'target' applied to standards. These are effectively variations on the idea of attainable standards, and are fairly self-explanatory. Normal standards are set at the expected level under normal conditions, whereas target standards are at the level that the organisation wishes to achieve under current conditions. Target standards may also be linked to the idea of target costing that will be examined in Chapter 5.

ideal and attainable standards and actual results

The link between ideal and attainable standards and the actual results is reflected in the difference between strategic and operational management.

Strategic management is concerned with long-term planning and decision making.

Operational management centres around the day-to-day activities taking place within an organisation. The way in which these types of management may rely on different standards can be illustrated by the following diagram:

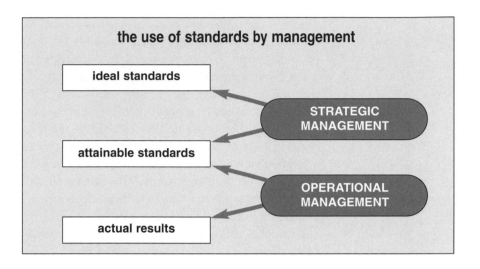

Strategic management can examine ways of moving what is attainable closer to the ideal over the longer term, whilst operational management is more concerned with moving the actual results closer to what is attainable in the short term. Total Quality Management (see pages 152-154) is one technique that can be used to bring the actual results closer to the ideal level.

IDEAL STANDARDS AND THEIR IMPLICATIONS

the tendency for dual standards

When an organisation implements a standard costing system, the way that the standard is set will affect the interpretation of the variances. If an ideal standard is used, with no allowances for wastage or inefficiency then the variances for material usage and labour efficiency will tend to be adverse. This in turn will mean that managers will come to expect adverse variances, and that action will only be taken when the variances are outside what they consider to be a reasonable tolerance level. If the use of an ideal is extended to setting material cost and labour rate standards by using the cheapest prices and the lowest labour rates then the managers will become used to finding that all the variances recorded are adverse. They will tend to ignore the adverse variances that are reasonably small, and concentrate their attention on the larger variances. In this way they will have started to operate a system of informal **dual standards**, whereby the standard that is set is not the one that it is expected will be achieved.

This has important implications when standard costing is used to help a business with its planning. Where standards set at an ideal level are used for planning purposes then the result will always be inaccurate. For example when using ideal standards to specify the amount of materials or labour time that will be required, the resources will tend to be under-estimated. This could result in lower production being achieved than was planned, or that additional resources are needed to complete the required production. This is because the ideal standards do not incorporate any allowance for the wastage or inefficient working that will always occur to some extent. Managers may get around this problem informally by adding an additional amount into their resource requirements. They are then effectively using their own version of a standard. The same situation will occur with material prices and labour costs, so that unless an amount is added to the standard when the anticipated production is costed, the result will almost invariably be under costing.

the dangers of informal standards

It could be argued that making such adjustments as described above is just a logical extension of the setting and use of standards. But problems could arise if different managers had different ideas of what tolerance levels were acceptable. The use of **exception reporting** whereby results are only reported if they are outside an agreed range is universally recognised as a useful management tool, and can form part of the wider technique of **management by exception**. This is where management time is concentrated on situations in which the actual results vary from the plans. Both these techniques can only work effectively if there is genuine agreement about the level at which results should be reported and acted upon instead of ignored. A situation could develop where not just informal dual standards were in operation, but a range of standards was in use by different managers for different purposes.

---

practical example

Consider the following situation:

The production scheduler may add an allowance of say 10% to the standard usage of materials when planning the amount to be bought for a production run and requisitioning the goods. The production supervisor may consider that a usage variance of up to 8% from standard is reasonable. The production manager views a tolerance level of 5% as being within an acceptable range.

If the variance is reported at 6% then the production supervisor may feel that he/she has performed well, whereas the production manager is expecting answers from him/her as to why the usage is so high. Meanwhile the excess purchases of raw material are sitting in the stores!

This situation would not be a good demonstration of how to use standard costing and variance analysis as a form of responsibility accounting. In order to make different managers responsible for different variances they must be clear as to exactly what standards they are expected to achieve. This can be difficult enough with the impact of the interdependence (interrelationship) of variances, without the additional confusion created by having different informal versions of the standards in existence.

ideal standards and motivation

A further area that is influenced by the way that standards are set is that of **motivation**. As discussed earlier, variances resulting from a system where standards are set at an ideal level will generally be adverse. Whether linked to a reward system or not, targets will only tend to work well if they are considered fair and achievable. It cannot be easy to motivate staff at any level to perform well if all you can measure is by how far they have fallen short of the standard on each occasion. The natural human reaction may be to feel that since the standards cannot be achieved there is no point in even attempting to work efficiently. The standards may be felt to be irrelevant by the staff – hardly the atmosphere of cost-consciousness that most businesses would like to develop!

The use of ideal standards will also effectively prevent businesses from setting up a traditional labour bonus system based on paying a percentage of time saved compared with the standard time. It will be clear that if the standards are set at an ideal level, then there will never be any time saved, and therefore no bonus is likely to be payable.

ATTAINABLE STANDARDS AND THEIR IMPLICATIONS

Setting standards at an attainable level should avoid most of the problems identified with setting ideal standards, and most businesses using standard costing opt for some version of attainable standards. Where the standards are carefully set, the resultant variances should typically be a mixture of adverse and favourable, as the organisation will tend to sometimes exceed the standard and sometimes not quite achieve it.

Not everybody considers what is 'attainable' as being the same thing, and there will be no standard that will be considered fair by everyone. It could be thought of as a range rather than a single point. If standards are set following consultation within the organisation there will always need to be some compromise as different managers and employee groups argue from their own perspectives. There are common problems arising from encouraging participation in the setting of both standards and budgets. While standards which are set by making use of the expertise of a range of participants will tend to be more easily accepted and 'owned', the conflicting needs and desires of the personnel involved can make the standard setting process long and difficult.

BASIC STANDARDS AND THEIR IMPLICATIONS

Maintaining standards at a 'basic' level will tend to have several disadvantages. Since the standard was set some time ago its relevance may be questionable, and large variances will tend to become normal. This will mean that comparison is most useful if it is based on the **trend** in variances and this procedure will enable managers to identify with ease the way in which costs have changed over a long period.

A clear disadvantage of using basic standards is that the standards themselves may not be comparable with current conditions, and the individual variances may be virtually meaningless. The impact of inflation and changes in working practices will mean that the standard cannot be used as either a target or an estimate of expected cost levels. For these reasons basic standards are rarely used as the only standard by an organisation, but may be used alongside variance analysis which is based on more current data to obtain a longer term view of changes which have occurred.

INTERPRETING VARIANCES

The interpretation of variances, and the taking of appropriate action will be influenced by the way in which the standard was set. We will now examine some of the other issues that need to be considered in interpreting variances and taking appropriate action. The steps involved can be seen illustrated in the diagram on page 122, which is then discussed further.

is the variance significant? – control limits

The first issue to consider is whether the variance is significant enough for any action at all to be worthwhile. The idea of tolerance levels was mentioned earlier, and it is important to establish how large a variance should be in order to justify an investigation into its cause followed by appropriate action. Since any investigation or action will have a cost implication (at least in terms of management time), it would not make sense to do this unless there was an expected benefit that would justify it. **Control limits** within which a variance is acceptable may therefore be set by the organisation (see the diagram on the next page). These limits will quickly identify the variances which need investigating.

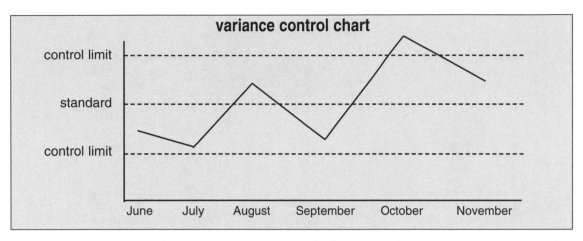

Variances are recorded chronologically from left to right on the chart, either individually or cumulatively. The control levels are agreed in advance. If a variance moves beyond these limits then investigation will be needed and appropriate action can be taken. In the chart shown here the control limit is exceeded in October.

The cumulative effects of variances must also be taken into account. The **trends** in variances that individually are small and may be considered immaterial may point to a situation that requires action. If, for example, efficiency levels amongst the direct labour force are very slowly decreasing then some action (perhaps retraining) will be needed to avoid excess costs occurring over a long period.

modifying standards

An important question to ask is:

'Is the variance due entirely to the way the standard was set, or is there a current situation that needs investigating?'

If a poorly set standard is creating a variance out of an otherwise acceptable situation, the most logical approach will be to amend the standard at the next opportunity. Resetting the standard will also be the most appropriate action if there is a long-term change to costs, otherwise 'false' variances will arise in future.

short-term changes

The cause of the variance will dictate whether or not action is required. If the variance is caused by a temporary change that will automatically right itself then clearly no action is needed other than to check later to see that it has. Examples of this could be:

- a price variance caused by a change to another supplier because the normal supplier was temporarily out of stock
- a machine breakdown causing excess wastage of material

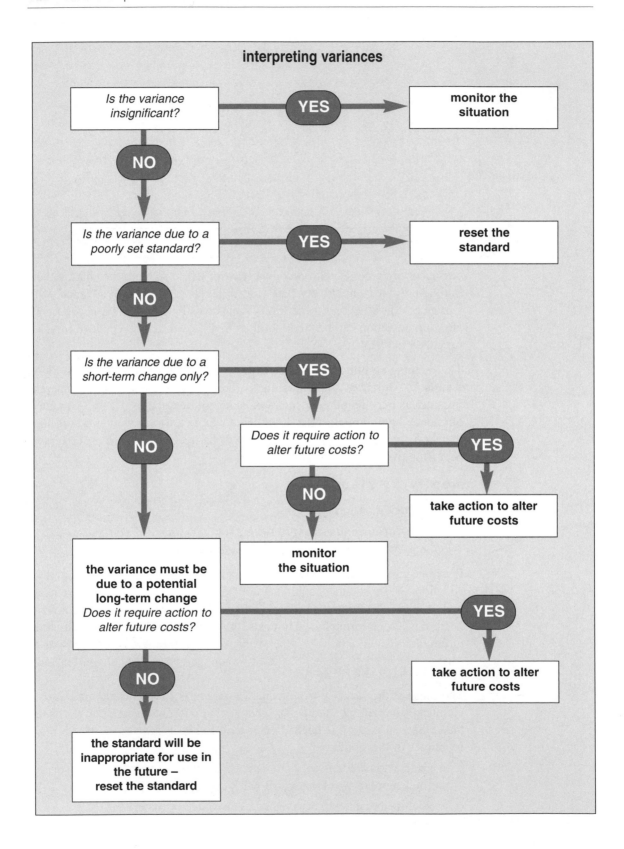

If, however, the variance is caused by some temporary change that may recur often enough to cause concern, then action should be taken either to prevent such changes or to alter the standard if the changes are uncontrollable.

An example of this could be individual batches of material that cause excessive wastage. A change of supplier may be a solution, but if all suppliers are having a similar quality problem due to some common situation then the issue may simply need to be acknowledged by monitoring the variances to ensure that they return to their expected level in future. If the material in this example were coffee beans that were affected by poor weather in the world's main coffee growing regions then it would clearly make some sense to monitor the situation over the coming seasons.

long-term changes

Sometimes variances are the result of situations that are potentially long-term. Perhaps there has been a change in working practices or wage rates resulting in different costs, and if the managers consider the situation is acceptable then it would be logical to reset the standards. The same would apply to a general price change that is seen as reasonably permanent and uncontrollable. If, however, a price rise could be avoided by changing suppliers, then there would be no need to alter the standards, provided that managers considered that this was the best solution.

INTERPRETING SPECIFIC DIRECT VARIANCES

At this stage it is worth looking back at the direct variances that we have examined, and making sure that we can link possible causes with each variance. We will now discuss each variance in turn. The total variances are not examined here, since the causes of these will be based on the causes of the appropriate sub-variances.

direct material price variance

The key to interpreting any variance is to remember what it is measuring. Here (as the variance title clearly tells us), the variance is concerned with the **price** of materials. We can therefore ignore any issues that are not related to price. Some of the reasons for price variances include:

- world-wide price changes (due to specific supply / demand issues or general inflation or deflation)
- change of supplier
- change of quality of material (better quality usually, but not always, costing more)
- changes in quantity purchased (obtaining better or worse quantity discounts)

Some of these reasons could also affect other variances. As noted earlier, these situations are sometimes referred to as the 'interdependence of variances'. The example often quoted is higher priced, better quality material creating an adverse material price variance, but also generating less wastage and therefore contributing to favourable material usage variances. Possibly even favourable labour efficiency variances could also arise if the material is easier to use.

direct material usage variance

Usage of material is concerned with how much material is used compared with the standard quantity that would be expected. Perhaps the most obvious example is the amount of wastage being higher or lower than expected. This could also be linked to material quality, or to skill level of labour or to poor machine maintenance.

However, the general assumption that a favourable variance is always 'good news' and that an adverse variance is always bad does not always apply for usage variances.

Sometimes any usage variance could be an indicator of a problem. For example, if making concrete products a favourable usage variance for cement may mean that the mix is too weak and the final products will not be strong enough.

Another situation where a favourable variance could be an indicator of a problem is if the final product is undersize or underweight. This could occur in both manual operations and automated ones. For example, tins of paint may be only 95% filled by a machine that is poorly calibrated. The system would record a favourable usage variance, but legal action could result from the quantity of paint not being as described on the tin.

Sometimes usage variances are due to a deliberate decision made in response to the available material. For example, additional sugar may need to be added to a fruit drink mixture if the fruit used was less sweet than usual.

As with other variances, it is always important to examine the circumstances and any additional information provided before making a judgement.

direct labour rate variance

The labour rate variance is concerned with how much the rate of pay costs the organisation. Here the background splits into two main situations:

- using the planned labour force, but paying a different rate, and
- using a different labour force than planned, often causing a different rate to be paid.

When using the planned labour force, the cost of labour could be different to standard for any of the following reasons:

- a pay rate change (usually a rise) that was either not built into the standard, or is more or less than the expected pay rate change
- bonuses paid at more or less than the expected amount; if bonuses are included in the standard rate the amount will be based on an expected average level
- more or less overtime being paid than expected; this depends on whether the overtime premium is charged to direct costs or overheads – if it is charged to overheads it would not be reflected here
- a change in costs of employment – for example national costs like employers' national insurance contributions, which are normally incorporated in labour costs

Sometimes the labour rate variance will be linked to a change in the labour force being used, for example:

- a higher or lower grade of labour being used than planned, or trainees being used instead of fully trained operatives; this could also link to other variances including labour efficiency and material usage
- contractors or agency staff being used instead of the normal employees; these are often more flexible in terms of contracts, but usually cost a higher rate (including a charge to the agency where appropriate)

direct labour efficiency variance

This variance focuses on the time spent by the labour force in producing the output. The direct labour idle time variance can also be calculated where information is available, and some of the following also applies to this variance. More or less time spent could relate to how long individuals spend on the work, or to more or less people being used.

Although efficiency often appears to be entirely in the control of the labour force and their managers, there are also outside influences that can result in variances. The range of causes for labour efficiency variances include:

- level of training of staff
- quality of materials
- availability of materials or components (for example awaiting a delivery)
- efficiency of machinery including breakdowns (ranging from hand held tools to production lines)
- working conditions (for example excessive heat or cold)

looking beyond the obvious

We saw in Chapter 2 that some causes can link to more than one variance – for example a cheap, poor quality material causing a favourable price variance but an adverse usage variance. However quality is not always in line with the price. A cheap material may be of better quality than more expensive material, or the opposite may be true. You should also consider carefully comments made by managers who may be trying to avoid the blame for poor performance. A production manager could try to justify poor usage by blaming the quality of cheap materials (and therefore the purchasing manager's fault) whereas the problem may really be something else. You should therefore consider all possibilities.

Case Study

1.850

1.600

DRINK-COCOA LIMITED
CALCULATING AND INTERPRETING VARIANCES

Drink-Cocoa Limited manufactures and distributes cocoa. One of its main products is Chocco-Smooth, a cocoa blended from Foro and Trino beans. Chocco-Smooth is sold in 1 kilogram packs. Budgeted production is 10,000 one kilogram packs.

You work as an Accounting Technician reporting to the Finance Director.

The company operates an integrated standard cost system in which:

* purchases of materials are recorded at standard cost

* direct material costs are variable

* production overheads are fixed and absorbed on a unit basis

* production costs include labour costs for maintenance and setting up of the machines

The actual results for November are as follows:

		Actual
Production (1 kilogram packs)		9,500
Direct materials (Foro beans)	4,000 kilograms	£12,800
Direct materials (Trino beans)	6,000 kilograms	£8,400
Direct packaging materials (foil)	110 square metres	£550
Fixed production overheads		£7,500
Total cost		£29,250

The standard cost card for production of 1 kilogram of Chocco-Smooth cocoa is:

	Quantity	Unit price	Total cost
Product: 1 kilogram of Chocco-Smooth			£
Direct materials (Foro beans)	500 grams	£3 per kilogram	1.50
Direct materials (Trino beans)	500 grams	£1.50 per kilogram	0.75
Direct packaging materials (foil)	0.01 square metres	£10 per square metre	0.10
Fixed production overheads			0.65
Standard cost			3.00

required – part one

(a)   Calculate the following variances for November:

   (i)   direct material (Foro) price variance

   (ii)   direct material (Foro) usage variance

   (iii)   direct material (Trino) price variance

   (iv)   direct material (Trino) usage variance

   (v)   direct packaging material (foil) price variance

   (vi)   direct packaging material (foil) usage variance

(b)   Prepare an operating statement reconciling the actual material cost of producing 9,500 one kilogram packs of Chocco-Smooth with the standard material cost of producing 9,500 one kilogram packs.

(c)   Calculate the fixed overhead expenditure variance and the fixed overhead volume variance.

solution – part one

(a)

   (i)   Direct material (Foro) price variance

    Actual cost of £12,800 compared with standard cost of actual quantity purchased (4,000 x £3) = £800 adverse

   (ii)   Direct material (Foro) usage variance

    Standard cost per kg of Foro = £3
    Total number of kgs used = 4,000
    Total number of kgs which should have been used = 9,500 x 0.5 = 4,750
    therefore variance = (4,750 - 4,000) x £3 = £2,250 favourable

   (iii)   Direct material (Trino) price variance

    Actual cost of £8,400 compared with standard cost of actual quantity purchased (6,000 x £1.50) = £600 favourable

   (iv)   Direct material (Trino) usage variance

    Standard cost per kg of Trino = £1.50
    Total number of kgs used = 6,000
    Total number of kgs which should have been used = 9,500 x 0.5 = 4,750
    therefore variance = (4,750 - 6,000) x £1.50 = £1,875 adverse

   (v)   Direct packaging material (foil) price variance

    Actual cost of £550 compared with standard cost of actual quantity purchased (110 x £10) = £550 favourable

   (vi)   Direct packaging material (foil) usage variance
    Standard cost per metre of foil = £10
    Total number of square metres used = 110

Total number of square metres which should have been used =
9,500 x 0.01 = 95
therefore variance = (95 -110) x £10 = £150 adverse

(b)

Actual total direct material cost			£21,750
Variances	Favourable	Adverse	
Direct materials (Foro) price		£800	
Direct materials (Foro) usage	£2,250		
Direct materials (Trino) price	£600		
Direct materials (Trino) usage		£1,875	
Direct materials (foil) price	£550		
Direct materials (foil) usage		£150	
Total variance	£3,400	£2,825	£575
Standard total direct material cost of actual production *(working 1)*			£22,325

Working 1

(£1.50 + £0.75 + £0.10) x 9,500 = £22,325

(c) Fixed overhead expenditure variance

Actual expenditure = £7,500
Budgeted expenditure = £6,500 (based on £0.65 x 10,000 budgeted kilos)
Variance = £1,000 adverse

Fixed overhead volume variance

Actual volume = 9,500
Budgeted volume =10,000
Variance: 500 units (adverse) x absorption rate of £0.65 per unit = £325 adverse

Additional data

You have been given the following information about Foro and Trino cocoa beans.

- Foro beans are a higher quality and provide a richer flavour whereas Trino beans are considered lower quality and tend to be bitter in taste. The cost of Foro beans is set by the market and recently the price has risen sharply due to a poor harvest. The purchaser has to take the price quoted on the market. The quality of the beans was as expected.

- An automated mixing machine broke down which led to more Trino beans being added to the mix. The breakdown has been blamed on the loss of maintenance personnel due to a lower than market pay rise.

- The price of Trino beans is set by the market and the price has recently fallen due to a good harvest. The purchaser has to take the price quoted on the market. The quality of the beans was as expected.

- In order to maintain the quality of the cocoa blend, the percentage of Foro beans should not fall below 45% of the weight of the blend.

required – part two

Using this information, prepare a report to the Production Director stating:

- possible reasons for the Foro and Trino variances you calculated in part one
- whether the company could have taken any action and if so what action could have been taken
- how the direct materials usage variances for Foro beans and Trino beans are linked.

solution – part two

To:	Production Director	From:	AAT student
Subject:	Reason for variances		

Direct material (Foro) price variance

The price variance for Foro beans is £800 adverse.

This is due to the market price of beans increasing due to the poor harvest, meaning there is lower supply therefore the price increases.

The company could not have taken any action as the market sets the price.

Direct material (Foro) usage variance

The usage variance for Foro beans is £2,250 favourable.

This has been caused by the mixing process making an error and adding a greater amount of Trino beans to the mix. The result is that the company has saved money on the purchase of the beans, but the mix is outside of the range recommended to produce an acceptable quality blend. Therefore the customers may be unhappy. The company could have secured the maintenance personnel by paying a market rate, or outsourcing the maintenance.

Direct material (Trino) price variance

The price variance for Trino beans is £600 favourable.

This is due to the market price of beans decreasing due to a good harvest meaning there is a larger supply, therefore the price reduces. The company could not have taken any action as the market sets the price.

Direct material (Trino) usage variance

The usage variance is £1,875 adverse because the company used more beans than expected. This was because of the automated mixing machine breaking down. The company could have ensured that maintenance was undertaken to prevent the machine breaking down. The Foro usage variance (2,250 favourable) is favourable which offsets the adverse Trino usage variance (1,875 adverse). In financial terms the overall position is a gain of £375. However the quality of the mix may be a problem as the percentage of Foro beans is below 45%. The company may therefore lose customers or have returned goods.

ANALYSING DIRECT VARIANCES

As we have just discussed, one of the problems that can arise is that the standard itself may become less useful or out of date due to a variety of reasons. There could, for example, be world-wide price changes, or the organisation itself may have deliberately changed its working practices.

Sometimes we may be aware of the issue, but we do not wish to change the standard, perhaps because standard setting is not scheduled to take place yet, or maybe we are not sure of the ultimate impact of the change.

In these circumstances it is sometimes useful to sub-divide direct variances to identify

- the part of the variance caused by the situation that we are aware of (the uncontrollable part) and
- the 'real' variance that may be otherwise hidden (the controllable part).

Whatever the situation, the basic procedure is the same.

We have already seen that direct variances result from a comparison between
- standard data, and
- actual data

For example, the **direct material price variance** is the difference between the standard price of the actual material, and the actual price:

But if we have additional information that means that the original standard ought to be changed, we can create a new 'revised standard' to help make comparisons, as shown at the bottom of the chart on the next page.

Note that
- we have added the prices to help show how the process works
- the actual price has increased even further than the new standard price

Study the diagram on the next page.

We can break down the original variance of £50 into two parts:

1 The part of the variance that we know the reason for – the difference between the original standard and our now 'revised' standard; here it is £30 (adverse). This is the uncontrollable part.

2   The part of the variance that must be due to other factors – effectively the 'real' variance. This is measured by comparing the actual data with the new 'revised' standard; here the difference is £20 (adverse). This is the controllable part.

Both parts will always add back to the original variance (£30 + £20 = £50).

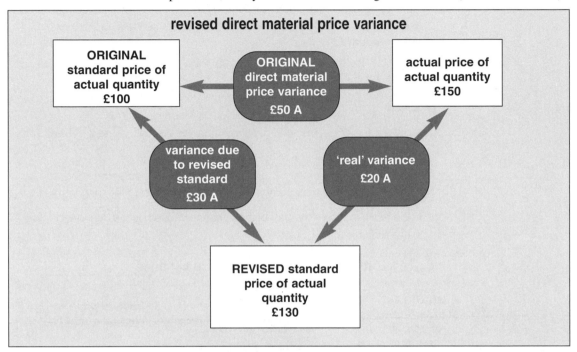

We can use the same technique for a variety of situations that can relate to any of the four direct variances that we saw in Chapter 2. Some of the main causes of change where this technique may be useful are:

relating to material prices
- inflation
- currency movements

relating to material usage
- new machinery or working practices
- untrained or better trained labour force

relating to labour rate
- pay rise

relating to labour efficiency
- new machinery or working practices
- untrained or better trained labour force

Before we examine specific situations, we will provide a further practical example to illustrate how the process works.

worked example: price changes

A company uses coffee beans to make its instant coffee.

The standard price of coffee beans is £10.00 per kilo, and this was set by using the published average trade price of coffee beans in January.

A trade publication has stated that the average trade price for coffee beans during May was £11.50 per kilo – the company has used this as the basis of the **revised standard.**

During May the company used 15,000 kilos of coffee beans, which cost £180,000 in total (ie an average of £12 per kilo).

required

Calculate the direct material price variance for the coffee used in May, and then analyse it into:

- the part of the variance – (the 'revised standard' variance) – caused by the movement in the average trade price of coffee in May (uncontrollable)

- the real variance – the part of the variance caused by the unknown factors (controllable)

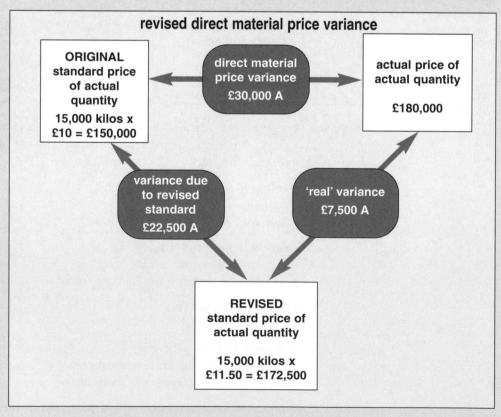

Analysis

This shows that while most of the original variance of £30,000 A (ie £22,500) is caused by the movement in average trade coffee prices, there is still an adverse variance of £7,500 that is not accounted for. This could be due to poor purchasing by the company or various other factors.

We will now look in more detail at how this technique can be used in other situations to analyse variances.

INFLATION

In Chapter 1 we examined the use of index numbers to record and forecast various data including inflation (see page 42). Cost inflation is usually taken into account when setting price standards. Whereas the retail price index (RPI) and the consumer prices index (CPI) are measures of general inflation, an estimate of specific inflation for the industry, or, better still, the specific material or labour index should be used where possible.

Where the allowance for inflation within the standard turns out to be incorrect, then the variances can be analysed into:

- the part caused by known price inflation
- the part due to other causes

Calculations may need to be carried out to determine what the price or rate would have been if the 'correct' allowance had been made for inflation. This can be done once the actual change in the appropriate index is applied to the 'pre-inflation' standard. The analysis of the price variance is then similar to that carried out based on seasonality, as shown in the Case Study that follows.

Case Study

MELTO PLASTIC MOULDINGS LTD: INFLATION AND THE ORIGINAL PRICE VARIANCE

Melto Plastic Mouldings Limited set its price standard for a high quality resin when the specific price index for the material was 180. The assumption was made that it would rise to 190 by the time the standard was in use, and therefore the standard decided upon was £38.00 per kilo to take this into account.

In reality the index rose to 186 by the time the standard was in use. During the month 2,000 kilos of the material were used, costing £80,000.

required

Calculate the material price variance, and analyse it into:

- the part of the material price variance due to the actual change in the price index
- the part of the material price variance due to other influences

solution

'Pre-inflation' standard price = £38.00 x (180 ÷ 190)   = £36.00 per kilo

Actual Index Adjusted Price Standard = £36.00 x (186 ÷ 180)   = £37.20 per kilo

(alternatively calculated as £38.00 x (186 ÷ 190) = £37.20)

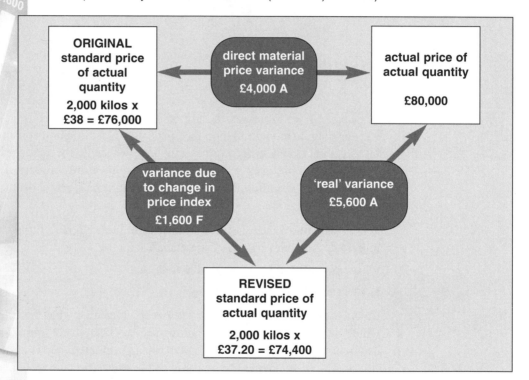

conclusion

This calculation shows that the original £4,000 adverse price variance masks a larger unexplained adverse variance of £5,600 when you take into account the fact that the rate of inflation has been lower than estimated, giving a favourable variance of £1,600.

labour rate indexation

A similar calculation can be made for the analysis of labour rate variances. Here the expected index change may be used as a guide to setting standards. Sometimes the actual wage rise agreed by an employer may be more significant than the actual change in the index when analysing the rate variance.

Case Study

1.850

1.600

MELTO PLASTIC MOULDINGS LTD: LABOUR RATE INDEXATION

For the period January to April the appropriate regional wage rate index was expected to rise from 290 to 300, and the standard wage rate was set by Melto Plastic Mouldings at £9.00 per hour to take account of this change. In reality the relevant grade of employees received a pay award averaging 4%.

During April the section of the labour force worked 24,000 hours, and were paid a total of £216,960.

required

Calculate the labour rate variance, and analyse it into the part due to the actual pay award, and the part due to other influences.

solution

'Pre-inflation' standard rate = £9.00 x (290 ÷ 300)   = £8.70 per hour

Actual Pay Award Adjusted Standard Rate = £8.70 + 4%   = £9.048 per hour

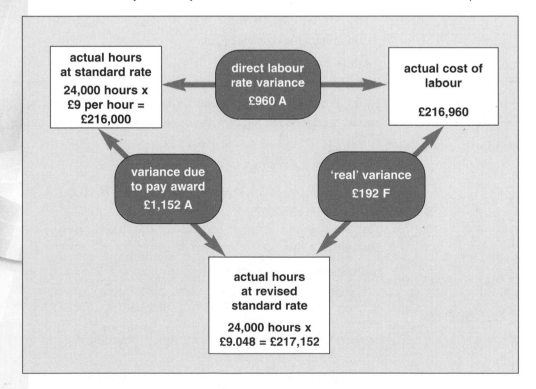

conclusion

This indicates that the pay award accounts for more than the original rate variance.
A smaller favourable variance appears to arise from other controllable causes.

ACCOUNTING FOR STANDARD COSTS AND VARIANCES

If standard costing is used by an organisation, the double-entry accounting system must also reflect the use of standard costing. This can be achieved by

- entering the actual cost figures into the relevant cost accounts as normal, and then

- entering the variances into the same cost accounts, with a double entry to the income statement, probably through a variance account

This will mean that the cost accounts will now contain the standard costs for the actual production level. These figures will then be used in the manufacturing account and income statement, with the variances also shown in the income statement.

An extract from the income statement could therefore look like this:

	£
Revenue	xxx
less cost of sales (at standard cost)	(xxx)
less adverse cost variances	(xxx)
add favourable cost variances	xxx
Gross Profit (actual)	xxx

To show how the accounts could be built up to arrive at this position, let us use an example showing how the direct labour could be accounted for.

worked example

Suppose the standard direct labour cost for the actual production was based on 500 labour hours at £10 per hour = £5,000.

If the actual labour cost was £5,600, based on 480 hours, then we could calculate the variances:

Direct labour rate variance

(480 hours x £10) – £5,600   = £800 A

Direct labour efficiency variance

(500 hours x £10) – (480 hours x £10)   = £200 F

These variances account for the total direct labour variance of £600 A.

Labour costs will normally be collected in the Work in Progress Account (as you will have learned in your earlier studies), and this account would be built up with the following entries relating to labour:

Work in Progress Account

Actual Labour Costs		Direct labour rate	
(from payroll account)	£5,600	variance	£800
Direct labour efficiency variance	£200		

This would mean that the net effect of these labour entries in this account equals £5,000 – the standard cost of labour.

The double entries for the labour variances would usually be collected in a variance account, along with the other variances, before being transferred to the income statement (profit & loss account) at the period end.

Variances Account

Direct labour rate variance	£800	Direct labour efficiency variance	£200
		Income statement	£600

Note that the effect is that:

- adverse variances are debited to the income statement (increasing costs and reducing profit) and
- favourable variances are credited to the income statement (reducing costs and increasing profit)

This applies to all cost variances, materials, labour and overheads.

journal entries

While the journal entry will depend on the exact names of the accounts used (which can vary), the principle is always the same. The ultimate aim is for:

- adverse variances to be debited to the income statement and credited to the relevant cost account, and
- favourable variances to be credited to the income statement and debited to the relevant cost account

The journal entries that reflect the variances in the above example would be as follows:

Account	Debit £	Credit £
Work in progress account	200	
Variances account (or income statement)		200
(the direct labour efficiency variance)		
Variances account (or income statement)	800	
Work in progress account		800
(the direct labour rate variance)		

A COMPREHENSIVE VARIANCE ANALYSIS CASE STUDY

In Chapter 2 we examined direct cost variances, and we have just seen how these can be analysed into controllable and non-controllable variances.

In Chapter 3 we studied fixed overhead variances and their implications.

In the following Case Study we combine the techniques from these three chapters.

Case Study

DELTA PRODUCTS LIMITED: VARIANCE ANALYSIS

Delta Products Limited manufactures a single product, and uses standard absorption costing for planning and monitoring costs. The standard cost of each unit produced is as follows, based on the budgeted production level of 5,000 units per month.

Direct Materials	150 litres @ £1.25 per litre
Direct Labour	5 hours @ £8.00 per hour
Fixed Overheads	5 hours @ £8.50 per hour

The fixed overheads are absorbed based on the standard direct labour hours for the production level achieved.

In September the following data is available on actual production level and costs incurred:

Production Level	5,500 units produced
Direct Materials	820,000 litres were used, costing £1,020,000 in total
Direct Labour	26,000 hours were taken, costing £208,000 in total
Fixed Overheads	Total expenditure on fixed overheads was £222,800

required

1   Calculate the standard cost of the actual production of 5,500 units.

2   Calculate the following variances, and use them to reconcile the actual costs incurred with the standard cost of the actual production.

- Direct Material Price Variance

- Direct Material Usage Variance

- Direct Labour Rate Variance

- Direct Labour Efficiency Variance

- Fixed Overhead Expenditure Variance

- Fixed Overhead Volume Variance, divided into

- Fixed Overhead Capacity Variance

- Fixed Overhead Efficiency Variance

3   It has been discovered that since the standards were set:

(a)   new production methods have improved standard material usage by 1%, and

(b)   the material price index that relates to the direct materials has fallen from 175 to 173.6.

Neither of these changes was anticipated by the standards.

You are to analyse the Direct Material Price Variance, and the Direct Material Usage Variance into the parts of the variances caused by these factors and the parts caused by other influences, which are controllable.

solution

1   Standard cost of one unit

Direct Materials	150 litres @ £1.25 per litre =	£187.50
Direct Labour	5 hours @ £8.00 per hour =	£40.00
Fixed Overheads	5 hours @ £8.50 per hour =	£42.50
		£270.00

Standard cost of 5,500 units £270.00 x 5,500 units = £1,485,000.

2 **The direct cost variances can be calculated as follows:**

- Direct Material Price Variance

  (820,000 litres x £1.25) - £1,020,000 = £5,000 FAV

- Direct Material Usage Variance

  £1.25 x ([150 litres x 5,500 units] − 820,000 litres) = £6,250 FAV

- Direct Labour Rate Variance

  (26,000 hours x £8.00) - £208,000 = £0

- Direct Labour Efficiency Variance

  £8.00 x ([5 hours x 5,500 units] − 26,000 hours) = £12,000 FAV

Using the format explained in Chapter 3 to calculate the fixed overhead variances, the diagram appears as shown below:

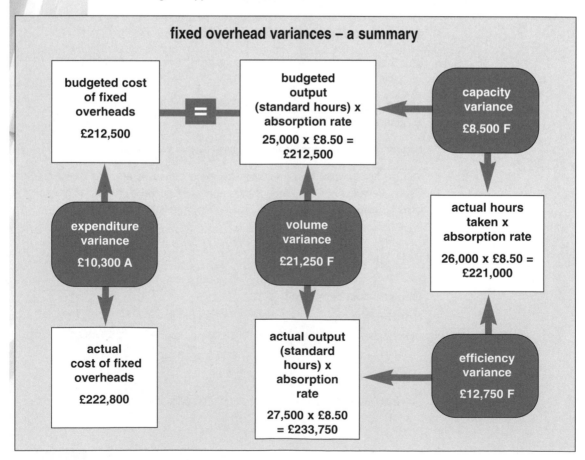

fixed overhead variances – a summary

Reconciliation

	£	£	£
Standard cost of production of 5,500 units			1,485,000
Direct Variances:			
Direct Material Price Variance		(5,000) F	
Direct Material Usage Variance		(6,250) F	
Direct Labour Rate Variance		0	
Direct Labour Efficiency Variance		(12,000) F	
			(23,250)
Fixed Overhead Variances:			
Expenditure Variance		10,300 A	
Capacity Variance	(8,500) F		
Efficiency Variance	(12,750) F		
Volume Variance		(21,250) F	
			(10,950)
Actual Cost of Production (£1,020,000 + £208,000 + £222,800)			£1,450,800

3 The revised standard price per litre = £1.25 x (173.6 ÷ 175) = £1.24

The 'revised' standard price for the actual quantity used, taking account of the movement of the price index would be:

820,000 litres x £1.24   =   £1,016,800

The Direct Material Price Variance of £5,000 F can therefore be divided into:

- Price Variance due to index movement:

   Actual Quantity at Standard Price – Actual Quantity at Revised Standard Price

   (820,000 litres x £1.25) - £1,016,800   =   £8,200 F

- Price Variance due to other influences

   Actual Quantity at Revised Standard Price – Actual Quantity at Actual Price

   £1,016,800 – £ 1,020,000   =   £3,200 A

The 'revised' standard usage for the actual production level, based on the new production methods would be:

5,500 units x 150 litres x 99%   =   816,750 litres

The Direct Material Usage Variance of £6,250 F can therefore be divided into:

- Usage Variance due to new production methods:

Standard Price x (Standard Usage – Revised Standard Usage)

£1.25 x ([5,500 units x 150 litres] – 816,750 litres) =   £10,312.50 F

- Usage Variance Due to other influences

Standard Price x (Revised Standard Usage – Actual Usage)

£1.25 x (816,750 litres – 820,000 litres)   =   £ 4,062.50 A

Chapter Summary

- Standards can be set at an Ideal, Attainable, or Basic level. There are also variations in attainable standards, called 'normal' standards and 'target' standards.

- The level at which a standard is set has implications for interpretation of variances, and the behaviour of employees.

- Actions to be taken resulting from variances will depend on materiality, whether the causes are short or long term, and how controllable they are.

- Actions to be taken can be divided into those that will change future costs or those that will require adjustment of the future standard.

- Variances can be analysed to determine the variance caused by specific factors such as inflation. These can then be excluded from the original variance to highlight the variance due to other factors.

- Accounting for standard costs and variances usually involves entering variances into the relevant cost accounts, along with the actual costs. The other entry for the variance is ultimately the income statement (profit & loss account) where adverse variances are always debited and favourable variances credited.

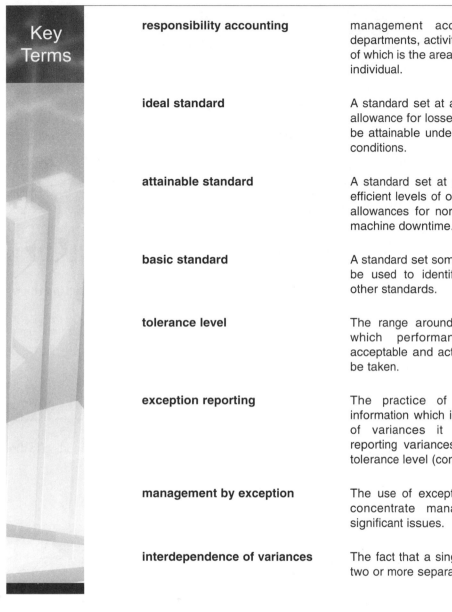

Key Terms

responsibility accounting	management accounting based on departments, activities or functions, each of which is the area of responsibility of an individual.
ideal standard	A standard set at a level that makes no allowance for losses, and which can only be attainable under the most favourable conditions.
attainable standard	A standard set at a level that assumes efficient levels of operation, but includes allowances for normal loss, waste, and machine downtime.
basic standard	A standard set some time ago which can be used to identify trends or develop other standards.
tolerance level	The range around the standard within which performance is considered acceptable and action does not need to be taken.
exception reporting	The practice of reporting only the information which is significant. In terms of variances it could involve only reporting variances outside the agreed tolerance level (control limits).
management by exception	The use of exception reporting to help concentrate management efforts on significant issues.
interdependence of variances	The fact that a single cause may create two or more separate variances.

Activities

4.1   The following statements were compiled by a trainee accountant:

(a)   All variances should always be thoroughly investigated.

(b)   Using standards set at a basic level may help to identify long-term trends in costs.

(c)   In order to motivate staff, standards should generally be challenging yet achievable.

(d)   One advantage of setting up a standard costing system is that an atmosphere of cost-consciousness is generated.

(e)   Responsibility accounting means that the accountant is responsible for calculating all the necessary variances.

(f)   If a variance has been caused by a short-term change that will naturally right itself then there is probably no need to adjust the standards.

(g)   Interpretation problems arising through the interdependence of variances would not exist if variances were calculated accurately.

Required

State whether each of these statements is true or false.

4.2   Heatit Ltd manufactures domestic radiators. You work as an accounting technician reporting to the Finance Director.

Heatit Ltd operates a standard cost system in which:

- direct material and direct labour costs are variable

- production overheads are fixed and absorbed on a labour hour basis

The budgeted activity and actual results for the month of April are as follows:

	Budget		Actual	
Production units (radiators)		5,000		5,200
Direct materials (steel)	20,000 sq mt	£30,000	21,320 sq mt	£30,914
Direct materials (paint)	500 litres	£2,500	505 litres	£2,600
Direct labour	2,500 hours	£27,500	2,650 hours	£31,800
Fixed overheads		£60,000		£58,500
Total cost		£120,000		£123,814

Required

(a)   Calculate the following variances for April:

   (i)   direct material (steel) usage variance

   (ii)   direct labour rate variance

   (iii)   direct labour efficiency variance

(b)   Complete the following sentence by selecting from the phrases shown below.

'An adverse variance is ………………………… the income statement (profit & loss account), and

a favourable variance is ……………………........... the income statement.'

Phrases: a debit to

              a credit to

              not shown in

4.3   Benson & Co was setting its standards for the next year at a time when the current average pay rate in the organisation was £7.00 per hour. At the time the appropriate regional wage rate index was standing at 140, and expected to rise to 145 in the next year. To take account of this expected increase in costs the new standard wage rate was set at £7.25 per hour.

In reality at the start of the year all employees received a pay award of 4.5%. The regional wage index moved to 150.

During week 12 the labour force worked 3,200 hours, and were paid a total of £23,744.

Required

(a)   Calculate the labour rate variance, and analyse it:

   (i)   by using the actual pay award data into the part of the variance due to the pay award, and the part due to other influences.

   and

   (ii)   by using the actual movement in the regional wage rate index into the part of the variance due to regional wage rate change and the part due to other influences.

(b)   State which analysis is most useful to managers and explain why.

4.4   The following budgetary control report has been provided for a liquid soap manufacturer.

	Budget		Actual	
Production units (bottles)		5,000		5,500
Direct materials (liquid soap)	1,250 litres	£7,500	1,400 litres	£7,700
Direct materials (plastic bottles)	5,000 units	£1,000	5,650 units	£1,017
Direct labour	150 hours	£1,650	175 hours	£1,663
Fixed overheads		£3,500		£3,750
Total cost		£13,650		£14,130

The following variances have been calculated:

Fixed overhead expenditure	£250
Direct materials (liquid soap) price	£700 F
Direct materials (bottles) price	£113 F
Direct materials (liquid soap) usage	£150 A
Direct materials (bottles) usage	£30
Direct labour rate	£262
Direct labour efficiency	£110 A
Fixed overhead volume	£350 F

Required

Calculate the standard (budgeted) cost of the 5,500 units produced, and complete the operating statement on the next page.

Standard cost for actual production			£
Variances	Favourable	Adverse	
Total variance			£
Actual cost of actual production			£

5 Measuring quality

this chapter covers...

In this chapter we examine a range of ideas and techniques that are connected with the concept of quality.

We start by learning what is meant by quality and value, and how this can vary in different circumstances, with examples in both products and services. We will also explain what is meant by total quality management, and how this idea is important in many organisations.

We will then see how we can measure the costs of quality, and how some of these costs are explicit and relatively easy to determine, while others are implicit within other costs.

Next we will examine the techniques of cost reduction, value engineering and value analysis. We will look at exactly what is meant by these terms as well as the practical aspects of implementing them.

Target costing is then studied, using practical examples so that both numerical and written tasks can then be attempted.

The final topic in this chapter is life cycle costing. We will see how it can be used for both new product ranges as well as investment in non-current assets. Discounted cash flow is an important tool when using life cycle costing, and this is demonstrated using case studies.

QUALITY AND VALUE

The terms 'quality' and 'value' are used in everyday language and generally taken to mean 'how good something is' and 'how much it is worth'. In this chapter, we will consider different ways of measuring how good things are and how much they are worth. We will also examine ways of making improvements in the quality and value of both goods and services.

quality

The quality of a product or service can be considered as its fitness for the customer's purpose.

Another definition is:

Quality is the degree of excellence of a product or service.

The two definitions go together. If we look for 'excellence' in a product or service, we are expecting it to be completely satisfactory for its purpose, as far as the customer is concerned.

quality and customer satisfaction

For a product or service to be of high quality, it does not necessarily mean that it uses very expensive materials or highly skilled staff to provide it. What is important is that it **satisfies the customer**. This means that the product or service must:

• be fit for the purpose for which it is purchased

• represent value for money to the customer.

In modern consumer-led societies, customers have access to a wide choice of products and services and make greater demands on suppliers. It is therefore increasingly important for businesses to pay more attention to the requirements of consumers. For example, there is fierce competition for market share between the main supermarket chains in the UK. If they all sell similar products at similar prices, the quality of the service they provide becomes a factor. Attention turns to reducing queues at the tills, providing in-store restaurants and other ways of increasing customer satisfaction.

The way in which customer satisfaction is to be achieved by ensuring that goods are fit for their purpose will depend on the type of product. For example, customers may look for:

• **low prices**

    Some products such as disposable razors and plastic ballpoint pens will be expected to have a short life. Customers expect them to be cheap and they may be made from cheap materials, provided they still work.

- **durability**

   Products such as computers and cars are expected to last much longer and remain reliable throughout their useful life.

- **uniqueness and craftsmanship**

   In certain businesses, expensive raw materials and highly skilled work are an integral part of the value of the product to the customer, for example in hand-made jewellery or furniture.

- **prestige or status**

   Products which represent value to the customer in terms of prestige or status are expected to have expensive packaging, designer labels and high prices, for example perfumes and fashion products.

quality in services

There will also be different ways of considering and measuring quality in the provision of services, depending upon the type of service. Here, customer satisfaction is dependent on customer experience. For example, the features they may look for include:

- **an efficient service**

   Where the service involves answering queries or giving advice, customers expect accurate information, given within a reasonable time. Efficient travel services (rail, bus or air) should run on time. These aspects of a service can be measured against targets.

- **friendly and helpful staff**

   These aspects are also likely to be very important to customers, but are more difficult to measure.

- **a clean and comfortable environment**

   Wherever customers have to visit a service provider or wait for service, for example at a clinic or at a railway station, the environment is an important factor.

quality and value

It can be seen that quality and value to the customer go hand in hand. An organisation can make improvements to the quality of its products or services by reducing the numbers of sub-standard products, responding to customers' demands and by getting things 'right first time'. This is referred to as **quality management**.

In the above discussion, we have concentrated on value to the customer, taking into account both **value in use** and **prestige value**. However, from the point of view of the producer or provider there are other important values to consider. In any organisation, whether profit-making or non-profit-making, control of costs is essential. One 'value' to be put on a product or service is therefore the **cost** of making it or providing it. For profit-making businesses, the selling price or market value is equally important.

In conclusion, the **value** of a product or service can be considered as having four main aspects:

1	value in use (fitness for purpose)	. . . for the customer
2	esteem or prestige value	. . . for the customer
3	cost of production or provision	. . . for the provider
4	exchange value (market value)	. . . for the provider

enhancement of value

Looking at the four aspects of value listed above, it is clear that, from the point of view of the producer or provider, it is desirable to add to the exchange market value of a product or service without increasing the cost. This means that the value in the view of the customers must be enhanced, so that they are prepared to pay a higher price.

In order to **add value**, it is necessary to analyse what customers expect and what they are prepared to pay for. Customers buying a product such as a car may be prepared to pay more for additional features. In service provision, the customers' experience could be improved, perhaps by having more luxurious surroundings, as in first class travel. Enhancement of value without increasing selling prices may be necessary where competitors offer similar products or services to customers, as in the example of supermarket chains described at the beginning of this chapter.

Adding value to a product or service while keeping costs down can only be achieved by careful monitoring of performance within the organisation. We will study ways to measure performance in detail in Chapters 6 and 7.

examples

1   List the features of an AAT Tutorial text which give it value to the customer.

2   List the features of an expensive, famous brand watch which give it value to the customer.

3   List the features of a clothes dry cleaning service which contribute to the quality of the service.

suggested answers

1   the AAT text

As the customers for this book are almost certainly AAT students, it is expected that they require:

-   the content of the text to cover the required material for the units

-   the content to be complete and clearly explained

-   that the layout of the book makes it easy to use

-   that there are no errors in the book

-   that the paper and binding of the book will be of a suitable standard to last the course, without making the book too expensive

2 the watch

Like any other watch, reliable and accurate time-keeping are important for its value in use. In addition, with this type of watch, the brand name adds value in the form of esteem value, as does the fact that it is known that the watch is expensive. Reducing the selling price may therefore detract from its value to the customer. The design and construction should be of a higher standard than cheaper watches, and more expensive materials on the outside of the watch also add value.

3 dry cleaning

In a dry cleaning service, customers would be looking for:

- efficient cleaning and pressing

- no errors resulting in lost items or damage to clothes

- value for money

- convenient time and place to leave and collect clothes

- quick service

- helpful staff

We will now consider in more detail some methods which can contribute to the management of performance and enhancement of value.

TOTAL QUALITY MANAGEMENT

Total Quality Management (TQM) means that quality management becomes the aim of every part of an organisation.

The basic principle is one of continuous improvement, in order to eliminate faulty work and prevent mistakes. Mistakes carry a cost:

- wastage of materials
- idle time
- the cost of reworking
- the loss of customer goodwill, resulting in lost sales
- the cost of replacements
- the cost of dealing with customers' complaints

The concept of continuous improvement and getting more 'right first time' will reduce these costs. Other costs will be incurred in quality management, but the intention is that in the long term the organisation will benefit.

implementing TQM

If TQM is to be introduced, it must become the philosophy of everyone in the organisation, and apply to every activity, including administration, purchasing, sales, marketing and distribution, as well as production. Training and motivation of staff is essential, so that an attitude of seeking improvement is encouraged. Everyone should be allowed to put forward ideas. Groups of employees may form 'quality circles' and have regular meetings to discuss their ideas for quality improvements.

Each person within an organisation has customers. These may be *internal* users of his/her work – ie colleagues – as not everyone deals directly with the external customers. If the quality of the work for the next immediate user is monitored, mistakes will be reduced throughout the organisation.

The involvement of all staff of an organisation means that many different types of knowledge and skills are being used. These may be in engineering, design, information technology, materials handling, office management and many other areas. Specialist consultants may also be needed from outside the organisation.

the costs of quality

The costs relating to quality management can be grouped under four headings:

1   prevention costs

2   appraisal costs

3   internal failure costs

4   external failure costs

Prevention and appraisal costs are increased when improvements are made, whereas failure costs will be reduced. We will look at each of the four categories in turn.

Prevention Costs are the costs associated with preventing mistakes and faulty output. They include the costs of:

• design improvements, to reduce numbers of rejects

• systems improvements for services

• the development and maintenance of quality control equipment

• the administration of quality control

• training employees in quality control and new methods of working

Appraisal Costs are the costs associated with assessing quality. They include the costs of:

• inspection of goods inwards and raw materials received

• inspection of work-in-progress

• performance testing of finished goods

• appraisal of the quality of services

Internal Failure Costs are the costs of mistakes within the organisation. They include the costs of:

• investigation and analysis of failures

• re-inspection

• losses due to scrapping sub-standard goods or selling them at lower prices

• losses due to faults in the raw materials purchased

• production delays

• reviewing product design and specification after failures

External Failure Costs are the costs of mistakes which result in sub-standard products or services reaching the external customer. They include the costs of:

• running a customer complaints department

• liabilities in relation to faulty products

• repairs and replacements

• loss of customer loyalty

the benefits of Total Quality Management

Organisations which develop a culture of TQM and continuous improvement expect that the costs will be outweighed by the benefits. The benefits include:

• reduction of Internal Failure Costs

• reduction of External Failure Costs

• improved reputation and goodwill of customers

• increased sales

• better motivated staff due to improved job satisfaction

• reduction of staffing costs in some areas (typically in middle management, as senior management develops closer links to the operational workforce)

Case
Study

MOTORCO PLC: TYPES OF COST OF QUALITY

This Case Study is based on Motorco Plc, a large car manufacturing company.

You are required to consider the effect of a number of events.

Identify, for each one, which of the costs of quality (prevention, appraisal, internal failure, external failure) would be affected by the event and state what the effect would be.

the events

1   There is a breakdown of one of the machines which carries out an automated process on the production line.

2   It is found that a particular model has a fault which involves recalling all cars of that type sold so far.

3   In the design of a new model, it is decided that the number of parts in the seat fixing can be reduced, to simplify construction and reduce errors.

4   The company has reduced the number of different suppliers from which materials are purchased.

5   The company has entered long-term contracts with major suppliers of components, and the contract terms include guarantees of the quality of components by the suppliers.

6   The company has introduced a more detailed inspection of the paint finish on all cars.

7   The detailed inspection of paint finish has revealed that one particular colour results in more defects.

suggested analysis of the events

1   Internal failure costs would increase, due to production delays and investigation of the breakdown.

2   External failure costs would increase, due to the cost of repairs, any claims relating to the fault, and possibly loss of customer loyalty resulting from the bad publicity. Internal failure costs would also increase in the form of investigation, review of the product design, repairs and re-inspection. Prevention costs would also increase, as the fault must be eliminated from future production.

3   Prevention costs would be incurred in the change of design, but both internal and external failure costs should be reduced as a result, if errors are avoided.

4   The appraisal costs due to inspection of raw materials received should be reduced if the procedures can be simplified with fewer suppliers.

5   The appraisal costs due to inspection of raw materials can be reduced if the supplier takes this responsibility.

6   Appraisal costs of the inspection will increase, but both internal and external failure costs resulting from defects should decrease.

7   Internal failure costs will be incurred in investigating the defects in this colour paint, in repainting and re-inspecting the cars. There may also be additional prevention and appraisal costs in eliminating the defects when the cause has been found.

Case Study

1.850

1.600

ISIS PLC: THE ACTUAL COST OF QUALITY

situation

ISIS plc manufactures clothes for a number of UK retail stores. The company has unfortunately allowed its quality systems to slip in recent years.

The fabric supplies are not inspected before cutting and making up the garments.

The finished garments are inspected, and on average 120 items per month are found to have fabric faults. Of these, 20 have to be scrapped. The remainder are sold as seconds at a discount of £15 on the normal price.

A further 40 garments per month are returned by retailers because of fabric faults, which have been missed by the inspectors in the factory. The retailers do not pay for these and they are not replaced. Some retailers do not reorder from the company.

The returned garments are all sold as seconds at the reduced price.

The variable cost of manufacture is £48 per garment.

A management consultant suggests that ISIS should:

1   Identify the costs of quality, in money terms where possible and state in which of the four types of cost of quality each cost should be categorised.

2   Think about and suggest ways in which improvements could be made.

solution

1   The costs of quality and types of cost

- The cost of scrapping 20 garments is the cost of making them, which is:

   20 x £48 = £960 per month.

   This is an internal failure cost.

   Note: We use the variable cost of making the garments, because the fixed costs (by definition) are not increased by making additional items.

- The cost of selling the faulty goods as seconds is £15 per garment, as this is the reduction in contribution from the discounted selling price. The cost of seconds found on inspection is:

   100 x £15 = £1,500 per month.

   This is an internal failure cost.

- The cost of selling the other faulty goods, which are returned by retailers, as seconds is:

   40 x £15 = £600 per month.

   This is an external failure cost, because the faulty goods went out of the factory. Additional external failure costs will result from the lost orders from retailers and loss of reputation amongst customers, but we do not have sufficient information to measure these.

2 how can improvements be made?

The situation could be improved by inspection of the fabric as it is received. This would give rise to appraisal costs. An alternative would be to negotiate contract terms with the supplier to include guarantees regarding the quality of the fabric. Immediate action could be taken to improve the inspection of finished goods and avoid sending faulty goods to retailers. Although this alone would not reduce the total number of substandard goods, it would avoid the external failure cost of lost goodwill and future sales.

MEASURING THE COSTS OF QUALITY

In order to calculate the costs of quality, it is necessary to have recorded the necessary data, such as:

* the numbers of defects,
* the costs of inspection procedures,
* the time spent on repairs and re-working, and so on

This data would not usually be recorded by traditional accounting systems. In a typical system, 'normal' losses would have been allowed for in the costs of production. Wastage of material and scrapping of defective units are then treated as being an unavoidable part of the cost of producing the good output. Costs of inspections and re-working would be included in overheads and not separately identifiable.

New demands are therefore put upon accounting information systems by the introduction of quality management: unless the data is collected, the costs (and benefits) cannot be calculated.

implicit and explicit costs of quality

In the ISIS plc Case Study, information was available which enabled us to give numerical values for certain costs of quality, in particular the costs of scrapping items and of selling them at reduced prices. These failure costs are examples of **explicit costs** of quality. With suitable data, many of the costs of Prevention, Appraisal, Internal Failure and External Failure can be separated out and given in money terms.

However, some costs could not be recorded or given in money terms, although they are equally important. These were the costs of lost future trade and damage to the company's reputation. These are examples of **implicit costs**.

Implicit costs of quality, which are not recorded in the accounting system, include:

* costs which cannot be separated out from other costs, eg the disruptive effects of re-scheduling production when internal failures have occurred

- costs which represent the loss of future benefits (these are called 'opportunity costs'), such as lost sales because customers are dissatisfied

Explicit and implicit costs are explored in more detail in the Case Study which follows.

Case Study

CLAIR LIMITED: EXPLICIT COSTS AND IMPLICIT COSTS

situation

Clair Ltd manufactures double glazed windows and doors, and has a division which installs them in customers' houses.

Clair Ltd buys in the glass sealed units and the locking mechanisms ready made, as well as purchasing the raw materials to make the frames.

When the glass units and locks are received, they are checked for any obvious faults. However, some less obvious faults may be found only when the locking mechanisms are fitted into the frames in the factory and the glass units are put in by the installers.

Defects may also occur in the frames: these are inspected on completion, but further problems may be found by the installers or customers. For example, the frames may not be the exact size required or the locks may not align properly when windows are fitted. If problems arise on installation, they cause delays which upset customers and disrupt the work schedule. If customers have any problems with the products, Clair Ltd's installers have to go back to carry out repairs or replacements.

Clair Ltd's managers feel that it is important to guarantee the quality of both their products and their installation service, but they realise this has a cost. The company records the numbers of:

- purchase returns, ie glass units or locks returned to suppliers
- defective frames, found on inspection before leaving the factory
- products returned to the factory by installers, whether before they are actually installed or later, when they have to be replaced

They also record the costs of:

- inspection of glass units and locks when received
- inspection of finished frames
- the time taken by installers to carry out repairs and replacements.

required

1   Give three examples of explicit costs of quality which should be identified by the management of Clair Ltd.

2   Give two examples of implicit costs of quality, of which Clair Ltd's managers should be aware, but which are not recorded.

solution

1   **Examples of explicit costs of quality include:**

- the variable cost of making frames which are then scrapped at any stage

- the variable cost of making replacement products

- the costs of inspections of purchases or production

- the labour costs of repairs and replacements after installation

2   **Examples of implicit costs of quality include:**

- the loss of potential sales when new doors and windows are seen being repaired or replaced

- the costs associated with the disruption of installers' job schedules when products are found to be faulty: although total time taken could be recorded, it is difficult to separate out different reasons for inefficiency – also the workers may be de-motivated by problems, or may rush their work, reducing the quality of installation

assessing quality

In assessing quality standards, the emphasis is on fitness for purpose and value to the user. Important ways of measuring quality are therefore related to external customer satisfaction, such as the numbers of goods returned or customer complaints. Inside the organisation, quality control and inspection procedures will use measurements which depend on the type of work being carried out. In the Motorco Case Study (see page 154), for example, the number of defects in the paintwork was a measure of quality.

In order to measure the quality of a product or service, it will be necessary to plan in advance in order to collect the relevant data. As we have seen above, the numerical data needed in order to calculate the costs of quality would not normally be available from a traditional accounting system. The same applies to the measurements needed in order to assess quality.

Considerations of quality and value therefore make new demands on information systems, so that the necessary data is collected. In the next chapter, we will be considering in more detail how quality can be assessed.

quality at any cost?

Before we finish our study of quality, it is worth noting that it may not always be worth achieving 100% quality output with zero defects. There may occasionally be justification for a low level of defects if the total cost of defects is lower than the implementation of a system that guarantees zero defects. However all costs must be considered before such a decision is made.

COST REDUCTION

cost reduction programmes

The aim of standard costing and budgetary control is to keep costs within pre-determined targets. By contrast, the aim of a cost reduction programme is to reduce costs from their previously accepted levels without reducing the value of the product or service.

For example, the value to the customer of the packaging of plain biscuits is that it prevents deterioration or breaking of the biscuits. It may be possible to achieve this with cheaper materials. On the other hand, the superior packaging of expensive chocolates may be important to consumers as chocolates are often given as a gift and the packaging is a sign of perceived quality. Cutting the costs here could reduce the value of the product.

To succeed, cost reduction programmes need the full support of senior management and the co-operation of all other employees. It is essential to plan for cost reduction throughout all areas of the organisation. It may be possible to reduce certain costs with no effect on the product or service at all, for example by reducing the wastage of power for lighting and heating.

approaches to cost reduction

In planning for cost reduction, it is important to ensure that the measures taken will reduce costs in the long term.

Initially, the costs to be considered are likely to be variable costs, because most fixed costs will already have been paid or contracted for a time period.

The only fixed costs which it may be possible to reduce immediately are the 'discretionary' fixed costs. Discretionary fixed costs are those which can be changed by managers. They are the costs of items where there is a choice about the level of expenditure, so that the level can be reduced within a shorter timescale. Examples of discretionary fixed costs include:

- advertising
- non-essential training and staff development
- research and development.

Cutting discretionary costs may increase profits in the short term, but could be damaging in the long term. Reducing spending on advertising and product development may lead to loss of market share. Cutting down on training and staff development will result in a less skilled workforce, inefficiency and possibly a high labour turnover. Care must be taken to plan cost reduction programmes, so that the savings are not outweighed by the loss of profits in future.

In general, long-term cost reduction can be achieved by improving productivity and efficiency and making better use of all resources. Changes may be made to working practices in all sections of the organisation, in order to make procedures, and hence the use of materials and of people's time, more cost-effective.

methods of assessing possible cost reductions

Methods which may be applied include:

- **Work Study**
  This is used in manufacturing to determine:
  - the most efficient methods and procedures
  - the best layout of the factory or production line to reduce costs
  - the most efficient ways to use materials, labour and machinery to reduce waste

- **Organisation and Methods**
  This is used in administration to determine ways to improve office methods and procedures, including:
  - form design, office layout, workflows and communication
  - the benefits of computerisation
  - elimination of unnecessary procedures and paperwork

- **Variety reduction**
  This may involve:
  - reducing the product range
  - standardising the components used in different products.

Variety reduction means reducing the number of different products or components which pass through the system. Standardising the components used in different products can be very cost-effective. It can allow for greater use of automation and also economies through bulk purchasing. Cutting the range of products, however, must be balanced with customer needs. The value of all the products to the user must be maintained, or sales and goodwill will be lost.

For example:

- customers expect a range of cars with different features, but the majority of the components can be standardised
- domestic products such as kitchen appliances are produced in different colour finishes and different sizes, but the working parts can be standardised.

other methods of cost reduction

Other aspects of an organisation where planned cost reduction should be considered are:

- **finance costs**: the interest payable on loans and overdrafts, foreign exchange, the cost of capital tied up in stock and the timing of capital expenditure may offer scope for cost reduction
- **energy costs**: savings may be made by energy conservation
- **staffing**: numbers of staff needed and the skill levels required should be considered
- **consumables**: the control of purchases and of stocks of items such as stationery may need to be tightened to make savings
- **authorisation of expenditure**: all expenditure should be subject to proper authorisation at a sufficiently high level of management

Cost reduction programmes, like TQM, involve all staff and hence draw on each person's specialist knowledge of their own job. Production staff can suggest changes in processing to reduce waste, human resource managers can assist with analysing staffing costs, accountants can look at finance costs and so on. Additional specialists may be brought in from outside to solve specific problems or to carry out work study for example.

examples of employee suggestions . . .

- In a small factory, where production of sports cars is not automated, workers noticed that they were spending unnecessary amounts of time fetching small items such as nuts and bolts from central bins. Placing stocks of these items nearer to the actual work speeded up production.

- In a large factory, one employee operated a machine to screw two parts of a component together. He realised that one of the four screws used did not actually contribute any strength or have any purpose. By modifying the process and eliminating this screw, both time and materials were saved. The suggestion earned the employee a bonus.

VALUE ENGINEERING AND VALUE ANALYSIS

As stated above, cost reduction programmes must not result in reducing the value of the product or service to the user. The examples of employees' suggestions show that this can be achieved by improving the design of products or processes.

In order to ensure that value is maintained, what constitutes that value must be analysed:

- before production starts (this is **value engineering**)
- or when the product or service is already on the market (**value analysis**).

definitions of value engineering and value analysis

value engineering	Ensuring that new products or services are designed for quality but at low cost, by analysing how every part of the design enhances value.
value analysis	Analysing the value of every part of the design of an existing product or service, and questioning whether its function can be achieved some other way at lower cost.

The aim of both these processes is to build quality into the design of the product or service, while keeping the costs down. Relevant specialists in engineering, design and technology will be consulted.

Clearly it is easier to make alterations at the design stage than afterwards, the aim being to build in value but at lower cost. At the design stage, each part or feature of the product or system is looked at to check that it is necessary and that it contributes value.

In existing products or services, it is possible to analyse the value provided to the customer, and decide whether that level of quality can be kept or improved, when costs are reduced.

For example, the exact colour of a disposable razor may be of no importance to customers, whereas the exact colour of a sofa may be part of its value. Cheaper raw materials which may show colour variations may be acceptable for some products but not others.

practical aspects of value engineering and value analysis

Value engineering and value analysis must look at each product or service in great detail. Typical questions to be asked include:

- Can the function of this product or component be achieved some other way?
- Are all the functions of the product or service essential?
- Can the product be made lighter or smaller, thus using less material? (This may enhance its value.)
- Can components be standardised across a range of products?
- Can the design of the product or the processes involved in a service be modified to save time?

advantages of value engineering and value analysis

The potential advantages of these techniques to the producer or provider are:

- continuous improvements in design and methods
- more efficient use of resources
- higher profits
- enhanced reputation
- extended product life
- improved customer service through standardisation of components
- improved employee motivation

The potential advantages of these techniques to the customer are:

- prices may be reduced without loss of quality
- better design based on satisfying users' needs
- improved performance and reliability
- quicker delivery
- standard components for servicing

We have seen that cost reduction programmes should be planned for the long term. Value engineering and value analysis can be used as part of these programmes, so that the value of products or services to users is maintained or increased, even when costs are reduced.

examples of cost reduction and value analysis

■ In a hospital outpatients' clinic, the original system meant that each consultant remained in one room, seeing a succession of patients. Time was wasted while patients were prepared for the consultation. The system was changed to one in which two rooms were used and the consultant moved between them. While the consultant saw one patient, the next could be prepared in the other room. The service to patients was improved at reduced cost.

■ In a factory manufacturing cheap pottery mugs, the handles for the mugs were made separately and attached to the mugs before firing. A moulding process was then developed which allowed the mug to be produced with the handle. This speeded up production and reduced the number of rejects.

■ Products such as radios and telephones are often produced in a range of exterior designs but offering the same functions. The basic product can then be exactly the same, but housed in different casings. Costs can be reduced by manufacturing the working parts in large numbers, and the value to customers is maintained. This is an example of 'variety reduction'.

TARGET COSTING

Cost reduction programmes may be introduced as part of a general drive to increase profits. More specifically, they may be necessary in order to reach 'target costs' for a product or service.

Instead of looking at the costs of making a product and then determining the appropriate selling price, it may be more important to decide on the selling price first.

For products and services in highly competitive markets, selling prices are determined by market values. The market price is influenced both by the customers' view of the value of the product and by the prices charged by competitors for similar products. The product or service will not sell if prices are too high and therefore to obtain the desired market share, the producer must keep the price down. If the selling price is kept down, the costs must be driven down as well, otherwise no profit will be made. Starting from the selling price, **target costs** can be calculated and cost reduction programmes introduced to try to reach these targets.

As we have seen for cost reduction programmes in general, target costing is a team-based approach, involving employees from all sections of the organisation. The emphasis on market share and selling prices may mean that customers become part of the team, being consulted about their exact requirements for the product or service and the price they are prepared to pay.

The steps involved in **target costing** are:
- decide the level of **market share** the organisation wants to achieve for the product and the level of **profit** expected
- estimate the target **selling price** at which the product would be expected to achieve the desired market share
- subtract the organisation's required level of profit from the target selling price to give the **target cost**
- compare the actual costs with the target. For a product in the design stage, the projected cost would be compared with the target cost. If the costs are too high, then cost reductions must be found in order to meet the target. Alternative methods of production may have to be considered. Value engineering and value analysis may be used
- if it is impossible to reduce costs to the target level without affecting quality, then it can be seen that the product is not viable at the chosen selling price and profit level

Target costing can only be used in situations where there is sufficient information available about the market for the product or service. It must be possible to link selling prices with market share. The organisation must also have a specific target for contribution or profit as a percentage of sales.

Target costing may be used with Activity Based Costing (see Chapter 1). In Activity Based Costing, overheads are charged to a specific product according to how much use it makes of the activities within the organisation. Required cost reductions would be concentrated on the activities most used by the product in question. This method should result in real cost savings for that product. In contrast, charging overheads to products using apportionment and absorption does not give a realistic view of how the costs (and therefore any reductions in those costs) relate to a particular product.

advantages of target costing

The potential advantages of target costing to the producer or provider are:

- improved sales volumes and market share through competitive pricing
- good relationships with customers through consultation and a team-based approach
- achievement of a planned level of profit
- more efficient use of resources
- improvements in production methods
- involvement of all sections of the organisation, resulting in better coordination of functions

The potential advantages of target costing to the customer are:

- the required product or service obtainable at the right price
- more reliable service from the supplier resulting from better relationships
- prices reduced without loss of quality

All the advantages of value engineering and value analysis (see pages 162-164) are relevant if these methods are being used to achieve the target cost.

Case
Study

METTLE PLC: TARGET COSTING

situation

Mettle plc is a manufacturer of components for heavy goods vehicles. The market for these products is limited to a small number of large companies, which manufacture the vehicles. Mettle plc currently supplies only three customers and the loss of a single customer would therefore be a serious problem. Mettle plc will lose sales if its prices for components are not competitive.

The sales manager of Mettle plc has established a maximum price for a particular component, C34, above which the vehicle manufacturers will not buy from Mettle plc. This price is £350 per unit of C34. At this price, sales demand for the next year is expected to be 6,000 units of C34. Mettle plc has a target level of 18% operating profit on sales.

Note: here we are using target 'operating profit', which means that the 'total costs' will include non-production costs. In other cases, the 'target profit' may be based on a required level of contribution or of gross profit, depending on the costing method being used in the organisation.

required

Calculate:

(a) the expected total sales revenue from component C34 for the next year

(b) the target operating profit required by Mettle plc from the total sales of C34

(c) the total target cost for C34 for the next year

(d) the target operating profit per unit of C34

(e) the target cost per unit of C34

solution

(a) Expected total sales revenue from C34 = £350 x 6,000 = £2,100,000

(b) Target operating profit from C34 = 18% x £2,100,000 = £378,000

(c) Total target cost for C34 = £2,100,000 - £378,000 = £1,722,000

(d) Target operating profit per unit of C34 = £378,000/6,000 = £63

(e) Target cost per unit of C34 = £350 - £63 = £287

target costing and value engineering

We have seen that value engineering is used to ensure that quality is built into the design of new products without incurring unnecessary costs. Unnecessary costs are those which do not add value to the product. As a result of value engineering, the lowest cost for a particular design should be established. This technique is clearly a useful tool if target costing is being used. If the lowest cost for the design meets the target cost, then that design is acceptable. If not, then it is necessary to re-think the whole design and carry out value engineering again or to reconsider the original product specifications. Care must be taken to avoid wasting resources on a lengthy design process in which too many alternatives are considered.

Success is achieved using a combination of target costing and value engineering if the resulting product satisfies the needs of both the customer and the producer:

• the product satisfies the user's requirements (value in use and prestige value)

• the selling price is at a level that customers are prepared to pay

- the selling price attracts sufficient customers to meet the producer's target market share
- the costs are reduced to the target level, so that the producer's target profit level is reached

The following diagram illustrates the links between value engineering and the steps of target costing.

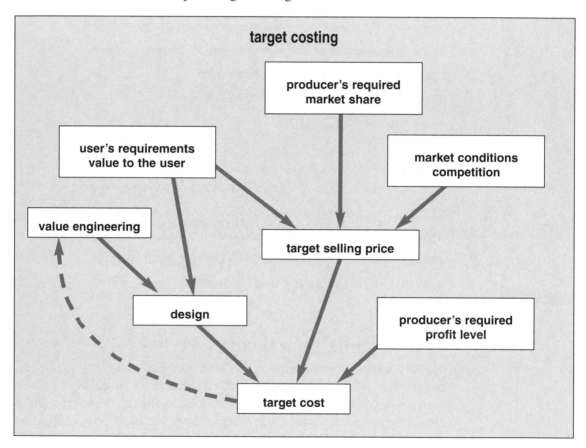

LIFE CYCLE COSTING

The life cycle of a product is a sequence of stages through which it passes, from the start of its development to the point at which it is no longer sold or supported by customer services. We use the term 'product life cycle' throughout this section, but all the ideas could equally well be applied to services.

Life cycle costing can also be applied to decisions relating to non-current assets (for example machinery). In that situation we would examine costs and savings over the life of the asset.

The length of a product life cycle can vary from a few years to 50 years or more. For example, products and services in hi-tech industries have short life cycles, whereas standard food products sell for many years.

Life cycle costing involves considering costs for the whole life cycle of a product instead of the usual short time periods. Target selling prices and target costs may result from a planning process covering the life cycle of the product.

As the product life cycle progresses, costs are accumulated in:

* research, development and design
* production
* selling and distribution
* customer services

When all these costs are considered, for many products, the costs of production represent a small proportion of the total. Research and development, followed by the detailed design of the product, may build up a very large part of the costs. Examples of such products include medicines, computer software and cars. In some cases, heavy costs are incurred at the end of the life cycle, when sales have ceased, for example in de-commissioning nuclear power stations.

Life cycle costing aims to collect together the costs of a single product over its entire life cycle. This means accounting for costs over a period of several years instead of a single year or less. Life cycle budgeting similarly involves planning for all the costs and revenues associated with the whole life cycle of the product.

problems of life cycle costing

There are considerable problems in establishing the life cycle costs of a product. Problems relating to the difficulty of forecasting (possibly five or more years ahead) include:

* predicting the length of the product life cycle and its various stages
* estimating future costs, taking into account inflation and the development of new materials and techniques
* estimating future demand for products, which may be affected by competition and by new developments
* allowing for possible costs caused by new legislation, for example on environmental issues

Other problems are related to the question of linking costs to particular products.

* production costs are the most likely category of costs to be recorded separately for individual products. It is much more difficult to link

research costs, for example, to specific products. For life cycle costing it is essential to be able to do this for all the costs incurred over the life cycle of the product.

life cycle costing and decision making

Research, development and design take place before the product goes into production. They also have a major influence on the other life cycle costs. Money spent on value engineering at the design stage can reduce production, marketing and customer service costs. On the other hand, a badly designed product will be more difficult to make, to sell and to maintain. This interdependence between the different stages of the life cycle is the main argument in favour of looking at the total cost of all the stages, rather than concentrating on just the production costs.

Budgeted life cycle costs and forecast sales volumes may be used for pricing decisions. The demand for a product will vary over its life cycle and the total sales revenue must cover the total life cycle costs. Forecasts of sales demands at different possible selling prices and expected costs for several years in advance are necessary to carry out the calculations for deciding on the best selling price. The chosen selling price, together with a required profit percentage, may be used for target costing. On the other hand, life cycle budget calculations may show that the product will not be profitable and therefore that expensive research and development work should not be carried out.

If life cycle budgeting and costing is being used, the accounting systems of the organisation must be designed to collect the relevant information. The costs of:

- research, development and design
- production
- selling and distribution
- customer services

must be collected separately for each product over its life, rather than being split down into monthly totals, for example. Of the costing methods studied in this book, activity based costing is likely to be the most appropriate. It can be seen that the four stages listed above represent groups of activities. Each one could be broken down into a number of separate activities, each with an appropriate cost driver. A particular product could then be charged for its usage of each activity (see Chapter 1, pages 11-13).

Once the life cycle of a product is completed, the actual costs and revenues can be compared with the life cycle budget in order to obtain information to help with future planning and decision making.

Case Study

AEROCAR PLC: LIFE CYCLE COSTING

situation

The managers of Aerocar plc are considering the possible development of a revolutionary kind of engine. The following forecasts have been made for the life cycle of this engine:

• research, development and design would take 3 years and cost £3million per year

• production and sales would take place over the following 4 years

• production costs would be £2million per year for 4 years plus £3,000 per engine

• selling and distribution costs would be £1million per year plus £1,000 per engine

• customer services would have to continue for 6 years and would cost £1.2million per year

• the total sales demand for the engine over the whole of its life cycle has been estimated for two possible selling prices:

Case 1: 12,000 engines at a selling price of £7,000 each

Case 2: 15,000 engines at a selling price of £6,000 each

required

(a) Calculate the total life cycle sales revenue at each of the possible selling prices.

(b) Calculate the total life cycle costs for:

Case 1: 12,000 engines

Case 2: 15,000 engines

(c) Calculate the total profit from the engine and the percentage profit on sales over its life cycle for each of the two possible selling prices.

Hint: Set out your answer in £millions, correct to 1 decimal place.

solution

(a) Sales revenue

12,000 engines at a selling price of £7,000 each gives sales revenue of

12,000 x £7,000 = £84,000,000 or £84.0million.

15,000 engines at a selling price of £6,000 each gives sales revenue of

15,000 x £6,000 = £90,000,000 or £90.0million.

(b) Life cycle costs

Case 1: 12,000 engines

	£million	£million
Research, development and design		
£3million per year for 3 years		9.0
Production		
£2million per year for 4 years	8.0	
12,000 engines at £3,000 each	36.0	44.0
Selling and distribution		
£1million per year for 4 years	4.0	
12,000 engines at £1,000 each	12.0	16.0
Customer services		
£1.2million per year for 6 years		7.2
		76.2

Case 2: 15,000 engines

	£million	£million
Research, development and design		
£3million per year for 3 years		9.0
Production		
£2million per year for 4 years	8.0	
15,000 engines at £3,000 each	45.0	53.0
Selling and distribution		
£1million per year for 4 years	4.0	
15,000 engines at £1,000 each	15.0	19.0
Customer services		
£1.2million per year for 6 years		7.2
		88.2

(c) Life cycle summary and profit calculation:

Selling price per engine	£7,000	£6,000
Total sales demand	12,000	15,000
	£million	£million
Total sales revenue	84.0	90.0
Life cycle costs	76.2	88.2
Life cycle profit	7.8	1.8
Profit percentage on sales	9.3%	2.0%

Notes

It can be seen that, according to these forecasts, the selling price of £7,000 per engine would be the more profitable option.

Suppose Aerocar plc uses target costing in conjunction with life cycle budgeting and costing, with a required profit percentage of 15% on sales. If the decision were made to use the selling price of £7,000 per engine, then the required profit would be 15% of the total sales revenue.

15% x £84million = £12.6million

Target total cost = £84million - £12.6million = £71.4million

Forecast total cost = £76.2million

The managers of Aerocar plc would have to look for £4.8million in cost reductions in order to meet this target. They would have to bear in mind that, if they cut back on the research phase, for example, the engine might cost more to produce. New forecasts for all the costs would need to be prepared.

LIFE CYCLE COSTING AND DISCOUNTED CASH FLOW

We were reminded in Chapter 1 how discounted cash flow (DCF) can be used to help make decisions regarding future costs and revenues. Since life cycle costing often relates to a substantial period of time (typically several years) it makes sense to make use of DCF techniques where appropriate.

Life cycle costing using DCF can be applied to decisions about products (by using the product life cycle) and to decisions about investment in non-current assets (by examining costs and savings over the life of the asset).

When we use DCF to make decisions we are usually making comparisons between two situations. In order to make valid comparisons we must bring the appropriate cost figures into our calculations. These are often called relevant costs. One way to remember what costs are relevant to any decision is that they are future incremental cash flows.

This means the costs are:

- future (not those costs that have already been incurred and cannot be changed by our decision),
- incremental (these are just the extra costs or savings resulting from the decision), and
- cash flows (always ignore non-cash items like depreciation).

Sometimes we can use just one DCF calculation to make our decision. This approach often suits situations where we are deciding to simply do something or not to do it. The first of the case studies that follows takes this approach, and is based on developing (or not developing) a new product.

The alternative approach is to use two DCF calculations. This is useful when we want to compare doing something in one of two ways. The second case study that follows uses this approach to compare two ways of investing in a non-current asset.

Examine these two Case Studies carefully and make sure that you can understand the logic that is being used.

Case Study

LIFE CYCLE PRODUCT COSTING

A company is considering developing and launching a new product into a fast moving market. The following data has been estimated, based on the project going ahead.

- Product development and testing would cost £6m immediately and a further £6m in one year's time.

- Marketing would cost £0.5m in one year's time, and a further £0.2m for each of the next two years.

- Variable unit costs would be £4, and each unit would sell for £10.

- Fixed production costs that relate only to this product would be £0.5m for each year of production. Production and sales will take place in the same year.

- The company already incurs fixed costs of £5m related to other products and these costs will continue.

- Sales will be as follows (based on the start of the project being year 0):

    Year 2   1m units
    Year 3   2m units
    Year 4   0.5m units

    There will be no sales after year 4.

The company's cost of capital is 5% and relevant discount factors are:

Year	Discount Factor
0	1.000
1	0.952
2	0.907
3	0.864
4	0.823

required

Using DCF, calculate whether the new product is worthwhile. Carry out calculations in £ thousands.

solution

The cash flows and present values are set out in the following table.

Year	Details	Cash Inflow £'000	Cash Outflow £'000	Discount Factor	Present Value £'000
0	Product development		6,000	1.000	(6,000)
1	Product development		6,000		
	Marketing		500		
	Net total year 1		6,500	0.952	(6,188)
2	Marketing		200		
	Sales Revenue	10,000			
	Variable costs		4,000		
	Fixed costs		500		
	Net total year 2	5,300		0.907	4,807
3	Marketing		200		
	Sales Revenue	20,000			
	Variable costs		8,000		
	Fixed costs		500		
	Net total year 3	11,300		0.864	9,763
4	Sales Revenue	5,000			
	Variable costs		2,000		
	Fixed costs		500		
	Net total year 4	2,500		0.823	2,057
				Net Present Value	4,439

Notice that the fixed costs that are already incurred are not relevant and are therefore not brought into the calculation. This is because they would not be altered by the decision on the new product – they remain the same regardless.

Based on the data given, the net present value is positive, so the project appears to be worthwhile.

<table>
<tr><td rowspan="2">**Case Study**</td><td></td></tr>
</table>

Case Study

LIFE CYCLE COST OF NON-CURRENT ASSETS

A company needs to replace its delivery vehicles. Each identical vehicle can be either leased or purchased, based on the following details.

- To lease a vehicle costs £12,000 per year for 5 years, payable annually in advance. This includes maintenance costs. At the end of the 5 year period the vehicle is returned to the leasing company.

- To purchase an identical vehicle costs £48,000 payable immediately. Maintenance costs are £2,000 per year, paid annually in arrears. The useful life of each vehicle is 5 years, and each can then be sold for a residual value of £5,000 at the end of that period.

The cost of capital to the company is 5%, and discount factors are as follows:

Year	Discount Factor
0	1.000
1	0.952
2	0.907
3	0.864
4	0.823
5	0.784

required

Calculate the discounted lifecycle cost of each option and recommend which has the lowest net present cost.

solution

Leasing

Year	Details	Cash Outflow £	Discount Factor	Present Cost £
0	Lease cost	12,000	1.000	12,000
1	Lease cost	12,000	0.952	11,424
2	Lease cost	12,000	0.907	10,884
3	Lease cost	12,000	0.864	10,368
4	Lease cost	12,000	0.823	9,876
			Net present cost	54,552

Note that as the payments are made in advance there is no payment required in year 5.

Purchase

Year	Details	Cash Outflow / (Inflow) £	Discount Factor	Present Cost £
0	Purchase	48,000	1.000	48,000
1	Maintenance	2,000	0.952	1,904
2	Maintenance	2,000	0.907	1,814
3	Maintenance	2,000	0.864	1,728
4	Maintenance	2,000	0.823	1,646
5	Maintenance	2,000	0.784	1,568
	Sale proceeds	(5,000)	0.784	(3,920)
			Net present cost	52,740

(2352)

The net present cost of purchasing each vehicle is lower, and therefore this should be chosen, based on these figures.

Chapter Summary

- Businesses can try to ensure that they keep their customers and remain profitable, by making continuous improvements in the quality and value of their products or services.

- The quality of a product or service can be considered as its fitness for the customer's purpose.

- There are costs attached both to poor quality and to making improvements. These costs are grouped under the headings:
  - Prevention costs
  - Appraisal costs
  - Internal failure costs
  - External failure costs

- Some of the costs of quality can be recorded in accounting systems and calculated in money terms. These are called 'explicit' costs of quality. Other costs are 'implicit' costs, which cannot be quantified.

- The intention of quality management is that the additional costs of getting more 'right first time' will be outweighed by the benefits.

- The value of a product or service for the customer is:
  - its value in use (fitness for purpose)
  - its esteem or prestige value

- The value of a product or service for the producer or service provider is:
  - its cost of production or provision
  - its exchange value (market value)

- The value of a product or service can be maintained or enhanced, while at the same time costs are reduced. A careful analysis of value assists with these aims.

- In value engineering (for new designs) and value analysis (for existing designs), the question: 'Can the same (or better) value to the user be achieved some other, cheaper way?' is asked about every part of the design. If this can be done, then:
  - the organisation should be able to increase its sales and profitability
  - customers will benefit from the availability of more efficiently designed products and services

- Cost reduction programmes may be used in order to achieve **target costs** for a product or service. Target costs are calculated by starting from the chosen selling price for the product and deducting the organisation's required profit. If it proves impossible to reduce costs to the target level without affecting quality, then the product is not viable at this selling price.

- The chosen selling price for the product may be decided by considering the market value, taking into account the market share that the producer hopes to obtain.

- A pricing decision may be the result of **life cycle budgeting**, in which the costs and revenues for the whole life cycle of the product are taken into account. As a result of these calculations, cost reduction programmes may be implemented in order to meet targets for the **life cycle costs** of the product.

- Discounted cash flow techniques can be used in conjunction with life cycle costing. It can be used to analyse the net present value (or cost) of both products and non-current assets.

Key Terms	**quality**	the quality of a product or service can be considered as its fitness for the purpose for which it is to be used by the customer
	total quality management (TQM)	a concept that means that continuous improvement is sought in every part of an organisation, attempting to get everything right first time and eliminate mistakes and defects
	costs of quality	the costs incurred in making improvements to quality (prevention and appraisal costs) or as a result of mistakes and defects (internal failure costs and external failure costs)
	value	A product or service has value to the customer and also to the producer or provider: . . . *for the customer:* - value in use - esteem or prestige value . . . *for the producer/provider:* - the cost to produce or provide - exchange or market value
	enhancement of value	the value of a product or service to the customer is increased by adding desirable features, eliminating faults or reducing the selling price without loss of quality
	cost reduction	a positive approach to reducing costs in all departments of an organisation, without affecting the quality of output
	value engineering	ensuring that new products or services are designed for quality but at low cost, by analysing how every part of the design enhances value
	value analysis	analysing the value of every part of the design of an existing product or service, and questioning whether its function can be achieved some other way at lower cost.

target costing	setting targets for costs as *selling price less required profit* and if necessary using cost reduction to meet the target cost
life cycle costing	accounting for the costs of a product over its entire life from the start of development to the end of customer support

Activities

5.1 A Family History Society produces a quarterly journal containing members' contributions, articles and advice about researching family trees. The journal is posted to members. The committee circulated members with a questionnaire about possible changes to the journal. The answers showed members' opinions on various suggestions, including:

- Whether better quality paper should be used: 78% said No.

- Whether the number of pages should be increased up to the maximum for the same postage rate: 65% said Yes.

- Whether the journal should have a crossword: 94% said No.

- Whether the cover should be printed in colour: 86% said No.

Required

Referring to the case described above to illustrate your answer, explain the terms 'quality' and 'enhancement of value'.

5.2 The costs of quality are divided into four categories:

1 Prevention costs

2 Appraisal costs

3 Internal failure costs

4 External failure costs

Required

State the category to which each of the following types of cost belongs:

(a) investigation of faults

(b)   training production staff to use new equipment

(c)   the loss of customer loyalty due to poor quality goods

(d)   costs resulting from loss of production due to machine breakdown

(e)   inspection of raw materials when received

(f)   the cost of scrapping output

(g)   claims from customers relating to defective products

5.3   AB Ltd manufactures electronic gadgets, many of which are purchased to give as presents.

AB Ltd has carried out an investigation into the reliability of one of its products, an electronic personal organiser. Investigations show that 1 in every 2,000 organisers quickly develops a fault and ceases to work. It is estimated that 75% of these are returned to the company. A repair which costs the company £10 corrects the fault. The remaining 25% are not returned, but the customers will not purchase AB Ltd's products in future. It is estimated that the costs of advertising in order to replace these customers amount to £50,000 per year. Average sales of organisers are 2,000,000 per year.

Required

List the costs of quality in this case, stating the category of each and the amount where possible. Suggest how AB Ltd could improve this situation and what would be the implications in terms of costs of quality.

5.4   TV-D plc is a digital television company which provides customers who subscribe with a free digital decoder. The decoders are purchased from several suppliers and are delivered to customers' homes. Customers carry out their own installation, but can telephone a helpline for advice. TV-D plc does not inspect or test the decoders. If customers cannot receive the digital service after installation following telephone advice, or if reception fails later, TV-D plc assume the decoder is either faulty or incompatible with the customers' own equipment and replace it. Decoders collected back from customers are scrapped.

Speed of delivery of decoders is an essential feature of the service, as customers kept waiting may choose another company.

In a given period, TV-D plc records the following results:

*   New customers placing an order: 8,500

*   Existing customers from previous periods: 76,000

*   Replacement decoders delivered (to new and existing customers): 3,860

*   Cancellations of subscriptions (total for all customers and all reasons): 9,800

*   Total cost of customer helpline: £1,400,000

*   Total cost of delivery of decoders: £250,000

*   Purchase cost per decoder = £52

Required

(a) Explain briefly what is meant by the term 'explicit cost of quality', giving two examples from the case described.

(b) Explain briefly what is meant by 'implicit cost of quality', giving two examples from the case described.

5.5 PQR and Partners is a large firm of accountants with branch offices spread across several counties. In order to recruit suitable trainees, the firm needs to have a display stand, stocks of literature and several senior staff at every careers convention in the region. Currently, the staff involved take the stand and literature to the convention and set the display up before the starting time. Afterwards, they pack up and return everything to be stored in one of the firm's offices.

One of the staff involved has received an advertising leaflet from Splash Ltd, a company offering to store, transport, and set up the display, then pack it and return it to their own store afterwards. The leaflet points out that the firm's staff need then only attend for the actual opening hours of the convention, and that transporting displays for several firms in one van can save costs.

Required

Referring to the case described above to illustrate your answer, explain what is meant by 'cost reduction' and 'value analysis'.

5.6 The managers of Snaps plc expect to achieve sales next year of 25,000 units of a digital camera, the Digisnap. They have established a market price of £480 per unit. Snaps plc has a target level of 22% operating profit on sales.

Required

Calculate:

(a) the expected total sales revenue from the Digisnap for the next year

(b) the target operating profit required by Snaps plc from the total sales of Digisnap

(c) the total target cost for Digisnap for the next year

(d) the target operating profit per unit of Digisnap

(e) the target cost per unit of Digisnap

5.7   A company is considering purchasing a new machine that will reduce the labour required to manufacture its products. The details are as follows:

- The machine will cost £350,000, plus installation costs of £25,000 and will have a life of 4 years with no residual value.

- Running costs of the machine are £20,000 per year, payable in arrears.

- Labour costs are £12 per hour, and the machine would save 2 hours time in the manufacture of each unit (treat savings as being made annually in arrears).

- Production over the next 4 years is planned to be as follows, starting immediately:

- Year 1   4,000

- Year 2   5,000

- Year 3   5,000

- Year 4   6,000

The company's cost of capital is 5%, with the following discount factors:

Year	Discount Factor
0	1.000
1	0.952
2	0.907
3	0.864
4	0.823

Required

Using discounted cash flow, calculate whether investing in the machine appears to be worthwhile.

6 Measuring performance

this chapter covers...

In this chapter we commence our examination of using performance indicators to monitor and control businesses. In this chapter we mainly concentrate on the use of financial ratios, and then look at other forms of performance measurement in the next chapter.

We start by examining what performance indicators can tell us and learn some of the 'ground rules' that will help. We will see how making comparisons is invaluable, and how benchmarking can play its part in making sense of the data.

Next we will start our examination of ratios by looking at those connected with the Income Statement (Profit & Loss Account). From there we continue our study of ratios by examining some ratios that link the Income Statement with information displayed in the Statement of Financial Position (Balance Sheet). These ratios are typically concerned with how the resources of the business are used to generate profit. The last groups of ratios are those concerned with examining the Statement of Financial Position to understand issues like liquidity and financial stability.

We will then learn how to interpret ratios, and their limitations. Finally we will start to examine the numerical manipulation of ratios to answer some 'what if' questions that will help us in our studies.

MEASURING THE PERFORMANCE OF ORGANISATIONS

performance indicators

It is important to be able to measure the performance of an organisation in a way which allows managers to see where improvements can be made. In Chapters 2, 3 and 4 we have studied the analysis of cost variances. These are examples of performance measurements which can be used:

• to monitor the use of resources

• to help with control of the business

• to help with planning for the future

A list of variances for one cost centre for one period is not particularly informative. The usefulness of variances depends on being able to compare them with target levels, with the variances for other time periods or with those for other similar cost centres.

In this chapter we will consider different ways of measuring the performance of an organisation (or of a part of an organisation). For example, we can calculate profit as a percentage of sales, sales revenue per employee, the percentage of orders which are delivered late, and many other measures. An individual measurement is called a **performance indicator**. What we have seen above for variance analysis applies to any performance indicator.

A performance indicator may be used for:

• identifying problems

• controlling costs

• measuring the utilisation of resources

• measuring an individual's performance

• planning

Examples of performance indicators include:

• the direct materials usage variance, which may identify a problem relating to wastage of materials

• the administration cost as a percentage of turnover, which may help with control of costs

• the number of hours of machine down time, which is relevant to how well resources are being used

• profit as a percentage of turnover, which may indicate how well a company has been managed

• the number of product units rejected on inspection, which may help with planning production levels

The usefulness of a performance indicator depends on:

- comparing with standards, budgets or targets
- comparing with other periods of time
- comparing with other similar organisations

making comparisons – benchmarking

Comparing performance indicators with standards or targets includes **benchmarking**.

Benchmarks are standards or targets set for one or more areas of activity and should be related to what is important to the organisation.

Benchmarks may be:

- set internally and relate to a single aspect of the work, for example: all correspondence to be answered within three working days
- set by external bodies, for example government targets relating to pollution of the environment
- set (either internally or externally) with reference to similar organisations, for example the expected level of profitability calculated as an average for the industry

A single organisation may have a number of benchmarks, including all three types described above:

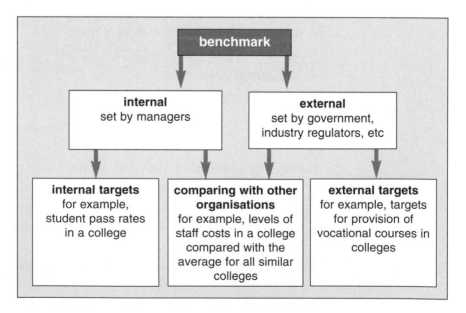

Measurement of how well an organisation (or part of an organisation) has performed in achieving these aims means that it has to record the necessary data to compare with the benchmark.

making comparisons – time series

Comparing the same indicator over a number of periods of time gives a Time Series. In Chapter 1 (pages 29-42) it has been shown how a time series may show a trend and possibly a pattern of variations around the trend. A performance indicator may show these features over a number of time periods, adding to the usefulness of the information.

For example, the number of customer complaints can be a useful performance indicator for an organisation. An overall downward trend in the number of complaints shows improvement, even if there are some fluctuations. An overall upward trend would indicate a problem to be investigated.

When items measured in money terms, such as Sales Revenue or Profit, are being compared over a number of years, it may be necessary to take out the effect of inflation. This can be done using index numbers, as shown in Chapter 1 and in Chapter 7.

making comparisons – consistency

Comparisons can give very useful information. However, we must be sure that figures being compared really are 'comparable'. In other words, they must have been prepared in a **consistent** way, so that we are comparing 'like with like'.

For example, the Net Profit figures for a business over a number of years can be compared provided that the same accounting policies have been applied throughout. A change in the policy for depreciation, for example, would affect the profit figures and they would not be comparable.

data for performance measurement

The diagram on the next page shows that there are different kinds of data that may be used for performance measurement.

Quantitative data is data which can be stated in numbers, and this can be split into:

- Financial or Monetary data which is in terms of money and
- Non-financial or non-monetary data, which is in terms of units other than money, such as numbers of hours for example.

Qualitative data is data which cannot be put in numerical terms. It can consist of people's opinions or judgements, for example the views of students about a teacher. Such data is used for performance measurement, particularly in appraisal schemes for types of work where there is no clearcut numerical measure of performance. A combination of quantitative and qualitative data is often used.

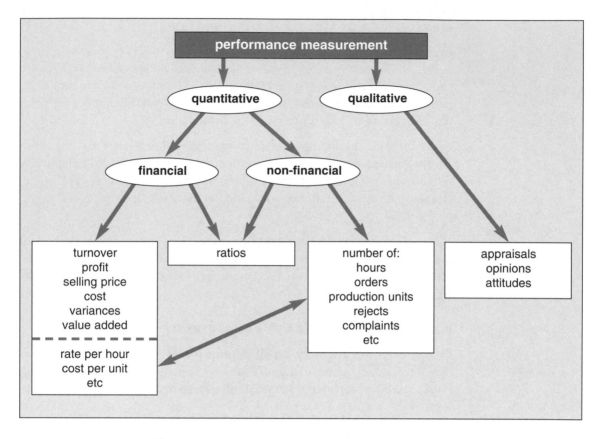

The examples shown in the diagram above include variances as an example of financial data. You have seen in your earlier studies that variances are given in money terms. The other point to note about variances is that each variance comes from two pieces of information and is the difference between them. An alternative way of comparing two pieces of information is to calculate a ratio or percentage, and this is one of the most common ways of arriving at a useful measure of performance. Percentages are particularly useful when comparisons are being made.

tutorial note – dealing with percentages

In order to express a ratio as a percentage, it is necessary to multiply by 100. This can be done using the % function on a calculator.

In all the formulas which follow, we have shown 'x 100' as well as indicating that the answer is a percentage by using the % sign.

When using these formulas:

either multiply by 100

or use the % button on your calculator.

Case Study

LITTLE LIMITED AND LARGE LIMITED: PERFORMANCE INDICATORS AS PERCENTAGES

Little Ltd and Large Ltd are companies which operate in the same industry. For a given period, we have the following data:

	Little Ltd	Large Ltd
	£000s	*£000s*
Turnover (Sales Revenue)	465	2,550
Gross Profit	185	895

At a glance, it is not easy to compare these figures because of the difference in size. If we calculate the gross profit as a percentage of turnover, we obtain more useful information for comparison:

Little Ltd   Gross profit percentage = $\dfrac{185}{465}$ x 100% = 39.8%

Large Ltd   Gross profit percentage = $\dfrac{895}{2,550}$ x 100% = 35.1%

We can then see that Little Ltd is translating a greater proportion of its turnover into gross profit than Large Ltd. This is an example of a performance indicator.

RATIO ANALYSIS

Ratio analysis generally refers to the calculation of a set of ratios or percentages using data from the financial and management accounts of a business. The income statement (profit and loss account) and the statement of financial position (balance sheet) are used in the analysis, which can then be used to evaluate the performance of the business, particularly by:

* comparing with budgets or targets
* comparing with other periods of time
* comparing with other similar organisations

In the case of limited companies, people outside the company can look at the final accounts and calculate ratios, for example when deciding whether to buy shares in the company. This analysis will add to the available information, but should not be used on its own.

In order to make meaningful comparisons between organisations or between time periods, the accounts must have been prepared on the same basis – applying the principle of consistency by comparing like with like. It is very difficult to achieve this, especially when using published accounts. In this case, it is essential to study the notes to the accounts, which may give important information about accounting policies and the breakdown of certain figures. Even so, details of the methods used may not be given and therefore the ratios calculated must be used with care.

The aim should always be to provide useful information for the purpose for which it is required. It is not sufficient to put figures into formulas (or into a computer program) without thinking of the factors that may affect them.

sources of data for ratios

In this chapter we consider the ratios which can be calculated from the Income Statement and the Statement of Financial Position of a business. We will do this in a number of stages:

1 We will consider first the ratios calculated from the Income Statement separately, before linking sales and profits with the Statement of Financial Position.

2 The key measure of profit in relation to the assets shown on the Statement of Financial Position is Return on Capital Employed.

3 Our third section on ratio analysis will include ratios relating to the current assets and current liabilities of the organisation.

The diagram below illustrates these groups of ratios and the sources of data for their calculation, and the stages in which we will look at them.

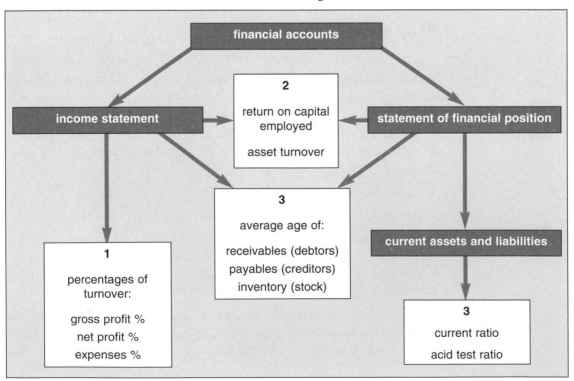

CALCULATION OF RATIOS: THE INCOME STATEMENT

In the Case Study comparing Little Limited and Large Limited, the calculation of gross profit as a percentage of turnover gives useful information. It shows what proportion of the turnover remains as gross profit, after the cost of sales is taken out. Little Ltd's gross profit percentage of 39.8%, for example, means that, out of every £100 of sales revenue, there is £39.80 gross profit. Large Ltd keeps only £35.10 gross profit out of every £100 of sales revenue.

Similar percentages can be calculated comparing each of the figures on a income statement with the turnover. These show what proportion or 'slice' of sales revenue is being used for each type of cost and how big a slice is kept in profits. (See the pie chart on page 194, which shows the breakdown of sales revenue in percentage terms for the Case Study Ayebridge Limited.)

Profit percentages are calculated on the basis of Turnover (Sales Revenue). This can be done for Gross Profit and Net Profit. In the accounts of a company, several versions of profit are given, before and after interest and tax. To measure the performance of the company, the 'Operating Profit' or 'Profit before interest and tax' is used for many ratios, because this is the profit from the main trading activities of the company. If management performance is being evaluated, the profit figure used should reflect the manager's area of responsibility. 'Controllable profit' is appropriate, and 'Revenue'. In the formulas below, the terms 'Sales' and 'Turnover' mean the same thing.

In assessment tasks, 'Sales Returns' are sometimes shown. In this case, the figure to be used for 'sales' in the calculation of ratios is the one *after* sales returns have been deducted, because this represents the actual sales achieved.

■   *gross profit margin (percentage)*   = $\dfrac{gross\ profit}{sales}$ x *100%*

■   *net profit margin*   = $\dfrac{net\ profit}{sales}$ x *100%*

■   *or operating profit margin*   = $\dfrac{operating\ profit}{sales}$ x *100%*

Profit percentages are indicators of the profitability of the business.

It must be remembered that the choice of methods for depreciation of assets and for inventory valuation can make a difference to profit figures.

Any other figure from the income statement can also be calculated as a percentage of sales, particularly if it appears to need investigation. For example, if selling expenses have increased from one period to the next, it may be useful to calculate for each period:

■ *selling expenses as a percentage of sales* = $\dfrac{selling\ expenses \times 100\%}{sales}$

■ *or any type of expense as a percentage of sales* = $\dfrac{expense \times 100\%}{sales}$

Similarly, if details of the costs of materials and wages are available, we can calculate, for any type of cost:

■ *cost as a percentage of sales* = $\dfrac{cost}{sales} \times 100\%$

Whether costs behave as fixed or variable costs in relation to activity levels (see Chapter 1) makes a difference to how we would expect the ratios to behave. A higher turnover figure often results from a higher volume of sales, which would mean that total variable costs would also be higher. Total fixed costs, however, would not be expected to change with the volume. In percentage terms, this means that we would expect:

• a variable cost to remain relatively stable as a percentage of turnover
• a fixed cost as a percentage of turnover to decrease as turnover increases

    For example, the direct materials cost of a product may be expected to be 12% of the sales revenue and this percentage would stay approximately the same for different numbers of units. On the other hand, if a fixed cost is £90,000 per year:

    compared with annual turnover of £900,000, the fixed cost would be 10%

    but compared with annual turnover of £1,200,000, it would be only 7.5%.

Calculation of the income statement ratios will show how the revenue from sales has been split between the elements of cost and the profit. The following Case Study illustrates this.

Case Study

AYEBRIDGE LIMITED: RATIO ANALYSIS OF THE INCOME STATEMENT

Ayebridge Limited is a manufacturer of electronic circuits used in domestic products. The following income statement for the year ended 30 June 20-3 includes some detail of the cost of sales.

Ayebridge Ltd: Income Statement for the year ended 30 June 20-3

	£000s	£000s
Sales		6,000
Less: Cost of Sales:		
Materials	800	
Labour	900	
Production overheads	1,700	
Cost of Sales		3,400
GROSS PROFIT		2,600
Selling and Distribution	813	
Administration	967	1,780
OPERATING PROFIT		820

required

Analyse the Ayebridge Limited income statement given above, using ratio analysis.

solution

Using the formulas listed on page 191, we obtain:

Gross profit margin (percentage) = $\dfrac{\text{Gross profit}}{\text{Sales}}$ x 100% = $\dfrac{2,600}{6,000}$ x 100% = 43.3%

This shows that 43.3% of the Sales Revenue remains as Gross Profit after the Cost of Sales has been deducted (see diagram on the next page).

The Cost of Sales therefore represents 100% – 43.3% = 56.7% of the Sales Revenue. In this example it is possible to calculate percentages for the three elements of the cost of sales, as follows:

- materials cost as a percentage of sales = $\dfrac{800}{6,000}$ x 100% =   13.3%

- labour cost as a percentage of sales = $\dfrac{900}{6,000}$ x 100% =   15.0%

- production overheads as a percentage of sales = $\dfrac{1,700}{6,000}$ x 100% =   28.3%

(Allowing for a rounding difference, these total the cost of sales percentage of 56.7%)

In order to draw any conclusions from these calculations, we would need more information for comparison. We would need the same format of income statement for Ayebridge Limited for other years, or as a budget for the year ended 30 June 20-3. Alternatively, we could compare Ayebridge's figures with averages for the industry or with those for other similar businesses, if available. The same applies to the remaining percentages:

- operating profit percentage = $\dfrac{820 \times 100\%}{6,000}$ = 13.7%

Each of the two categories of expense could also be calculated as a percentage of sales:

- selling and distribution as a percentage of sales = 13.6%

- administration as a percentage of sales = 16.1%
(Check that you can calculate these).

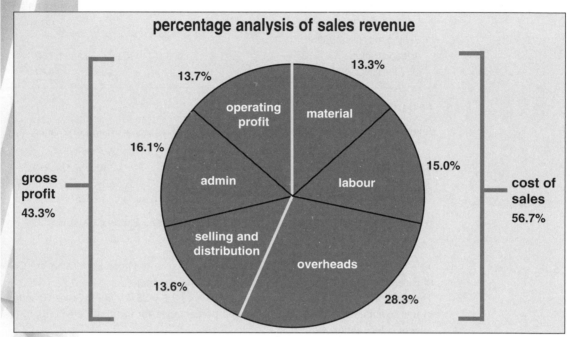

Case Study continued – comparison with the previous year

Consider the table below, which shows information for Ayebridge Limited for the year ended 30 June 20-2, together with answers from our calculations for the year ended 30 June 20-3.

	30 June 20-2	30 June 20-3
Gross profit percentage	41.0%	43.3%
Operating profit percentage	15.4%	13.7%

The Gross Profit percentage has therefore increased from 41% in the previous year, to 43.3% in the year ended 30 June 20-3. This improvement means that a lower proportion of the Sales Revenue has been used for Cost of Sales. This could result from increasing selling prices or from reducing costs. With more detailed information for the previous year this could be analysed further. Notice that we do not know whether the actual amount of gross profit has increased or decreased.

The Operating Profit percentage, however, has decreased from 15.4% in the previous year to 13.7% in the year ended 30 June 20-3. This means that a greater slice of the gross profit has been taken out in expenses. (Look again at the pie chart opposite). This could be because the expenses have increased, but it could also be due to a reduction in the total sales revenue, or both. Increased selling prices may reduce demand for the products, and this could result in lower total sales revenue, and a lower total amount of gross profit.

These comments show that the calculated percentages alone are not enough. To see exactly what has happened, we would need to look back at the original data as well.

Case Study

BEETON LIMITED: RATIO ANALYSIS OF THE INCOME STATEMENT

The following information relates to Beeton Ltd, a chain of retail stationery shops.
Note: whenever you are given data for different time periods, make sure you check which is the earlier and which the later time period. Here the earlier year is on the right, but this is not always so. If you do not check, you may discuss a completely opposite case!

Beeton Ltd: Income Statement for the year ended:				
		31 March 20-3		31 March 20-2
		£000s		£000s
Sales		4,500		3,600
Less: Returns		(300)		(200)
		4,200		3,400
Less: Cost of Sales				
Opening Inventory	450		410	
Purchases	2,896		2,250	
Less: Closing Inventory	(490)	2,856	(450)	2,210
GROSS PROFIT		1,344		1,190
Expenses:				
Selling and Distribution	157		128	
Administration	200	357	280	408
OPERATING PROFIT		987		782

required

Analyse the Income Statement, for each of the given years, by calculating (correct to one decimal place)

- the gross profit margin on sales   32%   35%
- the operating profit as a percentage of sales (operating profit margin) 23.5   21.7
- two other percentages to aid your analysis   64.4   66.2 .

Identify where possible the reasons for changes in the profitability of Beeton Ltd.

solution

Year ended:	31 March 20-3	31 March 20-2
Gross Profit Margin on Sales	32%	35%
Operating Profit margin	23.5%	23%
Expenses as % of Sales:		
Selling and Distribution	3.7%	3.8%
Administration	4.8%	8.2%

The **Gross Profit margin** on sales has decreased in the year to 31 March 20-3. This may be due to having to reduce selling prices in order to increase sales demand. It could also be caused by increases in purchasing costs, or a combination of these reasons. (Notice that we use the Sales figure after the Sales Returns have been deducted.)

The **Operating Profit margin** has increased slightly. It can be seen from the Income Statements and from the expense percentages that this level of operating profit margin has been maintained by a considerable reduction of Administration costs. This cost has been reduced by £80,000, even though sales have increased. The effect is to cut the Administration as a percentage of sales from 8.2% to 4.8%. The Selling and Distribution costs are at a similar level in relation to sales in both years.

RATIOS LINKING TURNOVER AND PROFITS TO THE STATEMENT OF FINANCIAL POSITION

So far, in this chapter, we have looked at sales and profits without considering the way that the business is being financed and the value of the assets being used. Managers need to ensure that the money invested in the business as capital is being used efficiently to generate sales and profits. We now consider ratios that can be used to assess how well they are doing this.

From your studies of financial accounting, you will be familiar with the idea that the Statement of Financial Position of an organisation represents the equation:

assets – liabilities = capital

and that the Capital represents the owners' interest in the business.
We can therefore look at the Statement of Financial Position from either side – as the net assets or as the capital provided by the owners.

- 'Assets' include both non-current (fixed) and current assets.
- 'Liabilities' include current and long-term liabilities.

Long-term liabilities, such as loans, can be viewed as a long-term source of finance for the organisation by rearranging the equation as:

non-current and current assets – current liabilities

= long-term liabilities + capital

This version of the equation will be used in calculating the Return on Capital Employed on the next page and examples will show how it works.

---

tutorial note

The Statement of Financial Position of an organisation shows its assets, liabilities and owners' capital on a specific date.

It is important to remember, when using a Statement of Financial Position for ratio analysis, and when interpreting the ratios, that the position shown on that date may not be typical. Transactions on the next day, such as a large payment to a Payable or the raising of a bank loan, will alter the position significantly. Always bear this in mind when calculating ratios using the Statement of Financial Position.

---

return on capital employed (ROCE)

By 'capital employed' we mean the money being used to finance the running of a business. This is normally represented by the owners' capital, together with any long-term liabilities such as loans that make more money available. We have seen above that the statement of financial position shows another way of looking at this, as the value of the non-current and current assets less the current liabilities.

Capital employed is the essential funding used by managers for the fixed assets, for keeping the business going and therefore for making sales and profits. It is important for investors to see that this funding is being put to good use. 'Return on Capital Employed' is a performance indicator that compares the profit with the amount of long-term finance being used by management.

Return on Capital Employed is a key ratio which therefore shows how well the management of an organisation has used the assets (or the resources shown on the statement of financial position) to generate profits.

To calculate ROCE, the profit is expressed as a percentage of the capital employed in the business.

The difficulty comes in deciding which 'profit' figure to use, and what is meant by 'capital employed'. If comparisons are being made, between companies for example, then the ROCE must be calculated in the same way for each company (as far as is possible from the available information).

The principle of comparing 'like with like' also means that the assets included in the capital employed must be those relevant to the profit being measured. Usually, the measurement of management performance would mean that the **Operating Profit** is used, and the Capital Employed would take account of the **assets used in the main activities of the organisation**.

For instance, if there is any income from investments, this would be excluded from the profit figure and the investment assets themselves would be excluded from the capital employed.

Allowing for such adjustments, the capital employed figure to use in straightforward cases is equal to the **Non-Current Assets plus the Net Current Assets**. By 'net current assets' we mean 'current assets less current liabilities'.

Referring back to the Statement of Financial Position equation on the previous page:

non-current assets plus net current assets

= non-current and current assets – current liabilities

= long-term liabilities + capital

We are looking at the 'capital employed' either as the assets being used to generate profits or the funds which are being used to finance those assets.

For our purposes in this unit, we therefore have the formulas:

$$ROCE = \frac{operating\ profit}{non\text{-}current\ assets\ +\ net\ current\ assets} \times 100\%$$

or

$$ROCE = \frac{operating\ profit}{capital\ on\ statement\ of\ financial\ position\ +\ long\text{-}term\ liabilities} \times 100\%$$

You may find the term 'Profit before interest and tax' instead of Operating Profit in some examples. A bank overdraft is normally shown as a current liability and, unless told otherwise, this is how you would treat it in an Assessment task. Some analysts, however, might argue that it is used as a semi-permanent form of finance and they would treat it as a long-term liability. This is an example of how a choice of method can make a big difference to the ratios. It is advisable to make your methods clear when calculating ROCE, because of the possible variations in the definitions.

You may be asked to calculate the 'return on net assets' instead of ROCE. This ratio is similar to ROCE, and you may be given a figure for 'net assets' to use.

JOHN KENT: RETURN ON CAPITAL EMPLOYED

John Kent is a sole trader who runs a plumbing business employing two other people. He financed part of the purchase of his vans with a long-term loan from his father. We have the following simplified statement of financial position:

Statement of Financial Position of John Kent as at 31 March 20-3		
	£	£
Non-current Assets:		
Vehicles at cost	50,000	
Less: provision for depreciation	12,500	37,500
Equipment at cost	6,800	
Less: provision for depreciation	1,200	5,600
		43,100
Current Assets	8,400	
Current Liabilities	(3,900)	
Net current assets		4,500
Long term loan		(30,000)
		17,600
Capital as at 31 March 20-3		17,600

required

Show the calculation of the Capital Employed as at 31 March 20-3 for John Kent from the above Statement of Financial Position using:

• Non-current assets plus net current assets

• Capital on Statement of Financial Position plus long-term liabilities

solution

• Non-current assets plus net current assets = £43,100 + £4,500 = £47,600

• Capital on Statement of Financial Position plus long-term liabilities

  = £17,600 + £30,000 = £47,600

Note: These two views of the statement of financial position give the same figure for Capital Employed (at 31 March 20-3).

Case Study

WING LIMITED: ROCE AND THE STATEMENT OF FINANCIAL POSITION OF A LIMITED COMPANY

This Case Study illustrates some of the features of a limited company statement of financial position, using a simplified version.

Statement of Financial Position of Wing Ltd as at 31 March 20-3		
	£000s	£000s
Non-current Assets (Net Book Value)		750
Current Assets	95	
Current Liabilities	68	
Net current assets		27
		777
Long term loans		150
		627
Capital and Reserves:		
£1 Ordinary Shares issued and fully paid		350
Reserves		200
Retained Earnings		77
		627

Note that the Statement of Financial Position total of £627,000 represents for Capital and Reserves:

- Share Capital which has been introduced into the company (by investors buying shares)
- Reserves, which represent amounts of capital or profits which have been set aside to be used in future
- Retained Earnings, which represents accumulated profits retained within the business (other than those set aside in reserves)

required

Determine the Capital Employed for Wing Ltd as at 31 March 20-3 and calculate the Return on Capital Employed. (Note: Operating Profit for the year was £233,100).

solution

Wing Ltd has long-term loans of £150,000 which are being used, along with the accumulated total capital, to finance the operating activities of the company. Therefore the Capital Employed is:

Statement of Financial Position total + Long term loans = £627,000 + £150,000 = £777,000

or Non-current Assets + Net Current Assets = £750,000 + £27,000 = £777,000

Applying the formula:

$$\text{Return on Capital Employed} = \frac{\text{Operating profit}}{\text{Capital employed}} \times 100\%$$

$$= \frac{£233,100}{£777,000} \times 100\% = 30\%$$

asset turnover

Asset Turnover is another important ratio which links the statement of financial position with the income statement. It measures how well the assets have been used during a period to generate sales revenue.

Asset Turnover is the number of times the value of the assets has been obtained in Turnover (Sales).

For example, an asset turnover ratio of 3 times would mean that, for every £1 of value in the assets, there had been £3 of sales revenue. Any improvement in asset turnover means that more sales revenue is being obtained per £1 value of the assets used. This can lead to improvements in the amount of profit and in ROCE, provided that the profit margin is not cut too much. We see below how asset turnover, operating profit margin and ROCE are linked.

Again there may be different definitions of the value of the assets, but we will use the non-current assets plus net current assets as above.

$$asset\ turnover\ =\ \frac{turnover}{non\text{-}current\ assets\ +\ net\ current\ assets}$$

WING LIMITED: ASSET TURNOVER

In the Wing Limited Case Study (see opposite), if the Turnover for the year ended 31 March 20-3 was £1,165,500, then:

$$asset\ turnover\ =\ \frac{£1,165,500}{£750,000\ +\ £27,000}\ =\ 1.5\ times$$

ROCE and operating profit margin

There is an important link between ROCE, Asset Turnover and the Operating Profit margin (ie Operating Profit as a percentage of Sales):

ROCE = operating profit margin x asset turnover

because

$$\frac{Operating\ Profit}{Non\text{-}current\ \&\ net\ current\ assets}\ =\ \frac{Operating\ Profit}{\cancel{Sales}}\ x\ \frac{\cancel{Sales}}{Non\text{-}current\ \&\ net\ current\ assets}$$

The sales (turnover) figure can be cancelled in the calculation of the right hand side of this equation (see lines).

The following diagram illustrates these connections:

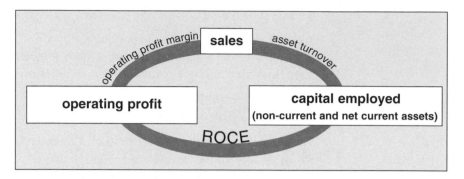

It is easiest to see this using the figures from the Wing Limited Case Study:

$\underline{£233,100}$ x 100% = $\underline{£233,100}$ x 100% x $\underline{£1,165,500}$ = 20% x 1.5 = 30%
$£777,000$ $£1,165,500$ $£777,000$

This relationship means that the ROCE can be increased either by improving the asset turnover or by increasing the Operating Profit Margin, or both. In other words, using the assets more effectively to generate sales or spending less of the sales revenue on operating costs can both improve ROCE.

Of course, if the asset turnover improves and the operating profit margin decreases, or vice versa, we need to investigate the effect on the ROCE. For Wing Limited, increasing the asset turnover to 2 times and keeping the operating profit margin at 20% gives:

ROCE = 20% x 2 = 40%.

If the operating profit margin dropped to 14%, however, the ROCE would go below its previous level of 30%, because 14% x 2 = 28%.

There is a further illustration of the calculation and interpretation of the ROCE and Asset Turnover in a Case Study later in this chapter (page 213).

CALCULATION OF RATIOS: CURRENT ASSETS AND LIABILITIES

An important aspect of the management of a business is the control of the current assets of inventory, receivables and cash.

Usually a certain level of inventory is necessary in order to avoid running out of inventory and losing production and sales. Keeping too much inventory, however, incurs additional costs of storage and means that the money tied up in inventory cannot be used for other purposes. Offering customers credit may boost sales, but it is important to collect the money from receivables within a reasonable time. Similarly, cash is needed on a day-to-day basis, but surplus cash should be invested in order to earn extra income. In each case a suitable balance must be achieved.

Control of the current liability of payables means taking advantage of the credit terms offered by suppliers, but making sure they can be paid on time.

The ratios usually calculated relating to the control of current assets and current liabilities are often referred to as 'working capital ratios'.

Working Capital is the part of the capital of the business which circulates between the inventory, receivables, cash and trade payables. These current assets and liabilities are constantly changing, unlike the non-current assets which change only occasionally.

The circulation of working capital is often illustrated by the Cash Cycle:

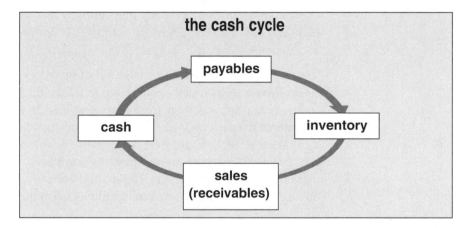

The diagram of the cash cycle above represents how suppliers provide inventory. When inventory is sold it results in an increase in receivables. When receivables pay, the cash increases. When suppliers are paid, the cash moves along to the payables. This decreases the payables' balance, but it will increase again when more inventory is provided . . . and so on.

calculation of working capital ratios: the current ratio

The current ratio compares the current assets with the current liabilities, to give an indication as to whether it should be possible to pay the current liabilities on time. We discuss below why it is important to consider how the balances of current assets and liabilities may be affected by the type of business, before drawing conclusions from the current ratio on its own.

$$\textit{The current ratio} \quad = \quad \frac{\textit{current assets}}{\textit{current liabilities}}$$

This is kept as a ratio and written in the form x : 1, where x is the answer obtained above. It shows the **number of times that the current liabilities are covered by the current assets**.

It is often said that the current ratio should be about 2 : 1, and this may be appropriate for some organisations. However, in certain types of business, the current assets are not expected to be so high in relation to the current liabilities. In a supermarket, for example, the level of receivables will be low in comparison to payables, and inventories are not held for long periods.

The ratio of 2 : 1 can be used as a guide for organisations where inventory does not sell so quickly and where sales as well as purchases are likely to be on credit. In a given case, look for comparisons (with other time periods or other similar organisations) rather than judging a single figure against this guideline.

Remember that the Statement of Financial Position shows the current assets and current liabilities on a particular date. A single transaction may change them considerably. More cash may or may not come in before current liabilities fall due. The guideline ratio of 2:1 allows some leeway for these uncertainties of timing.

The current ratio is affected by the level of inventory included in the current assets. Inventory is usually considered to be the least 'liquid' of the current assets, because it is further from becoming cash in most businesses. In the diagram of the cash cycle above, it can be seen that trade receivables are one step nearer to cash. Cash itself is the most 'liquid' current asset, because it can be used immediately to pay the suppliers (trade payables). The measurement of 'Liquidity' is important, because it indicates the ability of the organisation to pay its current liabilities when they fall due.

Case Study

A LTD, B LTD, C LTD: CURRENT RATIO

A Ltd, B Ltd and C Ltd are similar companies, which have current assets as shown:

	A Ltd £000	B Ltd £000	C Ltd £000
Inventory	170	100	50
Receivables	90	140	110
Cash at bank and in hand	40	60	140
	300	300	300

Each of the three companies has current liabilities of £150,000.

required
Calculate the current ratio for each of the three companies and compare the liquidity position of the three companies.

solution
For each company,
current assets = £300,000 and current liabilities = £150,000.
Each of the three companies therefore has a current ratio of 2 : 1.

However, A Ltd has built up inventory to a high level and we cannot be sure that these can easily be sold, in order to convert them into receivables and then into cash. When the inventory is taken out, A Ltd's current assets do not cover its current liabilities.
B Ltd has a better liquidity position, provided the receivables are well controlled.
C Ltd has the most liquid current assets and could pay most of its payables immediately.

calculation of working capital ratios: the quick ratio

The ratio which is usually used to measure liquidity compares the current assets *other than inventory* with the current liabilities, as follows:

$$\textit{Quick Ratio or Acid Test Ratio} = \frac{\textit{current assets} - \textit{inventory}}{\textit{current liabilities}}$$

This is based on the idea that inventory is the least liquid current asset. In some businesses such as supermarkets, however, inventory is very quickly turned into cash. As with all the ratios, the formula should not be applied as it stands without considering the particular situation.

As a guide, a level of 1 : 1 for the quick ratio is quoted, but a business with frequent cash inflows may operate satisfactorily on a lower quick ratio.

The aim is to check that the current liabilities are likely to be covered by cash or by current assets quickly convertible to cash.

Comparison with similar businesses gives more useful information, but it must be remembered that a single large transaction can alter the position significantly and the Statement of Financial Position may not be typical.

In most cases, the timing of cashflows in and out will be a vital factor. The quick ratio only indicates whether enough cash should 'normally' be available to pay the current liabilities when they fall due.

Case Study

A LTD, B LTD, C LTD:
CALCULATION OF THE QUICK RATIO

Referring to the data given for A Ltd, B Ltd and C Ltd in the last Case Study, we can calculate their quick ratios:

A Ltd: $\dfrac{300 - 170}{150}$ = 0.87, giving a quick ratio of 0.87 : 1

B Ltd: $\dfrac{300 - 100}{150}$ = 1.33, giving a quick ratio of 1.33 : 1

C Ltd: $\dfrac{300 - 50}{150}$ = 1.67, giving a quick ratio of 1.67 : 1

These calculations illustrate the discussion of the liquidity of the companies above.

WORKING CAPITAL RATIOS LINKING THE INCOME STATEMENT & STATEMENT OF FINANCIAL POSITION

We have seen above that an organisation needs to keep levels of receivables, payables and inventory that are appropriate for the type of business. Ratios used to measure these levels are usually calculated in terms of numbers of days or months, to estimate:

- the average time taken to collect money from trade receivables
- the average time taken to pay trade payables
- the average time that goods or materials remain in inventory

The limitations of these estimates are discussed below. The usefulness of the ratios is in making comparisons and identifying trends. For example, if the average time taken to collect money from receivables decreases over several time periods, this suggests that control of receivables is improving.

receivable collection

In the last Case Study, B Ltd has a high proportion of receivables and we noted that these should be well controlled. This means that the cash should be received within the time allowed by the normal credit terms for customers. It is possible to *estimate* the time being taken for customers to pay, by using the formula:

$$receivables'\ collection\ period\ = \frac{trade\ receivables}{credit\ sales}\ x\ 365\ days$$

A separate figure for 'Credit Sales' may not be available, and Total Sales would have to be used, although this is not appropriate if cash sales are a significant part of the total. Notice that the formula gives an average time, based on the closing receivables.

If customers are normally allowed two months' credit, for example, the receivables' collection period should not be much above 60 days (remembering that the closing receivables figure may not be typical). As usual, comparison over time is more useful and may show whether control of receivables is improving or not.

When making comparisons between organisations, remember that some businesses allow customers longer credit periods in order to increase sales.

In effect, customers are *borrowing from* the business, because sending goods without receiving payment is like lending money. Conversely, suppliers are *lending to* the business. It makes sense, therefore, to try to collect the money back from customers more quickly than paying amounts due to suppliers. However, suppliers who are not paid on time may refuse to supply goods or services in future.

payables' payment period

The **Payables' Payment Period** can be estimated in a similar way to the Receivables' Collection Period, but here it is credit purchases which are relevant.

$$payables'\ payment\ period = \frac{trade\ payables}{credit\ purchases} \times 365\ days$$

A separate figure for Credit Purchases may not be available, in which case Total Purchases or (less appropriately) Cost of Sales may have to be used.

Again, the formula gives an average, based on the closing trade payables figure, which may not be typical.

inventory holding ratios

Another step in the Cash Cycle can be estimated in terms of days: this is the length of time taken for inventory to be sold, or the average age of inventory. The inventory figure used in the formula may be the average of the opening and closing inventory, which is calculated in the usual way for an average (mean) of two items, by adding them together and dividing the total by 2:

$$average\ inventory = 0.5 \times (opening\ inventory + closing\ inventory)$$

If the opening inventory is not known, the closing inventory figure is used.

$$average\ age\ of\ inventory = \frac{average\ inventory}{cost\ of\ sales} \times 365\ days$$

or,

$$average\ age\ of\ inventory = \frac{closing\ inventory}{cost\ of\ sales} \times 365\ days$$

It can be argued that the closing inventory gives an equally good estimate. The average based on the opening and closing inventory may not be a fairer reflection, especially if the trade is seasonal. (See the discussion below.)

Note the correspondence between the pairs of figures used in the last three ratios:

- trade receivables are related to credit sales
- trade payables are related to credit purchases
- inventory is related to cost of sales

As an alternative to calculating the average age of inventory, we can look at the number of times per year that the inventory is 'turned over' or sold. This is called **inventory turnover** or **inventory turn** and is calculated as:

$$Inventory\ Turnover = \frac{cost\ of\ sales}{average\ inventory} \quad or \quad \frac{cost\ of\ sales}{closing\ inventory}$$

The result of this calculation gives the **Inventory Turnover as a 'number of times per year'**.

A higher inventoryturn indicates that inventory is moving more quickly, and this corresponds to a lower average age of inventory. The speed with which inventory should be sold depends on the type of business. For example fresh fruit must be sold within a few days, whereas non-perishable goods may be kept for longer periods. In some businesses, such as manufacturing ice cream, toys or fireworks, the level of inventories will vary considerably with the seasons. The statement of financial position date may happen to coincide with particularly high (or low)inventories and the inventoryturn will appear to be very slow (or fast) moving. Once more, we need more information about the business to be able to comment further.

ratios: the whole picture

We now look at a Case Study which incorporates a number of the ratios described so far in this Chapter. It shows how ratios can be used in business decision making.

Case Study

TUBS AND POTS LIMITED: RATIO ANALYSIS

Tubs and Pots Ltd supply plant holders to local garden centres. The company has now been offered a contract to supply a national chain of home and garden superstores. The following information shows extracts from the Statement of Financial Position and the Income Statement as forecast for the next year:

- on the basis of continuing with the current local trade ('Current Trade')
- on the basis of acceptance of the contract ('With Contract')

	Current Trade	With Contract
	£	£
Current Assets:		
Inventory	6,000	20,000
Trade Receivables	14,000	52,000
Cash at Bank	4,000	
	24,000	72,000
Current Liabilities		
Trade Payables	12,000	70,000
Bank Overdraft		7,000
	12,000	77,000
Sales (all Credit Sales)	70,000	204,000
Opening inventory	4,000	4,000
Purchases (all Credit Purchases)	40,000	140,000
Less: Closing inventory	(6,000)	(20,000)
Cost of Sales	38,000	124,000

required:

Task 1

Using the above information, calculate the following ratios for the current trade and for the acceptance of the contract:

1 Current Ratio

2 Quick Ratio

3 Receivables' Collection Period

4 Payables' Payment Period

5 Average age of inventory (using the closing inventory)

6 Gross Profit

7 Gross Profit percentage (on Sales)

Task 2

Identify the changes which will take place in the business of Tubs and Pots Ltd if the contract is accepted and comment on the findings.

solution

Task 1: calculation of ratios

Check that you can carry out these calculations, before looking at the workings at the end of the solution.

		current trade	with contract
1	Current Ratio	2.0 : 1.0	0.9 : 1.0
2	Quick Ratio	1.5 : 1.0	0.7 : 1.0
3	Receivables' Collection Period	73 days	93 days
4	Payables' Payment Period	110 days	183 days
5	Average age of inventory	58 days	59 days
6	Gross Profit	£32,000	£80,000
7	Gross Profit percentage (on Sales)	45.7%	39.2%

Task 2: analysis of ratios

The forecasts show that, with the contract, **sales** would increase to nearly three times the current level and the management of the company would need to consider whether such expansion within one year is feasible. There would also be higher **inventory levels** and the company would go into an **overdraft** situation. Building up inventories means that **purchases** are increased to more than three times the current level, which could have contributed to the need for an overdraft. Another reason for the overdraft could be purchases of non-current assets.

The indicators we have calculated show that both the **current and quick ratios** would be adversely affected by the contract, such that the current liabilities are not covered by the current assets. The **Receivables' Collection Period** increases to about 3

months with the contract, and the Payables' Payment Period to about 6 months. The adjustment to inventory levels would keep the **average age of inventory** about the same. With the contract, there is a decrease in the **Gross Profit Margin** (Gross Profit as a percentage of Sales).

The managers of Tubs and Pots Ltd need to investigate the risks attached to acceptance of this contract. If non-current assets are purchased, longer-term finance would be more suitable than an overdraft. They also need more working capital to avoid the problems with liquidity. The increased collection period indicates that the national chain would take longer to pay for the goods than the current customers. It appears risky to plan for a 6 month payables' payment period unless such terms have been agreed with the suppliers.

It would be important to consider the length and security of the contract. The forecasts given are for one year only and show that Gross Profit Margin would decrease. This could be caused by the national chain insisting on paying lower prices for the goods. Over a number of years it may be possible to improve on this, by reducing costs. Expansion on this scale would not be worthwhile unless the contract was secure for the long term. The management of Tubs and Pots Ltd should also consider the effect on their current trade with their local customers.

Workings		*current trade*	*with contract*
1	$\dfrac{\text{Current assets}}{\text{Current liabilities}}$	$\dfrac{£24,000}{£12,000}$	$\dfrac{£72,000}{£77,000}$
2	$\dfrac{\text{Current assets − Inventory}}{\text{Current liabilities}}$	$\dfrac{£18,000}{£12,000}$	$\dfrac{£52,000}{£77,000}$
3	$\dfrac{\text{Receivables} \times 365}{\text{Credit sales}}$	$\dfrac{£14,000 \times 365}{£70,000}$	$\dfrac{£52,000 \times 365}{£204,000}$
4	$\dfrac{\text{Payables} \times 365}{\text{Credit purchases}}$	$\dfrac{£12,000 \times 365}{£40,000}$	$\dfrac{£70,000 \times 365}{£140,000}$
5	$\dfrac{\text{Closing inventory} \times 365}{\text{Cost of sales}}$	$\dfrac{£6,000 \times 365}{£38,000}$	$\dfrac{£20,000 \times 365}{£124,000}$
6	Sales − Cost of sales	£70,000 − £38,000	£204,000 − £124,000
7	$\dfrac{\text{Gross Profit} \times 100\%}{\text{Sales}}$	$\dfrac{£32,000 \times 100\%}{£70,000}$	$\dfrac{£80,000 \times 100\%}{£204,000}$

FINANCIAL STRUCTURE RATIOS

The final group of ratios that we need to examine in this chapter relate to the financial structure of a business. This is about the way that the business is funded – how much of the capital employed is funded by the 'equity' of the business and how much is funded by loans (or similar) from outside the business. The equity of a limited company is the value owned by the shareholders.

Equity is shown in the statement of financial position (balance sheet) as the total of:

• ordinary share capital (the nominal value of the ordinary shares), plus
• the accumulated profit and other reserves that are owned by the ordinary shareholders

On some statements this forms a sub-total shown as equity, but on others you may need to calculate it yourself.

Some businesses may be funded entirely by equity, and this provides a very safe form of finance. All the profits generated will be owned by the shareholders, and they don't have to share it with anyone else. If profits are good then dividends can be paid, but there is no compulsion to do so.

Other businesses may obtain some of their finance from long term loans. While such loans may provide a cheap form of funding, interest will need to be paid regularly whether profits are made or not. Therefore too much finance in the form of loans can be a risky strategy, especially when profits are uncertain. A large amount of preference shares (whose holders are entitled to dividends regardless of profit) can also be risky for the same reason. The term 'fixed interest capital' is sometimes used to encompass both loans and preference shares.

There are two ratios that help us to examine the financial structure of businesses.

If we think of the sources of finance in the form of a simple pie chart, this will help us understand both these ratios.

Suppose the capital employed by a company is £1m, made up of loans of £0.4m and equity of £0.6m, as follows:

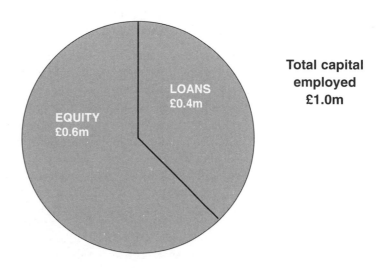

gearing ratio

This ratio (calculated as a percentage) shows how much of the total funding comes from sources that demand regular payments of interest or dividends.

It is calculated as:

$$\frac{(\text{Loans} + \text{Preference Share Capital})}{\text{Total Capital Employed}} \times 100$$

The higher the percentage, the higher the 'gearing' is said to be. A high gearing ratio will also mean that a low proportion of the capital employed is invested by the ordinary shareholders.

The gearing ratio based on the example above would be

$$\frac{£0.4m}{£1.0m} \times 100 = 40\%$$

This means that 40% of the finance comes from loans or preference shares (although there are no preference shares in this example).

debt to equity ratio

This ratio uses the same logic, but compares the 'fixed interest capital' directly to the equity instead of the total capital employed. It is also calculated as a percentage.

It is calculated as:

$$\frac{(\text{Loans} + \text{Preference Share Capital})}{(\text{Ordinary Share Capital} + \text{Reserves})} \times 100$$

The debt to equity ratio based on the above example would be

$$\frac{£0.4m}{£0.6m} \times 100 = 67\%$$

The debt to equity ratio will always result in a higher percentage than the gearing ratio when based on the same data.

For both these ratios, the higher the percentage the more fixed interest capital is being used. While many businesses will want to use some finance of this type, if the amount becomes excessive then it will make the structure very risky. This is because if operating profits fell below a certain level then the company would find it difficult to pay the large amounts of interest, and this could ultimately result in the collapse of the company.

We will now look at a long Case Study which gives practice in calculating and interpreting *all* the ratios. In assessments, it is usual for the tasks to concentrate on one aspect of performance, such as profitability or liquidity.

BAMBERDALE PLC:
COMPREHENSIVE RATIO ANALYSIS

Bamberdale plc is a large manufacturing company in the chemicals industry producing a range of different products. The following information is available for the years ended 30 September 20-2 and 20-3. (Note as before that the earlier year is shown on the right).

The term 'Debentures' under long-term liabilities in this example refers to long term loans, (which are often secured on the assets in a similar way to a domestic mortgage). For ease of working the information is shown in a simplified format.

Bamberdale plc Income Statement for the year ended 30 September

	20-3		20-2	
	£m	£m	£m	£m
Turnover		2,660		2,200
Opening Inventory	400		277	
Purchases	1,945		1,723	
Less: Closing Inventory	350		400	
Cost of Sales		1,995		1,600
Gross Profit		665		600
Selling and Distribution	120		105	
Administration	240	360	210	315
Operating Profit		305		285
Interest charges		25		20
Profit before taxation		280		265
Taxation		84		62
Profit after taxation		196		203

Bamberdale plc Statement of Financial Position as at 30 September:

	20-3		20-2	
	£m	£m	£m	£m
Non-current Assets at Cost	1,370		763	
Provision for Depreciation	770	600	500	263
Current Assets:				
Inventory	350		400	
Receivables	200		210	
Cash at Bank	26		97	
	576		707	
Current Liabilities:				
Trade Payables	236		224	
Taxation	84		62	
	320		286	
Net current assets		256		421
Long term liabilities:				
Debentures		200		160
		656		524
Financed by:				
Ordinary shares issued and fully paid		300		300
Retained Profits (reserves)		356		224
		656		524

required

Carry out an analysis of the ratios studied in this chapter (listed below) for Bamberdale plc and comment on the results.

The ratios to be analysed are:

1   Gross Profit Margin
2   Operating Profit %
3   Selling and Distribution % (of Sales)
4   Administration % (of Sales)
5   ROCE
6   Asset Turnover
7   Current Ratio
8   Acid Test Ratio
9   Receivables' Collection Period
10   Payables' Payment Period
11   Average age of inventory (use average inventory)
12   Gearing ratio
13   Debt to equity ratio

solution

The following indicators are calculated from the information given, using the formulas in this chapter. (Check that you can carry out these calculations, before looking at the workings at the end of the solution).

		30 Sept 20-3	30 Sept 20-2
1	Gross Profit Margin	25.0%	27.3%
2	Operating Profit %	11.5%	13.0%
3	Selling and Distribution % (of Sales)	4.5%	4.8%
4	Administration % (of Sales)	9.0%	9.5%
5	ROCE	35.6%	41.7%
6	Asset Turnover	3.11 times	3.22 times
7	Current Ratio	1.8 : 1	2.5 : 1
8	Acid Test Ratio	0.7 : 1	1.1 : 1
9	Receivables' Collection Period	27 days	35 days
10	Payables' Payment Period	44 days	47 days
11	Average age of inventory	69 days	77 days
12	Gearing ratio	23.4%	23.4%
13	Debt to equity ratio	30.5%	30.5%

comments

We can look first at the **original figures**, before considering the ratios. It is clear that, in the year ended 30 September 20-3, **Turnover** has increased, and so have the **Gross Profit** and **Operating Profit** figures. On the Statement of Financial Position, we can see that non-current assets have been purchased during the year, and there are also additional **long term loans** (debentures). Current assets have decreased, particularly the **Cash at Bank**. It seems that the extra loans have partly financed the new non-current assets, but cash has also been used for this. These assets have helped to generate higher sales and this has resulted in higher profits. However, the ratios will show how well the company has used its assets in comparison to the previous year, and what percentage of the higher sales has been translated into profits.

ratio analysis

1   **Gross profit margin** has decreased, which suggests that selling prices have been reduced (this could result in more demand for the products and therefore higher turnover). Alternatively, purchase costs may have gone up, or both.

2, 3 & 4 The **expenses** have increased approximately in line with turnover, being at similar percentage levels. Together with the lower gross profit margin, this has resulted in a decrease in the **operating profit percentage**. The increase in the amount of **administration** expenses could be investigated, as it might be expected that the majority of these costs would be fixed.

5   **ROCE** has decreased from 41.7% to 35.6%. This is due to the fact that the **capital employed** has increased. (The **operating profit** has also increased, but because we are dividing it by a much larger number, the resulting percentage has gone down). We saw that we can look at the capital employed from the point of view of the non-current and net current assets being used or the financing of those assets. The non-current assets being used in the year ended 30 September 20-2 were probably older and therefore the accumulated depreciation had

considerably reduced their value on the statement of financial position. In the following year, a significant factor is that there are **new non-current assets** included on the Statement of Financial Position as at *30 September.* There is no information as to whether these were acquired early or late in the year, which would make a difference to the amount of profit they could generate.

Looking at the increase in capital employed from the finance point of view, it is due to the £40m increase in **debentures** and the £132m increase in **retained profit** for the year ended 30 September 20-3.

6   The **asset turnover** has decreased slightly, but considering the effect of the additional non-current assets as discussed above, it seems that the company has continued to use its assets to generate sales at a similar level.

7 & 8   The **current and acid test ratios** have both deteriorated and may cause concern at these levels. The main reasons are the decrease in cash and the increase in **current liabilities**, particularly tax and trade payables. Some of the cash may have been used for the purchase of non-current assets. Cash will be required to pay the tax and dividends when they fall due and this could prove to be a problem.

9,10 & 11   There has been an improvement in the **collection of receivables** and **inventory** is being turned over slightly more quickly. The **payment period for trade payables** has changed only slightly and the net effect is that the circulation of working capital has been speeded up.

12 & 13   The gearing ratio and the debt to equity ratio have both remained static, because the additional loans have been matched by additional equity through retained profits. These levels are not high enough to increase risk, and this is confirmed by noting that the interest is a very small proportion of operating profit.

More general discussion of this case study could include some of the following points:

■   In general, the year ended 30 September 20-3 has been one of expansion for Bamberdale plc.

■   Sales have increased at a rate which corresponds with the expansion, and therefore to reverse the decline in profitability, opportunities for cost reduction should be investigated.

■   It will be important to review the ROCE in the next year, ending 30 September 20-4, to check that it does not continue a downward trend. The current year's decrease can be explained by the effect of increased capital employed and next year should see an improvement if the new assets generate sufficient profits.

■   The main problem at 30 September 20-3 is liquidity. At that date the company appears to need more cash. The improvement in collection of receivables is helpful, but the company may still have difficulty in paying its tax liability and the payables.

Workings (£m)	*30 Sept 20-3*	*30 Sept 20-2*
1 Gross Profit x 100%	665 x 100%	600 x 100%
Sales	2660	2200
2 Operating profit x 100%	305 x 100%	285 x 100%
Sales	2660	2200
3 Selling & Dist. x 100%	120 x 100%	105 x 100%
Sales	2660	2200
4 Administration x 100%	240 x 100%	210 x 100%
Sales	2660	2200
5 Operating profit x 100%	305 x 100%	285 x 100%
Capital employed	656 + 200	524 + 160
6 Turnover	2660	2200
Non-current & net current assets	600 + 256	263 + 421
7 Current assets	576	707
Current liabilities	320	286
8 Current assets – Inventory	226	307
Current liabilities	320	286
9 Receivables x 365	200 x 365	210 x 365
Credit sales	2660	2200
10 Trade Payables x 365	236 x 365	224 x 365
Credit purchases	1945	1723
11 Average inventory x 365	0.5 x (400+350) x 365	0.5 x (277+400) x 365
Cost of sales	1995	1600
12 Loans x 100	200 x 100%	160 x 100
Capital Employed	856	684
13 Loans x 100	200 x 100%	160 x 100
Equity	656	524

NOTES ON CALCULATION AND INTERPRETATION OF RATIOS

behaviour of ratios

The comments on the last Case Study are very detailed, but they are based on a few basic properties of ratios. It is important to be able to analyse the ratios by this method, as shown on the next page.

A ratio or percentage is calculated from two figures and shows how one amount relates to the other. There may be some other link between the two figures, for example:

Gross Profit = Sales – Cost of Sales

The gross profit margin shows what percentage of the sales is left after cost of sales is taken out. If the gross profit margin decreases, it means that the cost of sales is taking out a bigger part of the sales and therefore we conclude that either selling prices have been reduced or costs of sales have increased or both.

Each percentage is calculated by dividing one figure by another. Using the usual terms for fractions we could write this as:

$$\frac{Numerator \; x \; 100\%}{Denominator}$$

The percentage will **increase**:

either if the **numerator increases** relative to the denominator

or if the **denominator decreases** relative to the numerator.

The percentage will **decrease**:

either if the **numerator decreases** relative to the denominator

or if the **denominator increases** relative to the numerator.

In the Bamberdale Case Study, the ROCE decreased from

$$\frac{285 \times 100\%}{684} = 41.7\% \quad \text{to} \quad \frac{305 \times 100\%}{856} = 35.6\%$$

Although the numerator has increased, the much greater increase in the denominator has had the dominant effect and this is what has been highlighted in the discussion. If you find making comments on ratios difficult, try to see how this method applies to the other ratios in the Bamberdale Case Study.

Further examples of how percentages change:

■ $\frac{120 \times 100\%}{200} = 60\%$ and $\frac{130 \times 100\%}{200} = 65\%$

Here the numerator (on top) increases, the denominator (on the bottom) is unchanged, and the percentage increases.

■ $\frac{120 \times 100\%}{200} = 60\%$ and $\frac{114 \times 100\%}{180} = 63\%$

All figures decrease, but the decrease in the denominator dominates, causing the percentage to increase.

In an assessment on this unit, it is not likely that you would be expected to calculate and comment in detail on all the ratios as in the last Case Study. This is a comprehensive example to practise all aspects, but whichever aspect is examined, the basic method of interpretation can be used.

HINTS ON USING FORMULAS

In assessment tasks, you may be given information including, for example, a company's statement of financial position and have to answer such questions as:

* '*what* would the turnover have been *if* the asset turnover increased to 2 times?'
* '*what* would the operating profit have been *if* the ROCE reached a target level of 30%?'

We show below the method for carrying out these tasks, which are simple cases of 'What if?' analysis. This means calculating what will happen if certain conditions are satisfied.

In Chapter 8, there are more complex Case Studies illustrating 'What if?' analysis, where a number of conditions have to be satisfied at the same time.

In assessment tasks involving questions like those above, you often have to use *two* items of data to calculate *one* figure which you need. With ratio analysis, such calculations may involve using a given ratio and one of its parts to calculate the other part.

A general method to use for such questions is to write down the formula and insert the figures you are given. You should then be able to deduce the required amount.

Note: If you are not used to using equations, remember that you can move figures from one side of the '=' sign to the other, provided that you change

* addition into subtraction and vice versa
* division into multiplication and vice versa.

For example, in the Bamberdale Case Study, we could ask 'What would the Operating Profit have been in the year ended 30 September 20-3 if the ROCE had remained at 41.7%?'

First, write down the formula:

$$ROCE = \frac{operating\ profit \times 100\%}{capital\ employed}$$

Then insert the known figures:

$$41.7\% = \frac{\text{operating profit} \times 100\%}{£856m}$$

Then, moving £856m to the top left-hand side of the equation changes division to multiplication. The required Operating Profit is therefore:

$$41.7\% \times £856m = £356.95m$$

Your answer can always be checked by seeing that it satisfies the required condition. To check this answer: £356.95m ÷ £856m x 100% = 41.7%.

---

practical examples

See if you can work out the following:

1 If the Turnover is £98,000, what Gross Profit is required to give a Gross Profit Margin of 40%?

2 If the Operating Profit is £45,000 and this is 25% of Turnover, what is the Turnover?

3 If the Current Ratio is 2.2 : 1, and the Current Assets total £88,000, what is the total of the current liabilities?

solutions to examples

1 Gross Profit Margin = $\dfrac{\text{Gross Profit} \times 100\%}{£98,000}$ = 40%

   Therefore Gross Profit = 40% x £98,000 = £39,200.

2 Operating Profit = £45,000 = 25% x Turnover

   Therefore Turnover = £45,000 x 100 ÷ 25 = £180,000

3 $\dfrac{\text{Current Assets}}{\text{Current liabilities}}$ = 2.2

   $\dfrac{£88,000}{\text{Current liabilities}}$ = 2.2

   Therefore £88,000 ÷ 2.2 = Current Liabilities = £40,000.

(In each case the answer can be checked).

LIMITATIONS OF RATIO ANALYSIS

In the introduction to this section, it was emphasised that one set of ratios alone does not give very useful information. Ratios for other time periods or other organisations are useful for comparison, as are target ratios.

The principle of **comparing like with like** should be applied in ratio analysis, but this is not always straightforward. Some of the ratios can be defined in different ways, so the particular definition used should be made clear. Even so, detailed information may not be given, for example to split sales into cash sales and credit sales.

When using the **published accounts of companies**, it is not possible to guarantee that we are comparing like with like, as different policies (including those regarding depreciation, inventory valuation and goodwill, for example) will affect the results.

For any organisation, there is also the possibility that the Statement of Financial Position does not show a typical position, intentionally or otherwise. A single transaction the next day may make it look quite different. The Statement of Financial Position reflects the conditions for a particular season of the year and in trades with seasonal variations, this can make a big difference to the ratios.

Discussion of a particular case may include looking for ways in which the ratios could have been distorted. For example, high levels of spending on research, training or marketing may reduce profits in one period, but bring much greater benefits in a later period. The reverse is also true: cutting these costs may improve the profit ratios in the short term, but in the long term sales and profits would suffer.

When making comparisons over different time periods, the ratios are based on historical costs as shown in the accounts. If there has been inflation during the time periods, a better comparison can be made by making adjustments for this before calculating the ratios. (See Chapter 7, page 227).

Before drawing firm conclusions from ratio analysis, these limitations should be borne in mind. However, the analysis can give useful information, particularly in showing how items in the financial statements relate to each other and in identifying trends. In the next chapter, we consider other types of performance indicator, but again their usefulness depends on comparability.

Chapter Summary

- Numerical (quantitative) data can be used when measuring performance: this data may be in terms of money or other units.

- Opinions and judgements which are not numerical (qualitative) are also important when measuring performance.

- Comparisons are more useful than single sets of data, provided the data being compared has been prepared on a consistent basis, to compare like with like. Comparison may be made with standards, budgets or targets; with other periods of time; with other similar organisations.

- The methods and techniques used for performance measurement include Ratio Analysis - ie the calculation of percentages and ratios from the financial accounts.

- The techniques discussed in this chapter can give useful information, provided that the limitations of ratio analysis are kept in mind.

- The next chapter continues the study of performance measurement, with examples of alternative forms of performance indicator and consideration of methods applicable to various types of organisation.

Key Terms

performance indicator — an individual measurement used to evaluate the performance of an organisation or part of an organisation

benchmarking — the setting of standards or targets for the activities of an organisation

trend — the underlying behaviour of a series of figures over time

comparability — the principle of comparing like with like, that is comparing data prepared on consistent bases

quantitative data — data which can be measured in numerical terms, including financial and non-financial data

qualitative data — data which cannot be measured in numerical terms, such as opinions and attitudes

ratio analysis — the analysis of the financial accounts of an organisation by calculating ratios and percentages

gross profit margin (percentage) — $\dfrac{\text{Gross Profit} \times 100\%}{\text{Sales}}$

net profit margin — $\dfrac{\text{Net Profit} \times 100\%}{\text{Sales}}$

operating profit margin — $\dfrac{\text{Operating Profit} \times 100\%}{\text{Sales}}$

ROCE (return on capital employed) — $\dfrac{\text{Operating profit} \times 100\%}{\text{Non-current assets} + \text{net current assets}}$

asset turnover (number of times) — $\dfrac{\text{Turnover}}{\text{Non-current assets} + \text{net current assets}}$

current ratio — $\dfrac{\text{Current assets}}{\text{Current liabilities}}$

acid test or quick ratio	$\dfrac{\text{Current assets} - \text{inventory}}{\text{Current liabilities}}$
receivables' collection period	$\dfrac{\text{Trade receivables} \times 365 \text{ days}}{\text{Credit sales}}$
payables' payment period	$\dfrac{\text{Trade payables} \times 365 \text{ days}}{\text{Credit purchases}}$
average age of inventory	$\dfrac{\text{Average inventory} \times 365 \text{ days}}{\text{Cost of sales}}$
	or $\dfrac{\text{Closing inventory} \times 365 \text{ days}}{\text{Cost of sales}}$
inventory turnover (no. of times)	$\dfrac{\text{Cost of sales}}{\text{Average inventory}}$
	or $\dfrac{\text{Cost of sales}}{\text{Closing inventory}}$
gearing ratio	$\dfrac{(\text{Loans} + \text{Preference Share Capital}) \times 100}{\text{Total Capital Employed}}$
debt to equity ratio	$\dfrac{(\text{Loans} + \text{Preference Share Capital}) \times 100}{(\text{Ordinary Share Capital} + \text{Reserves})}$

Activities

6.1 Explain briefly what is meant by the following terms relating to performance measurement:

(a) Consistency *like with like*

(b) Benchmarking *setting standard*

(c) Qualitative data

6.2 The following information relates to Raven Ltd for a given period:

Sales revenue = £500,000,

Gross profit margin = 24%,

Operating profit = £50,000

Which of the following four statements is correct for Raven Ltd for the given period?

(a) Cost of sales = £620,000, Expenses = £170,000

(b)   Cost of sales = £70,000,   Expenses = £380,000

(c)   Cost of sales = £380,000, Expenses = £70,000

(d)   Cost of sales = £330,000, Expenses = £170,000

6.3   The following income statements relate to a small retail shop selling stationery and gifts:

Toni Jones Income Statements for the year ended:

	31 May 20-3		31 May 20-2	
	£000s	*£000s*	*£000s*	*£000s*
Sales		525		450
Less: Cost of Sales				
Opening inventory	50		30	
Purchases	408		335	
Less: Closing Inventory	(80)	378	(50)	315
Gross Profit		147		135
Less: Expenses:				
Administration	25		24	
Selling	38	63	30	54
Net Profit		84		81

Required

For Toni Jones for the given years, calculate:

(a)   Gross Profit percentage 28% 30%

(b)   Net Profit percentage 16% 18%

(c)   each expense as a percentage of Sales 4.76 5.33 7.23

Comment briefly on the original figures and on the percentages calculated. 5.24 6.66

6.4   Ace plc is an electrical goods manufacturing group and the information below relates to one of its subsidiaries, Jack Limited.

Jack Ltd: Summary Income Statement for the year ended 30 June 20-3

	£000s	£000s
Turnover		2,500
Less: Cost of Sales		
Opening Inventory	30	
Cost of Production	650	
Less: Closing Inventory	(90)	590
Gross Profit		1,910
Administration	780	
Selling and Distribution	505	1,285
Operating Profit		625

Jack Ltd: extract from Statement of Financial Position as at 30 June 20-3:

	£000s	£000s	£000s
Non-current assets	*Land and Buildings*	*Plant*	*Total*
At cost	900	2,000	2,900
Additions	-	1,000	1,000
	900	3,000	3,900
Accumulated depreciation	-	1,380	1,380
	900	1,620	2,520

Current Assets:		
Raw materials inventory	10	
Finished goods inventory	90	
Receivables	160	
Cash at bank	110	
	370	
Current liabilities	(50)	320
Net Assets		2,840

Required

(a)   Calculate the following ratios for Subsidiary Jack Ltd for the financial year

- Gross Profit margin
- Operating profit margin
- Return on Capital Employed (ROCE)
- Asset turnover
- The average age of receivables
- The average age of finished goods inventory (using average inventory)

(b)   The directors of Ace plc consider that ROCE and Asset Turnover are important performance measures, and Subsidiary Jack Ltd has failed to meet the group targets, which are:

Target ROCE   26%
Target Asset turnover   1.5 times

Identify one factor which may have affected the performance of Subsidiary Jack Ltd in relation to these targets in the year ended 30 June 20-3.

(c)   Calculate the Turnover which Subsidiary Jack Ltd would have obtained if it had achieved the target level of Asset turnover, using the Statement of Financial Position as given.

(d)   Assuming Subsidiary Jack Ltd maintained the same operating profit margin, calculate the ROCE which would have resulted from the Turnover calculated in (c) above. Assume that the Capital Employed is unchanged for Jack Ltd, as it is controlled at that level by Ace plc.

6.5   Using formulas, calculate the answers to the following:

(a)   If the Gross Profit Margin is 35% and the Turnover is £200,000, what is the Cost of Sales?

(b)   If the Inventory is £4,200, the Current Liabilities total £7,000, and the Acid Test Ratio is 0.9 : 1, what is the Current Ratio?

7 Measuring performance – further aspects

this chapter covers...

In this chapter we continue our study of performance measurement, and examine some additional aspects of the topic.

We start by using techniques to make more sense of financial indicators, such as adjusting using index numbers, and calculating averages. We will also learn how 'value added' can be calculated and used.

We will then examine non-financial indicators which are numerical, for example number of customer complaints or number of employee-days absence. We will then go on to discuss qualitative measures that are not expressed numerically, but may refer to attitudes and opinions.

The next section involves the measurement of productivity and efficiency. These terms will be explained and guidance provided on how they can be measured. This leads to the use of the control ratios of efficiency, activity and capacity which can be used to monitor aspects of production.

We will then examine performance measurement in service organisations, before going on to review the assessment of quality.

The balanced scorecard is a technique for grouping performance measurements under four categories (or 'perspectives'), and this idea is discussed and illustrated in the next section.

Finally we will examine how performance indicators can be developed and evaluated, and also see how managers' behaviour can be affected by the choice of indicators.

FINANCIAL INDICATORS

Data given in terms of actual amounts of money (or other units) is sometimes referred to as absolute data, and ratios or percentages as *relative* figures. We have included discussion of the financial indicators of absolute Turnover and Profit in the previous chapter, with ratios, because the most useful information comes from considering the absolute and relative figures together. Other financial indicators include selling prices, costs and variances. As before, the usefulness of these depends on:

- comparing with standards, budgets or targets
- comparing with other periods of time
- comparing with similar organisations

financial indicators: adjustment to real terms

In comparing financial data over periods of time, it may be necessary to 'deflate' the figures, that is take out the effect of inflation, so that the comparison is of 'like with like'. A suitable index is used to put all the data in terms of the value of money in the same year, often described as 'real terms'. This method is described in Chapter 1.

Financial data adjusted by using an index in this way, to obtain comparable figures, could then be used for the calculation and analysis of ratios, as illustrated in the Case Study that follows.

Case Study

TURNER LIMITED: ADJUSTING TO REAL TERMS

Turnover and Net Profit figures are given for Turner Ltd for the five years ended 31 December 20-1 to 20-5. A suitable index for Turner Ltd's industry is also given.

	20-1	20-2	20-3	20-4	20-5
Turnover (£000s)	435	450	464	468	475
Net Profit (£000s)	65	70	72	75	78
Industry Index	133	135	138	140	143

required

Calculate the Turnover and Profit in terms of year 20-5 values and comment on the results. Illustrate the results for the Turnover on a graph for the five years shown.

solution

To put each figure into 20-5 terms, it is divided by the index for its own year and multiplied by the index for 20-5, ie 143. (The base year is not used). For example:

Turnover Year 20-1 $\dfrac{435}{133}$ x   143 = 467.7

Turnover Year 20-2 $\frac{450}{135}$ x 143 = 476.7 and so on.

In year 20-5 terms:

	20-1	20-2	20-3	20-4	20-5
Turnover (£000s)	467.7	476.7	480.8	478.0	475.0
Net Profit (£000s)	69.9	74.1	74.6	76.6	78.0

The adjusted figures compare like with like in terms of the value of the pound, and the Net Profit still shows an increasing trend throughout, but the Turnover decreases in the last two years. The following graph shows both the original and adjusted turnover figures. (A similar graph could be drawn for the net profit).

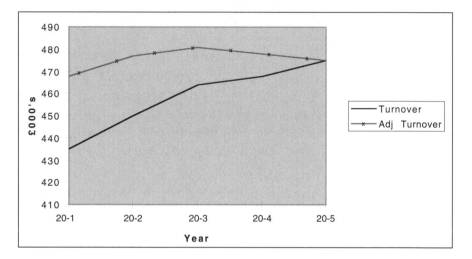

After adjusting the net profit and turnover to year 20-5 terms, we can calculate the net profit percentage, using the adjusted figures:

20-1   (69.9 ÷ 467.7) x 100% = 14.9%
20-2   (74.1 ÷ 476.7) x 100% = 15.5%
20-3   (74.6 ÷ 480.8) x 100% = 15.5%
20-4   (76.6 ÷ 478.0) x 100% = 16.0%
20-5   (78.0 ÷ 475.0) x 100% = 16.4%

This shows an increasing trend in the 'real terms' net profit percentage.

financial indicators: calculating averages

Although total amounts of money such as sales, profits and costs may be used for performance measurement, it is often more informative to calculate an average 'per employee', 'per hour', 'per unit of output' and so on. This is a simple calculation which relates the financial data to the size of the organisation in some way.

practical examples

1   If sales orders amount to £32million for the year and there are 16 sales representatives, then

Average sales orders per representative = £32m ÷ 16 = £2m

2   If materials cost £87,000 in total for output of 29,000 units of a product, then

Average cost of materials per unit = £87,000 ÷ 29,000 = £3

3   If training costs for the year total £171,000 and there are 450 employees, then

Average expenditure on training per employee = £171,000 ÷ 450 = £380

financial indicators: value added

The meanings of the words 'quality' and 'value' in relation to products and services are discussed in Chapter 5. On page 151, four aspects of the value of a product or service are listed:

1   value in use

2   esteem or prestige value

3   cost of production or provision

4   exchange value (market value)

The first two aspects are important to customers and will influence the fourth one: the market value. From the point of view of the business that makes the product or provides the service, the aim is to maximise the market value without increasing costs.

Turnover (sales revenue) is a measure of the market value of the output for a given period. Comparing this with the cost of inputs gives a measurement of the value added by the business as a whole.

'Value added' as a financial measure refers to the difference between the value of outputs and the value of inputs. It shows the increase in monetary value which has resulted from the work done and the use of assets within the organisation. For the calculation of value added, 'inputs' are defined as 'materials and bought-in services'. These have been brought into the organisation *from outside*. The monetary value of outputs is sales revenue or turnover, which is their value as they go to *outside customers*.

Value added = Turnover – (cost of materials used and bought in services)

The average value added per employee can also be used as an indicator of productivity within the organisation. (For more about productivity see later in this chapter.)

Case Study

TURNER LTD: VALUE ADDED

The following information is given for Turner Ltd for the year 20-5.

Turnover	£475,000
Number of employees	22
Cost of materials used	£100,000
Total cost of bought-in services	£155,000

required

Calculate the total value added and the value added per employee for the year 20-5 for Turner Ltd.

solution

Value Added = £475,000 – (£100,000 + £155,000) = £220,000
Value Added per employee = £220,000 ÷ 22 = £10,000

NON-FINANCIAL INDICATORS

A **non-financial indicator** is a measurement which is expressed in numbers, but not in money terms, the possible units being very varied: for example hours, transactions, units of product, customers and so on.

Non-financial indicators can take many forms, because they can be designed to measure aspects of any kind of work. They are useful in both manufacturing and service industries and can be applied in both profit-making and non-profit making organisations. They are particularly useful for measuring quality, which was discussed in Chapter 5.

Some examples of possible non-financial indicators are given below. Several indicators may be used together for the same activity. You may have other examples from the workplace.

In assessments, you may be asked to suggest how a particular aspect of the work of an organisation could be assessed.

Activity or aspect to be measured	Non-financial indicator
Automated production	Hours of machine down time
Absenteeism	Employee-days absence
Telephone helpline	Average time in seconds taken to answer calls
Quality of service	Number of customer complaints
Input of data to computer	Number of errors per 1000 inputs
Customer satisfaction	Number of repeat orders
Quality of output	Number of units rejected per 1000

Further examples of non-financial indicators will occur when different types of organisation are considered later in this chapter.

QUALITATIVE (NON-NUMERICAL) MEASURES

Some aspects of work are very difficult to measure in terms of numbers, for example: motivation of others, team working, helpfulness to customers.

When numerical indicators are not suitable, **opinions** and **attitudes** have to be recorded, perhaps by customer surveys. Surveys often ask customers to give ratings, say on a scale of 1 to 5, but these are only an aid to obtaining an overall view, not an accurate measurement.

Appraisal schemes within an organisation may involve collecting feedback from colleagues. For example, those present at a meeting may be asked their opinion as to the how well the person chairing the meeting carried out that task. Work relationships can affect the judgements given (and vice versa), so the usefulness of this feedback may be limited.

MEASUREMENT OF PRODUCTIVITY AND EFFICIENCY

The terms 'productivity' and 'efficiency' are used in various ways, but generally relate to how much output is being achieved from the inputs. Here we are referring to the productivity and efficiency of a whole organisation. (The efficiency of an employee or a group of employees can be measured by the labour efficiency variance or the efficiency ratio. The efficiency ratio is defined later in this chapter.)

Productivity is likely to be measured in terms of **units of output**, or related to quantity of output in some way.

For example, productivity could be measured by relating units of output to the number of employees or the assets used to produce them, by calculating: 'units of output per employee' or 'units of output per £ value of non-current assets'.

Efficiency implies that the measure should indicate the **value** of the outputs in relation to the inputs, because it is not 'efficient' to produce more units if they are worth less than their cost, for example if they cannot be sold. This suggests that the efficiency of the organisation as a whole is linked to **profits**, and how well resources have been used to generate the profits.

Measures of efficiency could therefore include Return on Capital Employed (ROCE) and operating profit margin, which we have studied in detail in Chapter 6. Where ROCE is used, a business with newer non-current assets, giving a higher capital employed, may appear less efficient than a similar firm with older assets. See the discussion in part two of the Case Study below. This Case Study also illustrates how the choice of performance indicators for productivity and efficiency will depend on the information available.

Case Study

LIDO LTD AND NEW LTD: PRODUCTIVITY AND EFFICIENCY

Lido Ltd and New Ltd are two companies owned by Wells plc. Lido Ltd and New Ltd are similar companies using the same accounting policies and both manufacture the same component, which is sold to the motor industry. The following information relates to the year ended 31 May 20-3 for the two companies:

	Lido Ltd	New Ltd
Units produced and sold	20,000	50,000
Number of employees	34	78
	£000s	£000s
Net book value of non-current assets	350	1,600
Net current assets	75	20
Capital employed	425	1,620
Turnover	640	1,600
Operating profit	128	256

required

1 Calculate for each company for the year ended 31 May 20-3 the following indicators:

- Units produced per employee
- Asset turnover
- Operating profit margin (percentage of turnover)
- Return on capital employed
- Operating profit per employee
- Units per £1,000 of NBV of non-current assets

State how each of these indicators might be relevant to the *productivity* or *efficiency* of the companies (abbreviated to 'P' and 'E' in the table below).

2 Explain briefly one reason why the productivity and efficiency measures calculated may give opposite rankings to the two companies.

solution

calculations		Lido Ltd	New Ltd	P or E?
1	Units produced ÷ number of employees	588	641	P
	Asset Turnover	1.51	0.99	E
	Operating profit as % of turnover	20.0%	16.0%	E
	ROCE	30.1%	15.8%	E
	Operating profit ÷ number of employees	£3,765	£3,282	P & E
	Units per £1,000 of NBV of non-current assets	57	31	P

comments

- *Units produced per employee* are a measure of output and therefore productivity.

- *Asset turnover* shows how efficiently the assets have been used to generate sales, so could be used to assess efficiency.

- *Operating profit margin* and *ROCE* are both measures of efficiency because they relate the value of outputs to inputs and resources used.

- *Operating profit per employee* could be said to relate to productivity as it compares the results of production with the number of employees; it is probably more suitable to measure efficiency because the profit figure is being used.

- *Units per £1,000 NBV of non-current assets* is an alternative measure of productivity, relating the output to the non-current assets used to produce it.

why are the ratings opposite?

2 Lido Ltd has higher Operating profit margin and ROCE, indicating that it is more efficient. New Ltd has higher productivity according to the units produced per employee, (although the units per £1,000 value of non-current assets was higher in Lido Ltd).

The reason for the different rankings is the *difference in the value of the* non-current *assets*. New Ltd has much higher value non-current assets, and would therefore have higher depreciation charges in the income statement. The result is that the efficiency measures of asset turnover, ROCE and operating profit margin are lower in New Ltd, whereas the output per employee is higher. The relative age of the assets could affect both productivity and efficiency measures. If the higher value is because New Ltd has newer non-current assets, particularly plant and machinery, this may also account for the fact that each employee can produce more output.

unit cost

Another way of comparing output with inputs is to calculate the *cost per unit of output*. This can be applied to products or services, provided the output achieved can be measured in some way.

The cost of inputs is divided by the number of units of output. This may be done for the total cost, or for some particular element of cost, for example

$$Production\ labour\ cost\ per\ unit = \frac{total\ cost\ of\ production\ labour}{number\ of\ units\ of\ output}$$

Comparing unit costs between similar organisations or divisions could be part of the assessment of efficiency, provided that the principle of comparing like with like is applied.

practical example

In a given period, the output of a division is 15,000 product units.

The costs of production are as follows:

Direct materials	£97,500
Direct labour	£63,750
Production overheads	£85,500
Total production cost	£246,750

Therefore, for these costs, the Unit Cost could be calculated as follows:

Direct materials:	£97,500 ÷ 15,000	=	£6.50 per unit
Direct labour:	£63,750 ÷ 15,000	=	£4.25 per unit
Production overheads:	£85,500 ÷ 15,000	=	£5.70 per unit
Total production cost:	£246,750 ÷ 15,000	=	£16.45 per unit

CONTROL RATIOS: EFFICIENCY, CAPACITY AND ACTIVITY

efficiency ratio

In the discussion above, 'efficiency' refers to an organisation's performance and this relates to its profitability. In this section, we consider the efficiency of the workforce (or a part of it) in terms of the hours used to produce the output. One performance indicator to measure this is the Labour Efficiency Variance studied in Chapter 2. The variance shows the difference between the *standard hours for actual production* and the *actual hours*, valued at the standard labour rate. The same two figures in hours can be compared in percentage terms instead of calculating the difference. This gives the efficiency ratio:

$$efficiency\ ratio\ =\ \frac{standard\ hours\ for\ actual\ production}{actual\ hours\ worked}\ x\ 100\%$$

If the ratio is exactly 100%, the employees have worked at the standard level of efficiency. If it is less than 100%, they have worked more slowly – this would result in an adverse variance. If it is more than 100%, they have worked more quickly than the standard – corresponding to a favourable variance.

activity ratio and production volume ratio

The standard hours for actual production can also be compared with the original plan for the period, the budgeted hours. This is an indicator of how actual output compares with the budgeted output and is known as the **activity ratio**. The formula is:

$$\frac{\textit{standard hours for actual production}}{\textit{budgeted hours}} \quad \text{X} \quad 100\%$$

This can alternatively be expressed in terms of volume of output and is known as the **production volume ratio**:

$$\frac{\textit{actual output}}{\textit{budgeted output}} \quad \text{X} \quad 100\%$$

capacity ratio

The third control ratio compares the actual 'capacity' which has been used with the planned amount.

Capacity (here being measured in terms of direct labour hours) is the amount of available resources being used. Full capacity would mean that all possible resources were being used. Budgeted capacity (probably less than full capacity) would be set in line with planned levels of production and sales.

The capacity ratio shows what proportion of the planned resources have actually been used. This is particularly important when there are significant fixed costs which have to be paid to make these resources available.

$$\textit{capacity ratio} = \frac{\textit{actual hours worked}}{\textit{budgeted hours}} \quad \text{X} \quad 100\%$$

Case Study

1.850

1.600

EAC LTD: CONTROL RATIOS

EAC Ltd produces a single product, for which the standard direct labour time is 2 hours per unit. For a given period, EAC Ltd budgeted for a total of 68,000 hours. The actual results for the period showed that 34,600 units were produced and the actual total direct labour hours worked were 71,000 hours.

required
Calculate the standard hours for the actual production in this case and hence calculate the three control ratios.

solution
The standard hours for the actual production of 34,600 units would be
34,600 x 2 = 69,200 hours.

Therefore, using the above formulas, the control ratios would be:

Efficiency Ratio = $\dfrac{69,200}{71,000}$ x 100% = 97.5%

Activity Ratio = $\dfrac{69,200}{68,000}$ x 100% = 101.8%

Capacity Ratio = $\dfrac{71,000}{68,000}$ x 100% = 104.4%

The control ratios for EAC Ltd, above, show that both the level of activity (output) and the resources used were more than planned in the budget, but the workforce were slightly less efficient than the standard. As in variance analysis, the reasons for the level of efficiency could be investigated and they may include external factors such as problems with supply of materials, not necessarily the fault of the employees.

PERFORMANCE MEASUREMENT IN SERVICE ORGANISATIONS

It is more difficult to measure the performance of a service organisation or department than one which produces tangible goods. Services cannot be checked before being provided in the same way as products can be inspected for faults.

The usual financial measures and ratios can be used for profit-making service organisations. (Non-profit-making organisations are considered in a later section of this chapter.)

Non-financial and qualitative measures, discussed earlier in this chapter, are often applicable to services. For example:

- Average waiting times for customers can be calculated and compared to a target.

- The number of customer complaints indicates the level of customer satisfaction.

- Analysis of customer opinions can be collected through surveys. Aspects such as 'Are the staff friendly and helpful?' can be judged in this way.

- Services can also be assessed by internal observation. Telephone services are monitored by supervisors listening to samples of calls, for example.

In assessment tasks, you may be required to identify or discuss suitable performance indicators for a service organisation.

The appropriate performance indicators to use depend on the type of service being provided and what its aims must be. From the organisation's point of view, financial indicators are likely to be important. If you then consider what features of the service would be important to customers, you can see which items of data are available to measure those features (see also 'developing a new indicator' later in this chapter.)

For example, in a Further Education College, comparisons of costs and incomes with budgets measure financial aspects. Customers' views may be more dependent on non-financial indicators such as average class size and pass rates or qualitative measures relating to the teachers and the classroom environment.

The *financial* and *customer* aspects or perspectives discussed in this section form part of the 'Balanced Scorecard', which can be applied to any kind of profit-making organisation, which is discussed later in this chapter.

ASSESSING QUALITY

In Chapter 5 we saw that the quality of a product or service depends on its fitness for the customer's purpose.

Customers' expectations may include prestige value with some products and services, as well as value in use. From the point of view of the supplier, quality must be provided at a reasonable cost. Quality management means aiming at continuous improvement and eliminating mistakes. If Total Quality Management is introduced, it must involve all employees in the organisation, not just those who deal with the external customers. Employees must treat colleagues as 'internal customers', and the same principles apply when supplying products or services to internal customers.

From the definition of quality, it is clear that performance indicators will include measures of customer satisfaction. Examples are:

- numbers of product units returned
- sales value of returns as a percentage of total sales
- numbers of warranty claims
- numbers of customer complaints

From the supplier's point of view, costs must be considered, for example:

- cost per unit of product or service
- cost of customer service department
- average cost of after-sales service per customer

Assessing the quality of tangible **products** is more straightforward than for services. Products can be inspected and compared to detailed product specifications. Samples can be tested to check their value in use. Quality can be measured by, for example:

- numbers of defects
- number of substandard goods as a percentage of units produced
- cost of reworking as a percentage of production cost

Performance measurement for **service** organisations has been discussed in the previous section. Assessing the quality of a service involves first deciding what customers expect from that service. There may be many aspects to this and these can be measured by, for example:

- customer opinions in response to surveys
- internal inspections or observations
- inspections or observations by external bodies
- non-financial indicators such as waiting times

Case Study

HERMES PLC: A QUALITY POSTAL SERVICE

Hermes PLC is considering introducing a rival postal service in the UK. The company is carrying out market research into customer expectations.

required

What would you consider to be the main features customers look for in a high quality postal service? How could the quality be measured?

solution

Suggestions of some of the features customers might want are:

• post to be delivered on time
• post to be delivered to correct address
• post to be undamaged
• postboxes to be conveniently placed
• post offices to be easily accessible
• short waiting times in post offices

Suggestions of ways these could be measured:

• percentages of letters delivered late
• numbers of returned letters or complaints (although mistakes may not be reported)
• numbers of damaged packets as percentage of total
• average distances between postboxes or numbers of postboxes per thousand households
• results of customer surveys or observations
• average post office waiting times calculated from observations

As can be seen in this Case Study, quality cannot be assessed unless systems are in place to record and analyse the necessary data. The general principles of **comparability** must also apply. Comparison over time and trend analysis is necessary to measure improvements resulting from quality management. In the Balanced Scorecard, which is explained in the next section, measurement of quality is part of the internal perspective.

THE BALANCED SCORECARD

The Balanced Scorecard is a way of viewing the performance of a profit-making organisation from four *perspectives*, relating to profits, customers, quality and development, as follows:

• **the financial perspective** is concerned with satisfying the shareholders or owners of a business and relates to profits. Suitable indicators include ROCE and profit margin.

- **the customer perspective** is concerned with customer satisfaction and loyalty. It relates to customers' views of the business and suitable indicators include delivery times and numbers or amounts of orders from previous customers.

- **the internal perspective** is concerned with technical excellence and consumer needs, which relate to quality. Suitable indicators are those which assess quality and value.

- **the innovation and learning perspective** is concerned with the need for continual improvement of existing products and the ability to develop new products to meet customers' changing needs, so it is related to development. Suitable indicators may include the percentage of turnover attributable to new products or a measure of research and development expenditure.

In a given case, you may be asked to identify ways of measuring these four perspectives. You will need to look for data available in the case study which you can connect with each aspect of the business and be prepared to develop new performance indicators. The next Case Study illustrates this type of task. Note particularly how the 'average delay in fulfilling orders' is calculated. The method is very similar to that used for the average age of inventory or receivables in Chapter 6. You need to be able to apply general principles like this in different situations.

Sometimes, a task is set the other way round: you are asked to say which perspective is being measured by a given indicator. It is important to read the tasks carefully and make sure you answer the right question!

Case Study

HSB LTD: THE BALANCED SCORECARD

You are employed by HSB Ltd, a company with several subsidiaries and you have been asked to apply the balanced scorecard to monitor the performance of the subsidiaries. The following information relates to Subsidiary H for the period ended 31 December 20-3. You also have available the financial accounts of Subsidiary H for the same year. Extracts are given here.

	£000s
Sales	3,500
Less: returns	70
Turnover	3,430
Operating profit	825
Analysis of turnover by products:	
Sales of new products	1,350
Sales of existing products	2,080
Turnover as above	3,430

Analysis of turnover by customers:

Sales to new customers	650
Sales to existing customers	2,780
Turnover as above	3,430
Value of orders placed for delivery during the year	4,250

required

Identify and calculate, from the available information, one performance indicator which you could use in monitoring each of the four perspectives in the balanced scorecard.

solution

Monitoring the balanced scorecard for subsidiary H for the year ended 31 December 20-3:

- The *financial* perspective could be measured by operating profit margin, which is $(825 \div 3,430) \times 100\% = 24\%$.

- The *customer* perspective could be measured by repeat custom as a percentage of sales, which is $(2,780 \div 3,430) \times 100\% = 81\%$.

- An alternative would be the average delay in fulfilling orders. The unfulfilled orders amount to £4,250,000 – £3,430,000 = £820,000 and this could be used as a fraction of turnover to calculate $(820 \div 3,430) \times 365$ days, giving 87 days as the average delay.

- The *internal* perspective could be measured by the percentage of sales returns, which is $(70 \div 3,500) \times 100\% = 2\%$.

- The *innovation and learning* perspective could be measured by the percentage of sales derived from new products, which is $(1,350 \div 3,430) \times 100\% = 39\%$.

PERFORMANCE MEASUREMENT IN NON-PROFIT MAKING ORGANISATIONS

Non-profit making organisations include charities and clubs as well as some public sector organisations. Without the objective of profit, there may be no single aim by which 'success' can be measured.

Performance indicators need to be designed to measure how well the organisation has achieved its aims. Much of the section on service organisations above applies to non-profit making organisations, many of which do provide services. Instead of profit, *value for money* is the main financial criterion. This is usually defined as:

- **economy**: controlling expenditure on costs

- **efficiency**: relating 'outputs' to inputs, meaning that obtaining more from the money spent shows greater efficiency

- **effectiveness**: relating 'outputs' to the aims of the organisation, so that achieving more of what it sets out to do shows greater effectiveness

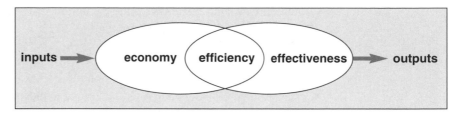

Economy can be measured in the same way as costs in businesses, by comparing with budgets and calculating variances for example.

A possible indicator for **efficiency** is the cost per unit, where units of output can be defined. For example, in a nursing home, the cost of a resident day could be calculated.

Effectiveness may be measured by comparison with targets or with other similar organisations.

Some aspects of non-profit-making activities can only be assessed by qualitative measures: opinions and judgements of experts, users or those who provide the funding. Representatives of government agencies or funding bodies may carry out observations or inspections, as in schools for example.

The general principles of performance measurement apply to these organisations as well as to businesses:

* comparability – comparing like with like
* comparison with standards, budgets or targets
* comparison with similar organisations
* comparison over time, to look for trends

EVALUATION AND DEVELOPMENT OF PERFORMANCE INDICATORS

In this chapter and in Chapter 6, we have studied a considerable number of commonly used performance indicators and also looked at possible measures to be used in different situations.

As well as the standard ratios, for which you are expected to know the methods, you need to be able to calculate averages, percentages or other ratios according to instructions given in a task. You may also be asked to evaluate an existing performance indicator or to develop a new one.

evaluating an existing indicator

If you are asked to discuss an existing performance indicator, you need to look at the kind of data that is being used, the way that the indicator is calculated and the aspect of the organisation that it is supposed to be measuring. A 'good' measure of performance should be based on relevant, unbiased data and calculated using a method that reflects the aspect being measured in a fair and meaningful way.

Questions to be asked include:

* what are the definitions being applied? For example, in measuring the percentage of orders delivered late, what is meant by 'late'?

* is the data collected by sampling and, if so, is there any possibility that it is biased? (See Chapter 1, pages 27-29, for a discussion of sampling).

* is the calculation based on items that the people being measured can influence? For example, people who can take action about costs, but are not responsible for any aspect of sales, should not be judged by looking at profits.

* does the indicator give a meaningful measurement of what it is supposed to be measuring? For example, it could be stated that only 2% of orders are delivered late. However, this may be achieved by cutting out final checks, so that many orders have missing or incorrect items. It may be more useful to measure the percentage of complete and correct orders delivered on time. It depends on the exact purpose of the measurement: is it intended only to assess the speed of delivery of orders, or is it part of the wider aspect of the quality of service to customers?

developing a new indicator

You may be asked in an assessment task to work out a way of measuring a particular aspect of the work of an organisation. You need to identify what you would mean by good or bad performance in that aspect of the work. This should help you find a way of measuring it. There may be some appropriate data available in the task, or you may have to suggest the type of data that would need to be recorded.

Throughout this chapter there have been various examples of performance indicators that are useful in certain situations.

EFFECTS OF PERFORMANCE MEASUREMENT ON BEHAVIOUR

The choice of performance indicator to use in a particular situation can affect the way people approach their work. It is important to make sure that the measurement of performance motivates employees to work efficiently and in the best interests of the organisation as a whole.

If the particular measure being used can be manipulated by workers, so that their performance looks good, it may encourage behaviour that is not in fact beneficial to the organisation as a whole. We learned in our study of standard costing that responsibility for variances may be allocated to individual managers, and that this may cause unhelpful behaviour.

Another example may be when using ROCE to evaluate performance. A capital investment in plant may be declined if the ROCE would deteriorate due to the increased investment. This may occur even though there may be significant benefits in using new plant, for example improved efficiency, quality, reliability and customer satisfaction.

If people take action to improve particular measures of performance in the short term, their behaviour may have adverse effects for the organisation later on. For example, profits may be improved by cutting down on training costs. Eventually, the lack of training may result in inefficiencies or mistakes, which will then reduce the profits. Looking at ways in which a performance indicator can be manipulated may be part of its evaluation, because the results are not useful or meaningful if they can easily be changed by such behaviour.

If targets are set in terms of a particular measure of performance, they should be:

- achievable, but encouraging improvement
- within the area of responsibility of the person being measured
- comparing like with like
- seen to be fair and meaningful

A system for assessing people's work is more likely to motivate them as part of the organisation 'team' if they can see that it is fair and that they can attain the required level by being efficient. The result should be to encourage behaviour that benefits the organisation as a whole.

You need to be prepared to discuss performance measurement in service industries as well as manufacturing. The Case Study that follows relates to the topics discussed above.

Case Study

BEST BUS LTD: PERFORMANCE MEASUREMENT

situation

Best Bus Ltd operates a single 'park and ride' route from a car park on the outskirts of Southtown to the town centre. The service runs on 360 days of the year, using 4 buses that were 3 years old when purchased second-hand for this route.

Car parking is free and each passenger buys a return ticket on the bus. The journey is 4 miles each way and the round trip of 8 miles is counted as one bus journey in the data below. There is a basic timetable for journeys, but, to speed up the service in peak periods, drivers may leave the car park as soon as their bus is full.

The following table shows information for the years ended 30 June 20-3 and 20-4, which were the first two years of operation of the route:

1	Best Bus Ltd data for the year ended:	30 June 20-3	30 June 20-4
2	Number of bus journeys	42,000	44,550
3	Number of return tickets sold	504,000	623,700
4	Return fare per passenger	£0.70	£0.90
5	Maintenance costs per year	£36,000	£36,800
6	Number of drivers	10	11
7	Gross profit margin	25%	36%
8	Net profit margin	4%	14%
9	Asset turnover	1.2 times	1.8 times
10	Working days per year		
11	Number of buses		
12	Miles per journey		
13	Average number of bus journeys per day		
14	Average number of passengers per journey		
15	Number of miles travelled		
16	Maintenance cost per mile		
17	Average number of bus journeys per driver		
18	Average number of miles travelled per bus		
19	Return on capital employed		

task 1

Calculate the performance indicators numbered 10 to 19 for each year and insert them in the table.

task 2

(a) The drivers claim that the improved profitability has been achieved because they have increased productivity. Identify **one** existing possible indicator of driver productivity and comment briefly on their claim.

(b) The Manager of Best Bus Ltd believes that a better service to customers will lead to increased profits. Identify and evaluate **one** existing indicator that may measure the quality of customer service.

(c) A bus users' group is concerned about safety. Identify and evaluate **one** existing indicator that may measure the safety aspect of this service.

(d) Develop **two** new indicators, one for **each** of the aspects discussed in parts (b) and (c) above. Your indicators may require the recording of data not shown above.

(e) Identify **one** indicator, which could encourage driver behaviour that would not be beneficial to Best Bus Ltd.

(f) Suggest **two** factors that may have contributed to the improved profitability of Best Bus Ltd and which are not related to driver behaviour or performance.

solution: task 1

10	Working days per year	360	360
11	Number of buses	4	4
12	Miles per journey	8	8
13	Average number of bus journeys per day	117	124
14	Average number of passengers per journey	12	14
15	Number of miles travelled	336,000	356,400
16	Maintenance cost per mile	£0.11	£0.10
17	Average number of bus journeys per driver	4,200	4,050`
18	Average number of miles travelled per bus	84,000	89,100
19	Return on capital employed*	4.8%	25.2%

*(net profit margin x asset turnover)

solution: task 2

(a) A possible indicator of driver productivity is the average number of journeys per driver. This has in fact decreased, even though the total number of journeys has increased considerably, because an extra driver has been employed. According to this measure the drivers' productivity has not increased. In any case, extra journeys per driver would not improve profitability unless they resulted in higher sales of tickets.

(b) A possible indicator of the quality of customer service is the average number of bus journeys per day, because more journeys should indicate that the service is more frequent. The limitation of this type of indicator is that an average does not give exact information as to whether the extra journeys were timed to satisfy customer demand. On its own this indicator does not show that passengers' waiting times have been decreased.

(c) A possible indicator of safety aspects is maintenance cost per mile. This has decreased very slightly in the second year, when it might have been expected to increase because the buses are one year older. Maintenance is an important aspect of the safety of the buses, but there are many other factors that passengers would want to take into account. On its own this indicator does not give much information about safety.

(d) New indicators: there are a number of valid answers in addition to the following suggestions (one required in each case).

Quality of customer service: numbers of customer complaints, passenger waiting times for buses, qualitative data collected in passenger surveys.

Safety: numbers of road accidents involving buses, number of injuries to passengers, time taken for action on driver reports of problems.

(e) The indicator 'average number of bus journeys per driver' may encourage drivers to leave the car park early, without waiting as instructed for passengers to fill the bus in peak periods. They may also rush the journey, allowing passengers less time to board and leave the bus. This behaviour would have safety and customer service implications, as well as financial effects on Best Bus Ltd's profits if unnecessary journeys were made.

(f) Factors that may have contributed to improved profitability include (two required):

- ticket prices have been increased
- the cost of fuel may have decreased
- the service has attracted more passengers because it has become more widely known in its second year or because car parking charges in the town centre have increased.

SUMMARY OF PERFORMANCE INDICATORS

In the last two chapters we have examined many performance indicators, and seen how they can be calculated and used. We will summarise examples of the indicators that you need to be able to understand and use, and group them under the main categories. Note that some indicators appear in more than one category.

Financial (Profitability, Liquidity, Efficiency and Gearing)

- Gross Profit Margin, Operating Profit Margin, any cost as a percentage of turnover
- Current ratio, quick ratio
- Receivables days, inventory days, payables days
- Gearing ratio, debt to equity ratio
- Value added

Control Ratios

- Labour efficiency ratio
- Capacity ratio
- Labour activity ratio

Indicators of Efficiency, Effectiveness and Productivity

- Efficiency: ROCE, Operating Profit Margin, Labour efficiency ratio
- Effectiveness: Percentage free from defects, average delivery times, services (eg trains) on time, percentage of students passing exams first time, average waiting times
- Productivity: Items manufactured per period (or per employee), operations per day, meals served per day

Quality

- Number of defects / returns / warranty claims / complaints
- Cost of inspections / repairs / re-working
- Prevention costs, appraisal costs, internal failure costs, external failure costs

Now would be a good time to check your understanding of all the above examples, and revisiting the relevant pages where necessary.

Chapter Summary

- Data which is collected for performance measurement may be quantitative (numerical) data in terms of money or other units, or it may be qualitative data consisting of opinions or attitudes. A combination of quantitative and qualitative data can be used. Appraisal schemes often use qualitative data.

- Comparisons are more useful than single sets of data, provided the data being compared has been prepared on a consistent basis, to compare like with like.

- The performance of organisations is measured using performance indicators to make comparisons with:
  - standards, budgets or targets
  - other periods of time
  - other similar organisations

- When making comparisons over time, index numbers are used to remove the effects of inflation from a series of data from different time periods.

- 'Value added', as a financial indicator, measures the difference in value between the outputs from an organisation and the inputs which come from external suppliers.

- Non-financial indicators are often in terms of time (such as machine hours or labour hours), but may be numbers of product units, transactions, errors and so on. They can be designed to measure specific aspects of performance in a particular organisation.

- Productivity and efficiency are both related to how much output is achieved from the inputs. Productivity generally refers to the quantity of output and efficiency to the value of output in relation to inputs.

- Unit cost is a financial indicator which can be applied to products or services, provided that units of output can be measured.

- Control ratios are based on direct labour hours and measure efficiency, capacity and activity in percentage terms.

- Non-financial and qualitative measures of performance are useful for service organisations, and should be designed to measure the aspects of the service which are important to customers.

- The quality of a product or service depends on its fitness for the customer's purpose and therefore suitable performance indicators include measures of customer satisfaction, which are often non-financial or qualitative measures.

- The 'balanced scorecard' looks at an organisation from the financial, customer, internal and innovation and learning perspectives and identifies ways of measuring each of these aspects of its performance.

- Financial performance measurement for non-profit making organisations is based on value for money, which is achieved through economy, efficiency and effectiveness.

- It is essential for fair and useful performance measurement that the indicators used are designed for the particular type of organisation, to measure how well it is achieving its aims and objectives. This must be planned in advance, as it can only be done if the necessary data is recorded during the period. The principle of consistency should be applied to both the collection and the analysis of data for performance measurement.

- Suitable performance indicators should be chosen to provide useful information and to motivate employees to improve efficiency. The choice of indicator should not encourage behaviour that is aimed at manipulating the figures and is not of benefit to the organisation.

Key Terms		
	performance indicator	an individual measurement used to evaluate the performance of an organisation or part of an organisation
	financial indicator	a performance indicator measured in money terms
	non-financial indicator	a performance indicator measured in units other than money
	quantitative data	data which can be measured in numerical terms, both financial and non-financial data
	qualitative data	data which cannot be measured in numerical terms, such as opinions and attitudes
	deflated series	a series of figures for different time periods from which the effect of inflation has been removed, to give comparison in 'real terms'
	value added	turnover less the cost of materials and bought-in services
	productivity	the aspect of the performance of an organisation which could be measured by the level of output
	efficiency	the aspect of the performance of an organisation which could be measured by relating the value of the output to the inputs
	unit cost	cost of inputs divided by the number of units of output
	control ratios	the efficiency, activity and capacity ratios
	efficiency ratio	$\dfrac{\text{standard hours for actual output}}{\text{actual hours worked}} \times 100\%$
	activity (or production volume) ratio	$\dfrac{\text{standard hours for actual output}}{\text{budgeted hours}} \times 100\%$
	capacity ratio	$\dfrac{\text{actual hours worked}}{\text{budgeted hours}} \times 100\%$
	balanced scorecard	the concept of performance measurement from the point of view of four perspectives: financial, customer, internal and innovation and learning

Activities

> Note: some of these activities include topics from Chapter 6 as well as Chapter 7. Assessment tasks are often structured to cover various aspects of performance measurement in this way.

7.1 Give two examples of each of the following:

(a) Financial quantitative performance indicators

(b) Non-financial quantitative performance indicators

(c) Qualitative performance indicators

7.2 You have the following information relating to a small charity and also inflation index numbers:

	Year 1	Year 2	Year 3
Income (£)	260,000	305,000	400,000
Expenditure (£)	200,000	240,000	330,000
Surplus (£)	60,000	65,000	70,000
Inflation index	115	123	130

Required

Restate the figures for year 1 and year 2 in year 3 terms and state whether or not the income and surplus are growing in real terms.

7.3 The following information is given for Exe Ltd for the year 20-3.

Turnover	£972,000
Output (product units)	67,500
Number of employees	54
Cost of materials used	£216,000
Total cost of bought-in services	£324,000
Total cost of inputs	£540,000

Required

Calculate for Exe Ltd for the year 20-3:

(a) total value added

(b) value added per employee

(c) material cost per unit

(d) total cost of inputs per unit

7.4 Wessit Housing Association is considering offering a contract for double-glazing its properties to one of two suppliers, Staylite Ltd and Temeglass Ltd. The following information has been extracted from the most recent annual report and accounts of the two companies.

	Staylite Ltd	Temeglass Ltd
	£000s	£000s
Sales	7,660	9,500
Gross Profit	3,467	4,522
Operating Profit	403	627
Interest charges	45	2
Non-current Assets (net book value)	600	800
Current assets	198	307
Inventory included in current assets	82	120
Current liabilities	182	156
Debentures	450	0
Share capital and reserves	166	951
Average number of employees	16	18

Required

(a) Calculate the following ratios for each of the two companies:
- gross profit margin
- operating profit margin
- return on capital employed
- current ratio
- quick ratio
- asset turnover
- sales per employee
- operating profit per employee

(b) Using the given information and the ratios you have calculated, comment on the profitability and financial position of the two suppliers.

(c) State which of the performance indicators you have calculated may be used to indicate how efficient the companies are.

(d) State which of the performance indicators you have calculated may be used to indicate the productivity of the companies.

(e) Explain the limitations of the above analysis, in particular from the point of view of Wessit Housing Association's decision about the contract.

(f) Suggest one further indicator which Wessit Housing Association should seek to obtain (not necessarily from the report and accounts) before making this decision.

7.5 CD Ltd makes a product which takes 6 hours per unit of direct labour time. In a given period it is planned (budgeted) that 14,700 direct labour hours will be worked.

During the period, the actual result is that 2,400 units of the product are made and the direct labour hours worked are 15,000 hours.

Calculate the Efficiency Ratio, the Capacity Ratio and the Activity Ratio for this period.

7.6 List and explain briefly the three aspects of 'value for money' which may be used as criteria in the performance measurement of non-profit making organisations.

7.7 Up-to-You Gym is a fitness centre, which obtains its sales income from membership fees, trainers' consultancy fees, sales of clothing and small items of equipment and sales of refreshments. During the year ended 30 September 20-4, there was considerable upgrading of the centre's equipment (non-current assets) and a drive to recruit more members by offering local firms group membership discounts for their employees. The following information is available for Up-to-You Gym for the years ended 30 September 20-3 and 20-4. (The total number of members in the year ended 30 September 20-2 was 580).

	30 Sept 20-4	30 Sept 20-3
Sales (£000s)	750	600
Costs (£000s)	520	430
Profit (£000s)	230	170
Number of new members	730	525
Number of returning members	470	175
Total number of members	1,200	700
Number of member visits	60,300	30,230
Number of employees	22	14
Total hours centre was open	4,368	3,698
Total days centre was open	364	360

Required

Using the above information, identify and calculate ONE appropriate indicator which may help to measure performance from EACH of the perspectives:

(a) The financial perspective

(b) The customer perspective

(c) The internal perspective

(d) The innovation and learning perspective

7.8 Scinso Soft Ltd has developed a product that softens skin and is claimed to produce the appearance of a youthful complexion. The product competes with many other products in the marketplace. The market leader is Laurelle plc, which sells to over 60% of the market. You have been given the following information about Scinso Soft Ltd and Laurelle plc for the year ended 31 May 20-0.

Income Statements		Scinso Soft Ltd	Laurelle plc
		£'000	£'000
Turnover		4,500	22,000
Cost of Production:			
Direct materials		1,200	3,300
Direct labour		750	2,200
Fixed production overheads		600	3,000
Total cost of sales		2,550	8,500
Gross profit		**1,950**	**13,500**
Selling and distribution costs		500	1,000
Administration costs		375	750
Advertising costs		250	10,000
Net profit		**825**	**1,750**
Other Information		Scinso Soft Ltd	Laurelle plc
Number of units sold	Units '000	600	2,200
Net assets	£'000	5,000	8,500

Calculate the performance indicators for Scinso Soft Ltd and Laurelle plc and complete the following table (give answers to two decimal places):

	Scinso Soft Ltd	Laurelle plc
Selling price per unit		
Material cost per unit		
Labour cost per unit		
Fixed production overheads per unit		
Gross profit margin		
Net profit margin		
Advertising cost as % of turnover		
Return on net assets		

8 Scenario planning

this chapter covers...

In this chapter we will examine and illustrate how scenario planning (or 'what if' analysis) can be used to develop future plans for an organisation.

We will start by discussing what the techniques mean in general terms, and illustrating them with a case study. We will then examine some specific situations that you may need to deal with, and see how the techniques are used.

The first specific situation that we will examine concerns the 'make or buy' decision. Here we will use our knowledge of marginal costing to develop our plans, and also consider some of the other important non-financial issues.

We then consider limiting factor decisions and will learn how to deal with:

- *more than one constraint for a single product, and*
- *product choice when there is a limiting factor*

In the next section we examine the marginal costing tools of contribution, break-even point and margin of safety. We will also see how an understanding of risk can be developed by examining the cost structure and using these indicators.

Next we will see how closure of a business segment can be analysed. This has some issues in common with the 'make or buy' decisions examined earlier.

Mechanisation is then considered and the three techniques that are applicable to this situation are illustrated. These are:

- *redrafting an income statement*
- *using discounted cash flow*
- *calculating net terminal value or cost*

Finally we will see how volume, price and cost adjustments can be built into scenario planning.

SCENARIO PLANNING OR 'WHAT IF?' ANALYSIS

In the last two chapters we have examined many possible ways of measuring the performance of an organisation. Problems may be highlighted by this process and the managers of the organisation will need to work out how performance can be improved. Useful information can be obtained by testing possible changes in 'what if?' analysis. This means recalculating *what* the results and performance indicators would be *if* the changes were made. The term 'scenario planning' is also used because a new scenario or situation is described. If analysis of the new situation shows satisfactory results, managers can plan the changes needed to reach that position.

You may have to prepare forecasts answering a number of 'what if?' questions at the same time. In your calculations, you need to account for all the effects of each change. For example:

- a change in closing inventory level will affect the cost of sales and hence the profit and also the inventory figure on the statement of financial position (it may, of course, simply be caused by lower or higher purchases)

- a change in receivables' collection period will affect the receivables figure on the statement of financial position

- a change in suppliers' credit terms will affect the payables' payment period and hence the payables figure on the statement of financial position

- changes in selling price or sales volume or both will affect the sales revenue and hence the profit

- changes in costs will affect the profit

- because the capital on the statement of financial position includes the retained profits for the year, any changes to the retained profit *will also change the capital employed*

- changes such as taking out or paying off loans will affect the capital employed

- **all the above changes** affect **the cash balance**, and therefore the revised figure is usually calculated as a balancing figure on the statement of financial position, after entering all the other revised figures

The following case study illustrates how scenario planning can be used to show the effects of changes in a situation and analyse the results. It is a more complex case study than you would be required to attempt in an assessment, but is worth studying carefully so that you can follow through all the implications.

We will then go on to examine some more specific situations where scenario planning can be used.

MEAD LTD: SCENARIO PLANNING

situation

Mead Ltd is a soft furnishings and interior design company. The operating statement for Mead Ltd for the year ended 30 April 20-3 and a statement of financial position as at that date are shown below.

The chief executive, Anna Mead is concerned about the company's liquidity and profitability. Suppliers are putting pressure on the company for quicker payment and the bank is concerned about the level of overdraft.

Anna Mead considers that better purchasing could achieve a 10% reduction in Purchase Costs and in Closing Inventory Value. She also wants to re-structure the company and reduce wages and salaries by 10%. She has set targets for the average payment periods as follows: trade receivables at 1 month and trade payables at 2 months.

Mead Ltd Operating Statement for the year ended 30 April 20-3

	£000s	£000s
Turnover		430.0
Less: cost of sales		
Opening inventory	64.5	
Purchases	218.0	
Less: closing inventory	(60.0)	222.5
Gross profit		207.5
Wages and salaries	91.0	
Depreciation	25.0	
Other costs	27.5	143.5
Operating profit		64.0

Statement of Financial Position as at 30 April 20-3

	£000s	£000s
Non-current Assets at Cost		250.0
Less: accumulated depreciation		75.0
		175.0
Current Assets		
Inventory	60.0	
Trade Receivables	72.0	
	132.0	
Current liabilities		
Trade Payables	54.5	
Bank overdraft	37.5	
	92.0	
Net current assets		40.0
		215.0
Long-term loans		(20.0)
		195.0

Financed by:

Ordinary shares issued and fully paid	120.0
Retained profits	75.0
	195.0

required

(a) Calculate the following ratios using the Operating Statement and Statement of Financial Position given above:

1 Gross Profit margin

2 Operating Profit margin

3 Return on Capital Employed

4 Asset Turnover

5 Average age of Trade Receivables in months

6 Average age of Trade Payables in months

7 Average age of Closing Inventory in months

8 Current Ratio

9 Acid Test Ratio

(b) Prepare a revised Operating Statement and Statement of Financial Position, which assume that Turnover remained the same, but all the changes suggested by Anna Mead had taken place. (Note that *additional* profits would increase the 'Retained Profits' figure on the Statement of Financial Position. The Cash at Bank can then be calculated as a balancing figure.)

(c) Calculate the set of ratios as in part (a) using your revised Operating Statement and Statement of Financial Position.

(d) Comment briefly on the results of your calculations.

solution

(a) 1   Gross Profit margin = (207.5/430.0) x 100% = 48.3%

2   Operating Profit margin = (64.0/430.0) x 100% = 14.9%

3   Return on Capital Employed = (64.0/215.0) x 100% = 29.8%

4   Asset Turnover = 430.0/215.0 = 2 times

5   Average age of Receivables = (72.0/430.0) x 12 = 2 months

6   Average age of Payables = (54.5/218.0) x 12 = 3 months

7   Average age of Closing Inventory = (60.0/222.5) x 12 = 3.2 months

8   Current Ratio = 132.0/92.0 = 1.4, i.e. 1.4:1

9   Acid Test Ratio = 72.0/92.0 = 0.8, i.e. 0.8:1

(b)

Revised Operating Statement for the year ended 30 April 20-3

	£000s	£000s
Turnover		430.0
Less: cost of sales		
Opening inventory	64.5	
Purchases (10% lower)	196.2	
Less: closing inventory (10% lower)	(54.0)	206.7
Gross profit		223.3
Wages and salaries (10% lower)	81.9	
Depreciation	25.0	
Other costs	27.5	134.4
Operating profit		88.9
Note additional profit 88.9 – 64.0 =		*24.9*

Revised Statement of Financial Position as at 30 April 20-3

	£000s	£000s
Non-current Assets at Cost		250.0
Less: accumulated depreciation		75.0
		175.0
Current Assets		
Inventory (10% lower)	54.0	
Receivables (1/12) x 430.0	35.8	
Cash at Bank (balancing figure)	7.8	
	97.6	
Current liabilities		
Payables (2/12) x 196.2	32.7	
Bank overdraft	-	
	32.7	
Net current Assets		64.9
		239.9
Long-term loans		(20.0)
		219.9
Financed by:		
Ordinary shares issued and fully paid		120.0
Retained profits (increased by £24,900)*		99.9
		219.9

Note how the additional profit has been added to the Retained Profits and the new Statement of Financial Position total calculated from this part of the Statement of Financial Position. The total is then entered in the top part and the balancing figure for Cash at Bank is the last figure to be entered.

(c) 1   Gross Profit margin = (223.3/430.0) x 100% = 51.9%

2   Operating Profit margin = (88.9/430.0) x 100% = 20.7%

3   Return on Capital Employed = (88.9/239.9) x 100% = 37.1%

4   Asset Turnover = 430.0/239.9 = 1.8 times

5   Average age of Receivables = 1 month as required

6   Average age of Payables = 2 months as required

7   Average age of Closing Inventory = (54.0/206.7) x 12 = 3.1 months

8   Current Ratio = 97.6/32.7 = 3.0, i.e. 3.0:1

9   Acid Test Ratio = 43.6/32.7 = 1.3, i.e. 1.3:1

(d)   The original figures show that Mead Ltd's customers are taking on average 2 months to pay, and the company is taking on average 3 months to pay its suppliers. The targets set by Anna Mead would bring cash in more quickly and satisfy the suppliers' demands. The Current and Acid Test ratios in (a) show that there may be a problem with liquidity.

The revised Operating Statement and Statement of Financial Position, together with the ratios calculated on them, show a better liquidity position, mainly due to the fact that the bank account is no longer overdrawn. The profit percentages have also improved, due to the reductions in costs.

The analysis shows that *if* all the conditions set out by Anna Mead could be achieved, with the same level of turnover, the position of Mead Ltd would be considerably improved. The current and acid test ratios look healthy and the overdraft has been replaced by a positive bank balance of £7,800. An additional £24,900 of Operating Profit results from the changes made.

functional analysis approach to decision making

Throughout our examination of scenario planning and decision making we will be using data from across the organisation, and looking at the impact of decisions throughout the organisations.

Suggestions for improvements and the solutions to problems are often made by managers throughout an organisation. Sometimes the cause and solution to a problem is initially unclear, and here functional analysis can help define the problem and provide a guide to its solution. Functional analysis is a decision making approach in which a problem is broken down into its component functions (accounting, marketing, manufacturing, etc). These functions are further divided into sub-functions until the function level suitable for solving the problem is reached.

For example, a manufacturing company may have a problem with shortage of cash. Initial investigation points to the holding of high levels of inventory as one of the main causes. The investigation now examines the manufacturing function to see why the inventory level is so high. It is discovered that the high level of inventory relates to raw materials and components. This is the responsibility of the stores and purchasing section. It is discovered that one specific (and expensive) component is being held in large numbers at the request of the production manager. This is because in the past production has been held up when deliveries of this component were delayed.

Now that the cause of the problem has been established, the problem can be resolved through the appropriate function. In this case the purchasing section can negotiate a new contract with the supplier to guarantee delivery dates in future. This would then take away the need for excessive inventory levels of the component.

MAKE OR BUY DECISIONS

One of the situations where scenario planning is useful concerns the possible outsourcing of production. This means having products made for you by an outside organisation instead of making them in-house.

If production was outsourced savings would normally be made of various manufacturing costs, but of course the cost of buying in a ready made product would be much greater than simply buying raw material. Great care must be taken to calculate which costs would be saved and which would remain.

variable costs

The general rule would be that any variable costs relating to the production that would not be taking place in-house would be saved, although any variable non-production costs (for example selling costs) would remain.

fixed costs

It is possible that some fixed costs may also be saved if they relate entirely to the production of the products to be made elsewhere. However fixed production costs that relate to several products, some of which continue to be made on site would not be saved in the short term. This is because if one product was no longer made on site these shared fixed costs would not change in total and would then need to be covered by the existing products.

other issues to consider

If a decision is to be made about outsourcing then various other commercial issues will need to be considered. These include:

- price – the agreed price must be guaranteed for an acceptable period of time, with any future increases within agreed limits
- quality – there needs to be sufficient reassurance that quality will be maintained when the production is in the control of another organisation

- supply – the manufacturing company must be able to offer guaranteed continuity of supply and timely deliveries
- commercial sensitivity – some products may be made to a 'secret' formula, or companies may wish to protect its brand by implying that its products are not made by anyone else

Once a decision has been made to cease manufacture of a product in-house it may be difficult to reverse in the future, especially if skilled staff and / or specialised equipment are required.

Case Study

TOUCAN LIMITED: MAKE OR BUY DECISION

situation

Toucan Limited, a soft drink manufacturer, currently makes two products in its factory. The first product is 'Wings', a high energy drink, and the second is 'SSSh', a calming and relaxing drink.

The following budgeted operating statement relates to the next year, and assumes that both products will be manufactured in-house. It is based on making and selling 1,000,000 units of Wings, and 1,000,000 units of SSSh.

	£'000	£'000	£'000
	Wings	SSSh	Total
Sales	750	500	1,250
Variable costs of production	200	230	430
Direct fixed costs of production	150	110	260
Shared fixed costs of production	150	100	250
Gross profit	250	60	310
Administration costs			80
Selling and Distribution costs			100
Operating profit			130

Consideration is being given to an option to buy in ready made SSSh units at £0.30 per unit. This would save both the variable costs of production and the direct fixed costs of production of that product. Shared fixed costs of production would remain the same in total. The number of units of SSSh sold would be unchanged.

If the decision were made to buy in the SSSh units, then the released manufacturing space could be used to increase the manufacture and sales of Wings to 1,200,000 units. The direct fixed costs of Wings production would be unchanged by this. Additional selling and distribution costs of £20,000 would be incurred by this increase in volume of Wings.

required

(a) Calculate the following data for each product, based on the current plan to manufacture both products in-house:

- Selling price per unit
- Variable production cost per unit
- Gross profit per unit

(b) Draft a revised budgeted Operating Statement, based on buying in ready made units of SSSh and increasing the volume of Wings units made and sold.

(c) Recommend whether, on the basis of your figures, the decision should be made to buy in SSSh. Note any factors that may risk the future business remaining in line with the budget if your recommendation were to be followed.

solution

(a)

Selling price per unit

Wings	£750,000 / 1,000,000	= £0.75 per unit
SSSh	£500,000 / 1,000,000	= £0.50 per unit

Variable costs per unit

Wings	£200,000 / 1,000,000	= £0.20 per unit
SSSh	£230,000 / 1,000,000	= £0.23 per unit

Gross profit per unit

Wings	£250,000 / 1,000,000	= £0.25 per unit
SSSh	£60,000 / 1,000,000	= £0.06 per unit

(b)

Revised Operating Statement

	£'000	£'000	£'000
	Wings	SSSh	Total
Sales	900	500	1,400
Variable costs of production / buy-in	240	300	540
Direct fixed costs of production	150		150
Shared fixed costs of production	250	___	250
Gross profit	260	200	460
Administration costs			80
Selling and Distribution costs			120
Operating profit			260

(c)

Recommendation

From the calculations, the total operating profit would increase from £130,000 to £260,000, and therefore the units of SSSh should be outsourced. However, factors that may make the business more risky in future include:

- whether sales of Wings can be increased by 20% as assumed
- whether the quality of SSSh can be assured
- whether the long term continuity of supply and price of SSSh can be assured

LIMITING FACTOR DECISIONS

You may need to deal with situations where production is reduced because of one or more 'limiting factors'. These could be, for example:

- shortage of materials – a short or longer term issue that may restrict production; tactics for dealing with this situation range from changing supplier to using up inventories, or even changing the product that is being made

- shortage of labour – this could restrict production, especially if the labour force is skilled; this could be tacked by overtime working, sub-contracting or outsourcing

- limited production capacity – based on the size or maximum throughput of the organisation's manufacturing plant; while long term solutions include outsourcing or investing in property and equipment, short term issues can sometimes be resolved by shift working or manipulating inventory levels

Dealing with one factor alone is relatively straightforward if there is only one product, and a given scenario should contain clear information on the calculations required. The next two topics to examine are:

- more than one constraint for a single product
- product choice when there is one limiting factor

dealing with a combination of limitations

There may be occasions when there is a limit on not just one resource, but a combination of two or more. This can also form the basis for an examination task, so you should make sure that you are able to carry out the necessary calculations.

The technique that we are going to use is quite logical. We will calculate which one of the limitations on our output is going to limit production most severely, and concentrate on that problem.

For example if we originally planned to make 5,000 units, but find that we only have sufficient labour for 4,800 units, and enough materials for 4,000 units, then materials is the most pressing problem. It would not make sense to bring in temporary staff while there was still a material shortage. If we can solve the material shortage problem, only then should we turn our attention to the labour limitation. The issue that most constrains the output (as materials does in this example) is sometimes known as the binding constraint.

product choice when there are limited resources

The final situation that we must be able to deal with when there are limited resources concerns selecting the most profitable products. The situation arises when it was originally planned to make a number of different products, but a shortage of some resource now makes the plan impossible. The resource that is preventing normal output is known as the limiting factor. The most common limiting factors are either materials or labour.

What we must do in these circumstances is to calculate which of our products gives us the most profitable use of the limited resources. The technique relies on marginal costing techniques, and even if the data is provided in a different form, you must first identify the variable costs for each product.

The full procedure to be adopted is as follows:

- Using marginal costing, calculate the contribution per unit that each different product generates. This is carried out by subtracting the variable costs per unit from the selling price per unit. Fixed costs are ignored.

- Identify the resource that is in short supply (the limiting factor), and how much of that resource is needed to make one unit of each different product. Divide the contribution per unit already calculated by the quantity of limited resource required to make a unit. This gives the contribution per unit of limiting factor.

- Rank the possible products according to the value of the contribution per unit of limiting factor. Starting with the product ranked highest, schedule the production so that the expected demand is met for this product. Then schedule the next highest-ranking product, and so on until the limited resources are used up.

This technique will ensure that the quantities of different products manufactured will make the most profit from the limited resources. This does mean that some products will be made in reduced quantities, or not made at all. This will leave the demand from some customers unsatisfied, and the technique does not address any further implications of this policy. For example a customer of a product that may have production suspended could also be a valuable customer of other products. Suspension of manufacture could result in the customer cancelling their orders and finding an alternative supplier for all their requirements.

The two Case Studies that follow show how the technique is used to schedule production so that the profit from using limited resources is maximised.

THE THREE COUNTIES COMPANY: CONTRIBUTION PER UNIT OF LIMITING FACTOR

The Three Counties Company manufactures three products, each using the same material. The budget data for quarter 2 (the next quarter) is as follows. (There is no budgeted finished goods inventory at the beginning or end of any quarter.)

Product	Demand	Costs per unit		
	(units)	Materials	Labour	Overheads
Gloucester	10,000	£25.00	£30.00	£60.00
Worcester	15,000	£50.00	£30.00	£60.00
Hereford	12,000	£15.00	£20.00	£40.00

The material costs £5.00 per kilo. Due to its short shelf life it must be used in the period that it is bought. The labour force is employed on a fixed contract that entitles them to a weekly pay of £350 for a guaranteed 40-hour week. The contract prohibits any overtime working. The overheads are a fixed cost.

The Gloucester sells for £125 per unit, the Worcester for £150 per unit, and the Hereford for £90 per unit.

It has just been discovered that there is a limit on the quantity of material that can be purchased in quarter 2 of 180,000 kilos.

required
Produce a revised production budget in units for quarter 2 that maximises profit.

solution
Since the labour force is paid a guaranteed week the cost of labour behaves as a fixed cost in this case study. Because overheads are also fixed, the only variable cost is material. This gives contributions per unit calculations as follows:

	Gloucester	Worcester	Hereford
	£	£	£
Selling Price per unit	125	150	90
less variable costs	25	50	15
contribution per unit	100	100	75

The quantity of material used for each product can be calculated by dividing the cost of material for a unit by the cost per kilo of £5.00. This quantity is then used to calculate the contribution per kilo of material (the limiting factor).

	Gloucester	Worcester	Hereford
Quantity of material per unit	5 kg	10 kg	3 kg
Contribution per kilo of material	£100 / 5	£100 / 10	£75 / 3
	= £20	= £10	= £25
Ranking	2	3	1

The ranking is derived directly from the contribution per kilo of material. Note that this ranking is different from both the contribution per unit and from the profit per unit if calculated under absorption costing. We now use the ranking to produce up to the demand level of first the Hereford, followed by the Gloucester, and finally the Worcester, using up the material until there is none left.

Product	Ranking	Production (units)	Material Required (kilos)	
Hereford	1	12,000	12,000 x 3 kg =	36,000
Gloucester	2	10,000	10,000 x 5 kg =	50,000
Worcester	3	9,400*	9,400 x 10 kg =	94,000
				180,000

* The quantity of Worcester that can be produced is calculated as follows:
First, the remaining quantity of material is calculated in kilos:
(180,000 – 36,000 – 50,000 = 94,000)
Then the number of units of Worcester that can be produced with that material is calculated: (94,000 kg / 10 kg each unit = 9,400 units).

In the next Case Study we will see how labour can be a limiting factor, and how we will tackle the problem.

Case Study

THE TWO CITIES COMPANY: CONTRIBUTION PER UNIT OF LIMITING FACTOR

The Two Cities Company manufactures two products, each using the same material and the same direct labour force.

The original budget data for month 6 is as follows. There is no budgeted finished goods inventory at the beginning or end of any month.

Product	Demand	Costs per unit		
	(units)	*Materials*	*Labour*	*Overheads*
Bristol	2,000	£70.00	£18.00	£80.00
Cardiff	2,500	£60.00	£12.00	£40.00

The material costs £10.00 per kilo. The labour force is paid on an hourly basis at £6 per hour, and can be called in to work as appropriate. They have no minimum agreed working week, and will be sent home if there is no work available. Because of the nature of the contract there is no overtime premium payable. The overheads are a fixed cost.

The Bristol sells for £178 per unit, and the Cardiff for £150 per unit.

Following negotiations with the company management regarding conditions of employment, a number of the direct labour workers have decided to withdraw their labour. This leaves a reduced number of employees willing to work normally. It is estimated that the maximum number of working hours available from those working normally is 7,100 hours in month 6.

required

Produce a revised production budget in units for month 6 that maximises profit.

solution

Due to the conditions under which the labour force operates, the labour cost behaves as a variable cost. The material cost is also a variable cost, since it will always vary in proportion to production levels. Note that even though there is no shortage of material, its cost is still used to determine the contribution figures. This gives contributions per unit calculations as follows:

	Bristol	**Cardiff**
	£	£
Selling price per unit	178	150
less variable costs:		
materials	70	60
labour	18	12
contribution per unit	90	78

The amount of labour time used for each product can be calculated by dividing the cost of labour for a unit by the labour hourly rate of £6.00. The direct labour time is then used to calculate the contribution per hour of direct labour (the limiting factor).

	Bristol	**Cardiff**
Labour time per unit	3 hours	2 hours
Contribution per direct labour hour	£90 / 3	£78 / 2
	= £30	= £39
Ranking	2	1

We now use the ranking to produce up to the demand level of first the Cardiff, followed by the Bristol, using up the labour hours until there is none left.

Product	Ranking	Production (units)	Labour Hours Required		
Cardiff	1	2,500	2,500 x 2 hours	=	5,000
Bristol	2	700	700 x 3 hours	=	2,100
					7,100

BREAK-EVEN ANALYSIS AND MARGIN OF SAFETY

You will be familiar with the use of marginal costing to calculate contribution, break-even point and margin of safety from your earlier studies. All these are important techniques for scenario planning and decision making.

In this section we will first remind ourselves of the calculations of these indicators, and then go on to see how they can help us understand the risk that a business is exposed to.

contribution

The contribution is:

Sales Revenue – Variable Costs

It can be calculated per unit or per period of time. The contribution can also be calculated as a percentage of the sales revenue – this is sometimes known as the PV (profit-volume) ratio.

worked example

Suppose a company sells 3,000 units per month for £6 each. Variable costs are £3.50 per unit, and fixed costs are £4,000 per month.

The contribution per unit is £6 - £3.50 = £2.50 per unit.

The contribution per month is 3,000 x £2.50 = £7,500 per month.

This can also be calculated as:

Monthly Sales	3,000 x £6	£18,000
Monthly Variable Costs	3,000 x £3.50	£10,500
Monthly Contribution		£7,500

The contribution as a percentage of sales revenue will be the same whether calculated per unit or per month:

Per unit (£2.50 / £6) x 100   = 41.67%
Per month (£7,500 / £18,000) x 100 = 41.67%

break-even point

The break-even point is the number of units, or the value of sales that would result in zero profit. It is calculated as follows:

Break-even point (in units)

$$\frac{\text{Fixed Costs}}{\text{Contribution per Unit}}$$

Break-even point (in sales value)

$$\frac{\text{Fixed costs}}{\text{Contribution per £ of Sales}}$$

The contribution per £ of sales is the same as the contribution as a percentage of sales, but expressed as a decimal.

To return to our example; a company sells 3,000 units per month for £6 each. Variable costs are £3.50 per unit, and fixed costs are £4,000 per month.

Break-even point (in units)   £4,000 / £2.50   = 1,600 units

Break-even point (in sales value)   £4,000 / 0.4167   = £9,600 sales value

Note that these two break-even figures are completely compatible; 1,600 units sold for £6 each gives a sales value of £9,600.

---

margin of safety

This measures how far the expected sales level is from the break-even sales level. It is often calculated as a percentage of the current sales level – showing what percentage drop in expected sales would result in a zero profit.

This calculation would be:

$$\frac{(\text{Budgeted Sales} - \text{Break-even Sales})}{\text{Budgeted Sales}} \times 100$$

It can be calculated using sales values or units, and the percentage results will be identical.

Using our example again; a company sells 3,000 units per month for £6 each. Variable costs are £3.50 per unit, and fixed costs are £4,000 per month.

Margin of safety (in units)
            (3,000 − 1,600) / 3,000   x 100   = 47%

Margin of safety (in sales value)
            (£18,000 - £9,600) / £18,000   x 100   = 47%

understanding risk

The margin of safety is a clear indicator of the risk that a business will fail to make a profit, by showing how far its sales would have to fall. In the above example the business has a low risk, since its sales would have to fall by 47% to reduce its profit to zero. The expected monthly profit in this example is:

Monthly contribution	£7,500
Less monthly fixed costs	£4,000
Monthly profit	£3,500

A business with different levels of fixed and variable costs might have a very different exposure to risk.

worked example

Suppose a business sells 3,000 units per month for £6 each. Variable costs are £1 per unit, and fixed costs are £11,500 per month.

Contribution would be £5 per unit x 3,000 units = £15,000 per month

Profit would be £15,000 contribution, less £11,500 fixed costs = £3,500 per month – the same as the last example.

Break-even point (in units) is £11,500 / £5   = 2,300 units

Margin of safety (in units) is (3,000 – 2,300) / 3,000 x 100   = 23%

This is much lower than the previous example, as this business has a riskier cost structure, with higher fixed costs and lower variable costs. The higher fixed costs need to be covered to break-even. If sales levels fall each unit lost will reduce profit by its contribution of £5, so that the profit is very sensitive to changes in sales level.

Case Study

DELTA LIMITED: USING MARGINAL COSTING

Delta Limited manufactures a skin cream and is considering how it can be more environmentally friendly. Scientists have developed a new product to replace Alpha's existing skin cream; the new product is a gel and takes up less than 10% of the volume and weight of the existing product.

You have been given the following information.

- current sales volume is 1.0 million units per annum and this is not expected to change.
- current fixed production costs are £0.8 million.

- current labour cost per unit is £1.25 which is completely variable.
- current material cost per unit is £2 and is completely variable.
- assume inventory levels are kept at zero.
- variable material cost of the new product will be £0.50 less per unit than the current cream.
- selling price will be increased from £7.50 to £8.50.
- fixed selling and distribution costs will reduce from £800,000 to £300,000.
- additional investment in assets will be £4 million which will be depreciated at £400,000 per annum.
- all other costs will remain the same.

required

(a)   Calculate the total annual increase in profit by completing the table below.

	Units	Price/cost	Total (£)
Additional revenue			
Savings on materials			
Reduction in selling and distribution costs			
Additional depreciation			
Additional annual profit			

(b)   Calculate the return on the additional investment.

(c)   The marketing department is concerned that the volume of sales may not reach 1.0 million. The finance director has asked for the break even sales volume.

Calculate:

- the fixed costs
- the contribution per unit
- the break even sales volume in units
- the percentage margin of safety

solution

(a)

	Units	Price/cost	Total (£)
Additional revenue	1,000,000	£1	1,000,000
Savings on materials	1,000,000	£0.50	500,000
Reduction in selling and distribution costs			500,000
Additional depreciation			- 400,000
Additional annual profit			1,600,000

(b) **Return on investment:**

£1,600,000 (as above) / £4,000,000 (investment) x 100 = 40%

(c) Fixed costs:

Production	£800,000
Selling & Distribution	£300,000
Depreciation	£400,000
Total	£1,500,000

Contribution per unit:

	Selling Price	£8.50
Less	Labour	£1.25
Less	Materials	£1.50
	Contribution	£5.75

Break-even sales volume in units:

$$\frac{\text{Fixed Costs}}{\text{Contribution per unit}}$$

£1,500,000 / £5.75 = 260,870 units

Percentage margin of safety:

$$\frac{(\text{Budgeted Sales} - \text{Break-even Sales}) \times 100}{\text{Budgeted Sales}}$$

(1,000,000 − 260,870) / 1,000,000 x 100

= 73.91%

CLOSURE OF A BUSINESS SEGMENT

The closure of an uneconomic part of a business requires careful planning. Particular attention must be paid to the cost savings that will be made, especially if there are costs which are currently apportioned to more than one part of the business. It will often be the case that all or part of these costs will continue after closure, and therefore need to be set against the income of the remaining part of the business.

If closure is undertaken then redundancy costs of employees will need to be calculated and taken into consideration. As these are a 'one-off' cost, the exact way that these are accounted for in the management accounts would depend on the company policy.

It is possible that the operation could be relocated overseas to make it more economic. This could relate to a manufacturing activity, and the products could then be transported to be sold to the same or new markets. This could either be based on outsourcing to an established foreign business, or by setting up an in-house operation in the new location.

The outsourcing model would be similar to the 'make or buy' decision that was discussed earlier in this chapter. The added risk factor would be currency exchange movements that could rapidly change or eliminate any profits.

Setting up a new operation in a foreign country would be a complicated project, although the planning would follow the normal procedures. The added complications of language, legal systems, tax and currency would have to be considered carefully.

Case Study

MINUTEMAN LIMITED:
CLOSURE OF A BUSINESS SEGMENT

Minuteman Limited is a watch manufacturer located in the UK. It currently manufactures two ranges of watches; a craftsman made traditional precision watch that sells to the premium market for £450, and an electronic fashion watch that is assembled from bought-in components and sells for £40.

The manager is concerned that the electronic watch is no longer profitable, and has obtained quotations from the Far East where these watches could be made for £15 each (including delivery).

The current factory is used for the manufacture of both watch ranges, and there is no likelihood of another use for the part currently used for assembly of the electronic watches.

The operating statement for the last quarter was as follows:

	Premium Watch	Electronic Watch	Total
	£'000	£'000	£'000
Sales	225	160	385
Materials and components	15	64	79
Direct labour	75	60	135
Fixed Factory Costs	45	32	77
Administration Costs	20	20	40
Selling and Distribution Costs	10	20	30
Operating Profit / (Loss)	60	(36)	24

The following information has been established:

• materials and components and direct labour are variable costs

• fixed factory costs relate to the whole factory, and have been apportioned based on sales value

• administration costs are fixed costs and would remain if the electronic watches bought in ready made

• selling and distribution costs are variable costs and would remain if the electronic watches were bought in ready made

• redundancy costs can be ignored

• this level of sales of both watches is expected to continue

required

(a)   Calculate, based on the last quarter:

• the numbers of each watch range that were sold

• the contribution per watch for each type of watch

(b)   Calculate the revised contribution per electronic watch if it were to be bought in ready made from the Far East.

(c)   Prepare a budgeted Operating Statement based on ceasing to manufacture the electronic watches in the factory, but buying them in ready made from the Far East.

solution

(a)   Number of watches:

Premium watch   £225,000 (sales value) / £450 (price each) = 500 watches

Electronic watch £160,000 (sales value) / £40 (price each) = 4,000 watches

Contribution per watch – working		Premium	Electronic
		£	£
Selling Price		450	40
less:	Materials and components	30	16
	Direct labour	150	15
	Selling and distribution costs	20	5
Contribution		250	4

(b)

	£
Selling Price	40
less: Bought in cost	15
Selling and distribution costs	5
Revised Contribution	20

(c)   Budgeted Operating Statement

	Premium Watch £'000	Electronic Watch £'000	Total £'000
Sales	225	160	385
Materials and components	15		15
Bought in watches		60	60
Direct labour	75		75
Fixed Factory Costs	77		77
Administration Costs	20	20	40
Selling and distribution costs	10	20	30
Operating Profit / (Loss)	28	60	88

Note that the fixed factory costs have all been allocated to the premium watch (since there is no other manufacturing taking place), and this reduces the profit recorded for this range. The overall profit has increased from £24,000 to £88,000.

However additional risks in terms of currency movements, price stability and quality control would need to be considered.

MECHANISATION

Mechanisation of a production operation usually involves

- spending considerable amounts of money on buying (or leasing) non-current assets, and subsequently maintaining and operating them

- reducing labour costs

This may mean that fixed costs increase (eg the operating costs and depreciation of the plant or machinery, and variable costs decrease (eg if labour costs are variable). This can therefore change the cost structure to a more risky one which is more sensitive to changes in the volume of output. This is the same idea that we examined in the section on break-even and margin of safety earlier in this chapter.

There are two main types of task relating to mechanisation:

- redrafting of an income (or operating) statement to determine the impact on profit

- using discounted cash flow (DCF) to establish the net present value of the mechanisation (or to establish the 'net terminal cost' that we will examine later)

redrafting an income statement

This type of task can use similar techniques and logic to the case studies that we have already seen in this chapter. Remember that depreciation is a proper cost to show in an income statement, so the additional depreciation change related to the non-current assets will need to be accounted for.

You may also be asked to carry out some contribution calculations and work out the break-even point and margin of safety as illustrated earlier.

The following Case Study will illustrate this type of task.

Case Study

EDDY'S READIES:
MARGINAL COSTING AND MECHANISATION

situation

Eddy's Readies Limited makes a range of prepared meals that are ready to be heated and eaten. The operation is currently labour intensive, and a large number of people are employed to prepare the meals in the factory, using traditional cooking techniques. These employees are brought in to work according to demand, and are therefore treated as a variable cost.

The manager has been investigating the purchase of automated production line equipment that would eliminate the need for the majority of employees. The purchase and installation of the equipment would cost £1,000,000, and would be depreciated at £200,000 per year.

The following income statement is based on the next year's operation, assuming the current working practices, and production of 1 million meals.

	£'000
Sales	3,950
less:	
variable material cost	1,800
variable labour cost	700
Contribution	1,450
less:	
fixed production costs	150
fixed administration costs	320
Operating profit	980

The net operating assets of the business are currently £1,500,000.

If the automated production line is installed:

• labour costs will reduce to £250,000 per year, regardless of the production level

• fixed production costs will increase by £160,000 per year, in addition to the depreciation expense

• other costs will be unchanged

required

(a) Calculate the current
- break-even point (in units)
- margin of safety as a percentage of sales
- return on net assets

(b) Show the revised income statement based on the installation of the automated production line.

(c) Calculate the revised
- break-even point (in units)
- margin of safety as a percentage of sales
- return on net assets

(d) Briefly comment on whether the automated production line would make the cost structure more or less risky.

solution

(a) Current position:

Break-even point

£470,000 / £1.45   = 324,138 meals

Working:

Fixed Costs: £150,000 + £320,000 = £470,000

Contribution per unit £1,450,000 / 1,000,000 meals = £1.45 per meal

Margin of safety as percentage of sales

$$\frac{(1,000,000 - 324,138) \text{ meals}}{1,000,000 \text{ meals}} \quad \text{x } 100 \qquad = 67.6\%$$

Return on net assets

$$\frac{£980,000}{£1,500,000} \quad \text{x } 100 \qquad = 65.3\%$$

(b) Revised income statement

	£'000
Sales	3,950
less:	
variable material cost	1,800
Contribution	2,150
less:	
fixed labour costs	250
fixed production costs	510
fixed administration costs	320
Operating profit	1,070

(c)   Revised position:

Break-even point

£1,080,000 / £2.15   = 502,326 meals

Working:

Fixed Costs: £250,000 + £510,000 + £320,000 = £1,080,000

Contribution per unit £2,150,000 / 1,000,000 meals = £2.15 per meal

Margin of safety as percentage of sales

$$\frac{(1,000,000 - 502,326) \text{ meals}}{1,000,000 \text{ meals}} \times 100 \qquad = 49.8\%$$

Return on net assets

$$\frac{£1,070,000}{(£1,500,000 + £1,000,000)} \times 100 \qquad = 42.8\%$$

(d)   Although the profit would be greater with an automated production line, the break-even point is higher, leading to a reduced margin of safety. Therefore if sales fell below the expected level the profit would fall more rapidly than under the existing cost structure. This makes the revised cost structure more risky. However if sales were to rise above the 1m expected meals then the revised cost structure would mean that profits would increase more rapidly due to the increased contribution per meal.

USING DISCOUNTED CASH FLOW

Discounted cash flow (DCF) techniques can be used to establish the net present value of a project to mechanise a manufacturing activity. This is the same technique that we used in Chapter 5 for life-cycle costing.

When using DCF to make a comparison – for example mechanisation or no mechanisation, we can

- ignore costs that are the same in both cases
- ignore non-cash costs like depreciation
- include both capital and revenue receipts and payments

Contrast this with the technique that we have just examined where we were calculating a profit figure – here we are only concerned with cash flows.

We can use the same data as the last Case Study to contrast the techniques.

Case Study

EDDY'S READIES: DISCOUNTED CASH FLOW AND MECHANISATION

situation

Eddy's Readies Limited makes a range of prepared meals that are ready to be heated and eaten. The operation is currently labour intensive, and a large number of people are employed to prepare the meals in the factory, using traditional cooking techniques. These employees are brought in to work according to demand, and are therefore treated as a variable cost.

The manager has been investigating the purchase of automated production line equipment that would eliminate the need for the majority of employees. The purchase and installation of the equipment would cost £1,000,000, and would be depreciated at £200,000 per year.

The following income statement is based on the next year's operation, assuming the current working practices, and production of 1 million meals.

	£'000
Sales	3,950
less:	
variable material cost	1,800
variable labour cost	700
Contribution	1,450
less:	
fixed production costs	150
fixed administration costs	320
Operating profit	980

The net operating assets of the business are currently £1,500,000.

If the automated production line is installed:

• labour costs will reduce to £250,000 per year, regardless of the production level

• fixed production costs will increase by £160,000 per year, in addition to the depreciation expense

• other costs will be unchanged

The company's cost of capital is 5%, and discount factors over the five year life of the project are as follows:

Year	Discount factor 5%	Year	Discount factor 5%
0	1.00	3	0.864
1	0.952	4	0.823
2	0.907	5	0.784

The automated production line will be paid for immediately and have no value at the end of the five year project. Assume that sales and costs remain at the same level for each of the five years, and occur at the end of each year.

required

Using the following table, calculate the net present value of the mechanisation project.

Year	Cash Outflow £'000	Cash Savings £'000	Discount Factor	Present Value £'000
0				
1				
2				
3				
4				
5				
	Net Present Value			

solution

Working:

Annual cash savings

Labour £700,000 - £250,000	£450,000
Less additional production costs	£160,000
Net cash savings	£290,000

Year	Cash Outflow £'000	Cash Savings £'000	Discount Factor	Present Value £'000
0	1,000		1.000	(1,000)
1		290	0.952	276
2		290	0.907	263
3		290	0.864	251
4		290	0.823	239
5		290	0.784	227
	Net Present Value			256

The net present value is a positive amount of £256,000, which means that based on these figures the mechanisation project appears to be worthwhile.

Note that in the calculation only cash figures which arise directly from the decision to mechanise (or not) are used. The case study therefore provided lots of data that was not needed for this technique. You may need to carefully select the data that you need to use in a DCF calculation.

calculating net terminal value or cost

In the technique that we have just examined, all cash flows have been adjusted to present values by using discount factors. The calculation of net terminal cost involves the opposite – adjusting all cash flows to a future point in time when the project will finish. This is carried out by effectively using compound interest to adjust the cash flows.

If the total net figure is a cost then it is described as 'net terminal cost', but if it is a positive figure it is described as 'net terminal value'.

worked example

Because we are converting costs to a future value, the years need to be based on how far they are from that future point. We will use the cash flows from the last case study to illustrate the calculations.

The interest factors at 5% are as follows (based on number of years to the end of the project).

Year	Interest factor 5%	Year	Interest factor 5%
0	1.00	3	1.158
1	1.050	4	1.216
2	1.103	5	1.276

The calculation would then be as follows:

Year	Cash Outflow £'000	Cash Savings £'000	Interest Factor	Terminal Value £'000
0 (5 yrs to end)	1,000		1.276	(1,276)
1 (4 yrs to end)		290	1.216	353
2 (3 yrs to end)		290	1.158	336
3 (2 yrs to end)		290	1.103	320
4 (1 yrs to end)		290	1.050	305
5 (0 yrs to end)		290	1.000	290
Net Terminal Value				328

What we are doing is showing what the total cumulative value of the project would be at the end date, incorporating interest costs. It is therefore equivalent to the amount left over if the money to invest was borrowed at 5% and all cash receipts were also invested at 5%.

Note that the net terminal value calculation results in a different numerical answer to the net present value calculation that we examined earlier.

In this example we have assumed that annual cash flows occur at the end of each year, but other timing assumptions could have been required.

ADJUSTING VOLUMES AND PRICES

A popular scenario task involves the adjustment of expected financial data to allow for changes in sales volumes and / or sales prices and / or costs. This is a problem best solved through the use of marginal costing, since these changes can be built into a financial model without the distortions that would result from using absorption costing.

The key is to remember that when adjusting an income statement:

- sales revenue is the result of both sales volume and sales price

- variable costs are based on the sales volume and the unit costs

- fixed costs will be unchanged (provided the volume is within the relevant range)

Changes in the income statement will also affect the net current assets of the organisation. Remember that the sales volume will be the same as the cost of sales volume. Therefore if no other changes are made (for example to inventory days or receivables days) then:

- inventory value will be affected by both sales volume and unit costs

- receivables value will be affected by sales volume and selling price

- payables value will be affected by both sales volume and unit costs

We can illustrate the arithmetic for volume, price and cost changes using the following example.

worked example

A product is currently sold for £10 each, and has variable costs of £3 each. Fixed costs are £2,500 per month. If expected monthly sales are 1,000 units, the income statement would be summarised as follows:

	£
Sales	10,000
Variable Costs	3,000
Fixed Costs	2,500
Operating Profit	4,500

Suppose that the elements of net current assets are currently as follows:

	£	
Inventory	6,000	(2 months' variable costs)
Receivables	30,000	(3 months' sales)
Payables	(9,000)	(3 months' variable costs)
Net current assets (exc cash)	27,000	

We will now assume that:

- selling price is reduced by 5%, and volume increases by 15%, and
- variable costs increase by 2%

The monthly income statement would now appear as:

	£
Sales (£10,000 x 95% x 115%)*	10,925
Variable Costs (£3,000 x 102% x 115%)*	3,519
Fixed Costs	2,500
Operating Profit	4,906

*These calculations could also be carried out by working out revised unit prices and costs and multiplying by revised volumes in units.

The net current assets would change to:

	£	
Inventory	7,038	(2 months' variable costs)
Receivables	32,775	(3 months' sales)
Payables	(10,557)	(3 months' variable costs)
Net current assets (exc cash)	29,256	

If these assumptions were valid, the operating profit would rise because the benefit of the increased volume would outweigh the reduced contribution per unit. The sales volume is therefore the main (or dominant) factor in this example. However the increased working capital requirements would also need to be taken into consideration.

We will now use a Case Study to explore some of these ideas further.

Case Study

VOLUMIZER LIMITED:
ADJUSTING VOLUMES AND PRICES

situation

Volumizer Limited is developing a new product and a colleague has prepared forecast information based upon two scenarios. The forecast income statement and statement of financial position for both scenarios are shown on the next page.

- Scenario 1 is to set the price at £18 per unit with sales of 60,000 units each year.
- Scenario 2 is to set the price at £12 per unit with sales of 120,000 units each year.

Forecast Income Statement	Scenario 1	Scenario 2
	£	£
Turnover	1,080,000	1,440,000
Cost of production		
Direct (Raw) Materials	300,000	600,000
Direct Labour	120,000	192,000
Fixed Production overheads	360,000	360,000
Total cost of sales	780,000	1,152,000
Gross profit	**300,000**	**288,000**
Selling and distribution costs	74,000	122,000
Administration costs	50,000	50,000
Operating profit	**176,000**	**116,000**
	Scenario 1	Scenario 2
Gross profit margin	27.78%	20.00%
Operating profit margin	16.30%	8.06%
Direct Materials as a percentage of turnover	27.78%	41.67%
Direct Materials cost per unit	£5.00	£5.00
Direct labour cost per unit	£2.00	£1.60
Fixed production cost per unit	£6.00	£3.00

required

Draft a report for the Finance Director covering the following:

(a) An explanation of why the gross profit margins are different, referring to the following:
- Sales price and Sales volume
- Materials cost
- Labour cost
- Fixed costs
- The dominant factor

(b)   An explanation of why the operating profit margins are different.

(c)   A recommendation, with reasons, as to which course of action to take.

solution

To: Finance director	Subject: Scenarios 1 & 2
From: Accounting technician	Date:

(a) Why are the gross profit margins different?

- Sales Price / Sales Volume

The sales price is 50% higher under Scenario 1, which will result in an increase in the gross profit margin. The sales volume under Scenario 2 is double that of Scenario 1. This only affects the gross profit margin percentage because not all the production costs are variable.

- Materials

The materials cost per unit is constant at £5.00 per unit, and therefore does not affect the gross profit margin. There is no economy of scale.

- Labour

Labour cost per unit is £2.00 for Scenario 1 decreasing to £1.60 for Scenario 2. The more units that are produced, the lower the labour cost per unit. This will improve the margin for Scenario 2. It may be because of economies of scale in production.

- Fixed costs

Fixed costs are constant in total, and so as the volume of production increases, the fixed cost per unit decreases. This will increase the margin for Scenario 2.

- Which is the dominant factor and why?

Scenario 2 sells twice as many units as Scenario 1, has the same material cost per unit, lower labour cost per unit, and lower fixed costs per unit. All of these would increase Scenario 2's margin. However, the margin is lower. This is due to the lower sales price per unit, which is the dominant factor.

(b) Why are the operating profit margins different?

The operating profit margins are different partly due to the reduction in gross profit for Scenario 2, and partly due to the increased sales and distribution costs in Scenario 2.

(c) Recommendation, with reasons, as to which course of action to take

Based purely on the forecast information, Scenario 1 is the best option creating the largest return. However, the sales volume is lower than Scenario 2, and so the market share is lower. It may be worth considering what the demand level would be if the selling price were set somewhere between £12 and £18 per unit, and modelling that scenario before making a final decision.

Chapter Summary

- Scenario planning (or 'what-if' analysis) involves developing and analysing plans to ascertain whether they provide viable alternatives to the current situation.

- Make or buy decisions involve using marginal costing to examine all costs and establish which ones would remain if the goods were outsourced. Other non-financial issues would also need to be considered.

- There may be limiting factors (eg lack of resources) that prevent manufacturing or selling the desired quantities. Techniques are available for establishing the 'binding constraint' and for making choices when there are several products.

- The marginal costing indicators of contribution, break-even and margin of safety can be used to analyse situations. These indicators can also be used to help assess the risk of a business plan.

- The consideration of the closure of a business segment involves examining all relevant costs as well as non-financial risks.

- Mechanisation can be tacked by using one or more of three techniques. These are redrafting an income statement, using discounted cash flow, and calculating net terminal value or cost.

- Volume, price and cost changes can be incorporated into a scenario, often by using information about cost behaviour.

Key Terms

contribution the difference between sales and variable costs; this can be calculated per period or per unit

break-even point the number of units or sales value that results in a profit of zero

margin of safety a measure of how far the expected position is from the break-even point; it is often measured as a percentage drop in sales

net present value

the net result of cash inflows and outflows at different points in time, converted into present value terms by using discount factors

net present cost

the net result of cash inflows and outflows at different points in time, converted into present cost terms by using discount factors; net present cost is always a net outflow

net terminal value

the net result of cash inflows and outflows at different points in time, converted into a future value at the end of the project by using interest factors

net terminal cost

the net result of cash inflows and outflows at different points in time, converted into a future value at the end of the project by using interest factors; net terminal cost is always a net outflow

dominant factor

the one change (out of several changes taking place) that has the major impact on the outcome of a scenario

Activities

8.1 The following information relates to Subsidiary Tay Ltd of Arch plc.

Tay Ltd Income Statement for the year ended 31 December 20-3

	£000s	£000s
Sales		6,200
Less: Returns		(200)
Turnover		6,000
Materials	350	
Labour	560	
Production overheads	450	
Cost of production	1,360	
Opening finished inventory	80	
Closing finished inventory	(170)	
Cost of Sales		1,270
Gross profit		4,730
Administration	440	
Customer support	600	
Selling and distribution	750	
Training	200	
Research and development	1,100	3,090
Operating profit		1,640

Notes:

1   Asset turnover is 1.5 times
2   Orders received in the year totalled £7,000,000
3   Production overheads included £45,000 for reworking faulty production
4   Turnover (£000s) is split: 4,800 for regular customers and 1,200 for new customers
5   Turnover (£000s) is split: 3,150 for new products and 2,850 for existing products

Required

Calculate for Tay Ltd for the given year:

(a) The capital employed, given that the asset turnover is 1.5 times

(b) Return on capital employed

(c) Operating profit margin (percentage of turnover)

(d) The average delay in fulfilling orders

(e) Develop and calculate **one** other possible measure of customer satisfaction other than (d) above

(f) Identify one way of manipulating the operating profit percentage and the ROCE

(g) Suggest and calculate **two** indicators that may help to measure performance from an internal perspective

(h) Suggest and calculate **one** indicator that would help to measure the innovation and learning perspective

8.2 Lambert Ltd is a wholesaler of office supplies. The operating statement for Lambert Ltd for the year ended 31 December 20-3 is shown below, together with a simplified Statement of Financial Position as at that date.

The managers of Lambert Ltd are considering improving the control of receivables and reducing the company's administration costs. They also think that inventories should be at a higher level at the end of the year. They require the Operating Statement and the Statement of Financial Position to be re-drafted to show what the results would have been if all the following conditions had been applied:

• the purchases and the closing inventory value had both been increased by £30,000

• the receivables' payment period had been reduced to 1 month

• the administration costs had been reduced by 15%

• if possible, the loan had been paid off at the end of the year

Lambert Ltd Operating Statement for the year ended 31 December 20-3

	£000s	£000s
Turnover		600
Less: Cost of Sales		
Opening Inventory	70	
Purchases	320	
Less: closing inventory	(30)	360
Gross profit		240
Administration Costs	100	
Selling and Distribution expenses	50	150
Operating profit		90

Lambert Ltd Statement of Financial Position as at 31 December 20-3

	£000s	£000s
Non-current Assets at cost		380
Less: accumulated depreciation		110
		270
Current Assets:		
Inventory	30	
Receivables	120	
Cash at Bank	10	
	160	
Current Liabilities:		
Payables	60	
Net current assets		100
		370
Long-term liability: loan		(50)
		320
Financed by:		
Ordinary shares issued and fully paid		200
Retained Profits		120
		320

Required

For Lambert Ltd for the year ended 31 December 20-3:

(a) Calculate the following ratios from the given data:

- the average age of inventory using closing inventory
- the Gross Profit as a percentage of Turnover
- the Operating Profit as a percentage of Turnover
- the Return on Capital Employed

(b) Re-draft the Operating Statement and the Statement of Financial Position according to the four requirements of the managers of Lambert Ltd.

(c) Calculate the same four ratios as in (a) for the revised data prepared in (b).

(d) Comment briefly on the results of your calculations.

8.3 Delta Limited is considering designing a new product, and will use target costing to arrive at the target cost of the product. You have been given the following information and asked to calculate the target cost for materials so that the purchasing manager can use this as a target in her negotiations with suppliers.

- The price at which the product will be sold is £50

- The company has firm orders for 20,000 units at a price of £50

- The fixed costs per unit are £16 per unit

- The labour requirement is 20 minutes at a cost of £18 per hour

- The required profit margin is 40%

- The material requirement is 200 grams per unit (ie 0.2 kilogram)

(a) Calculate the target cost per kilogram for the materials component of the product.

	£
Sales price per unit	
Profit margin	
Total costs	
Fixed cost per unit	
Labour cost per unit	
Maximum material cost per unit	
Target cost per kilogram	

(b) Complete the following statement:

The trade price per kilogram quoted on the supplier's price list is £50 per kilogram. The purchasing manager has negotiated a discount of 15%. The discount should be **accepted / rejected** because the £50 reduces to £ _____ which is **above / below** the Target cost.

(c) The minimum percentage discount needed to achieve the Target cost is:

8.4 Beta Limited will be replacing some machines in the next year and needs to decide whether to purchase or lease the machines.

The discount factors you will need are shown below.

Year	Discount factor	Year	Discount factor
0	1.00	3	0.864
1	0.952	4	0.823
2	0.907	5	0.784

(a) Calculate the discounted lifecycle cost of purchasing the machine based upon the following:

- Purchase price of £200,000
- Annual running costs of £16,000 for the next five years, paid annually in arrears
- A residual value of £80,000 at the end of the five years

Year	**0**	**1**	**2**	**3**	**4**	**5**
Cash flow						
Discount factor						
Present value						
Net present cost						

(b) Calculate the discounted lifecycle cost of leasing the machine for five years based upon the total annual costs of £50,000 paid annually in advance.

Year	**0**	**1**	**2**	**3**	**4**
Cash flow					
Discount factor					
Present value					
Net present cost					

(c) Based on the calculations it is best to **purchase / lease** the machine, which saves a present value of £ _____

Answers to activities

CHAPTER 1: MANAGEMENT ACCOUNTING TECHNIQUES

1.1 (a) The Management Accountant should have these on file.

(b) Trade Press, or Trade Association Database.

(c) Published on behalf of the Government, and reproduced in various printed and electronic forms.

(d) This internal data will probably be held by the Sales Manager, although the Management Accountant will also have a copy.

(e) These will be reported in the financial press, the trade press, and on the Internet.

(f) This is collected on behalf of the Government, and available through Censuses.

1.2 Based on the information given, activity based costing would appear to be most appropriate for the Radical Company. It is the only system that would cope with accurately costing the range of products outlined. For example the developments and design costs for items that are constantly updated are likely to be greater than those with unchanged specifications. Similarly the size of batches and lengths of production runs would have a cost impact that only ABC would recognise.

1.3 (a) (i) **Profit Statements Using Absorption Costing**

	Week 1 £	Week 1 £	Week 2 £	Week 2 £
Sales		24,000		40,000
Less cost of sales:				
Opening Inventory	–		5,000	
Cost of Production:				
Direct Materials	5,000		5,000	
Direct Labour	9,000		9,000	
Fixed Overheads	6,000		6,000	
Less				
Closing Inventory	(5,000)		–	
		15,000		25,000
Profit		9,000		15,000

(ii) **Profit Statements Using Marginal Costing**

	Week 1 £	Week 1 £	Week 2 £	Week 2 £
Sales		24,000		40,000
Less cost of sales:				
Opening Inventory	–		3,500	
Variable Cost of				
Production:	14,000		14,000	
Less Closing Inventory	(3,500)		–	
		10,500		17,500
Contribution		13,500		22,500
Less Fixed Costs		6,000		6,000
Profit		7,500		16,500

(b) The inventory valuation using absorption costing includes £6,000 ÷ 4,000 units = £1.50 per unit of fixed overheads, which is not included when using marginal costing. This means that the inventory of 1,000 units at the end of week one is valued at £1,500 more using absorption costing, and the profit recorded in week one is also £1,500 more. Marginal costing records a profit higher by £1,500 in week two, as the inventories fall by 1,000 units. Both systems show identical profits for the two weeks added together because the inventory level at the start of week one is the same as at the end of week two.

1.4 (a) As can be seen from the workings, this example has a regular trend, increasing by £10 each day, and seasonal variations that are consistent, with each set of 5 totalling zero.

(b) The forecast for week 4 is calculated as follows:

	Forecast Trend £		Seasonal Variations	Forecast £
Tues	2,130 + (3 x 10)	= 2,160	– 180	1,980
Wed	2,130 + (4 x 10)	= 2,170	– 100	2,070
Thurs	2,130 + (5 x 10)	= 2,180	+ 50	2,230
Fri	2,130 + (6 x 10)	= 2,190	+ 120	2,310
Sat	2,130 + (7 x 10)	= 2,200	+ 110	2,310

Workings

Week	Day	Sales £	5-Point Moving Average (Trend)	Seasonal Variations
Week 1	Tues	1830		
	Wed	1920		
	Thurs	2080	2030	+ 50
	Fri	2160	2040	+120
	Sat	2160	2050	+110
Week 2	Tues	1880	2060	–180
	Wed	1970	2070	–100
	Thurs	2130	2080	+ 50
	Fri	2210	2090	+120
	Sat	2210	2100	+110
Week 3	Tues	1930	2110	–180
	Wed	2020	2120	–100
	Thurs	2180	2130	+ 50
	Fri	2260		
	Sat	2260		

1.5 (a) As can be seen from the workings, this example has a regular trend, decreasing by 10 each quarter, and seasonal variations that are consistent, with each set of 4 totalling zero.

(b) The forecast for year 5 is calculated as follows:

	Forecast Trend			Seasonal Variations	Forecast
Qtr 1	270 – (3 x 10)	= 240		+ 100	340
Qtr 2	270 – (4 x 10)	= 230		+ 40	270
Qtr 3	270 – (5 x 10)	= 220		– 50	170
Qtr 4	270 – (6 x 10)	= 210		– 90	120

Workings

		Sales Units	Moving 4-point Average	Averaged Pairs (Trend)	Seasonal Variations
Year 1	Qtr 1	500			
	Qtr 2	430			
	Qtr 3	330	385	380	– 50
	Qtr 4	280	375	370	– 90
Year 2	Qtr 1	460	365	360	+ 100
	Qtr 2	390	355	350	+ 40
	Qtr 3	290	345	340	– 50
	Qtr 4	240	335	330	– 90
Year 3	Qtr 1	420	325	320	+ 100
	Qtr 2	350	315	310	+ 40
	Qtr 3	250	305	300	– 50
	Qtr 4	200	295	290	– 90
Year 4	Qtr 1	380	285	280	+ 100
	Qtr 2	310	275	270	+ 40
	Qtr 3	210	265		
	Qtr 4	160			

1.6 Price trend figures are:

Jan	Feb	March
£6.80 - £0.40 = £6.40	£6.40 + £0.10 = £6.50	£7.00 - £0.40 = £6.60

Price trend movement is +£0.10 per month

1.7 (b)

Working:

The cost per kilo is

January £20,000 / 2,000 kilos = £10.00 per kilo

March £25,000 / 2,140 kilos = £11.68 per kilo

This is an increase of 17%, giving an index of 117, when based on 100.

1.8 (a)
Working:
If an index of 100 represents a cost of £70, then a cost of £80 gives an index of (£80 / £70) x 100 = 114 (to nearest whole number).
The cost increase from January to April is (£80 - £72) / £72 x 100 = 11.11%

CHAPTER 2: STANDARD COSTING – DIRECT COSTS

2.1 (a) Direct material price variance

(610 sq metres x £25) - £15,400

= £150 Adverse

(b) Direct material usage variance

((300 windows x 2 sq metres) x £25) – (610 sq metres x £25)

= £250 Adverse

(c) Direct labour rate variance

(145 hours x £8) - £1,220

= £60 Adverse

(d) Direct labour efficiency variance

((300 windows x 0.5 hours) x £8) – (145 hours x £8)

= £40 Favourable

2.2 (c)

2.3 (d) This is an adverse variance.

2.4 (a)

2.5 Labour efficiency variance:
(5,000 units x 0.75hr x £10) – (4,000 hrs x £10)   = £2,500 A

Labour idle time variance:
(150 hrs x £10)   = £1,500 A

2.6 To calculate the total actual costs we can reproduce what is effectively a cost reconciliation.

Standard cost for actual production level: £95.40 x 1,060 =   £101,124

Add: Direct Material Price Variance	£1,585	A
Less: Direct Material Usage Variance	(£ 993)	F
Direct Labour Rate Variance	(£2,460)	F
Direct Labour Efficiency Variance	(£1,051)	F
Actual Cost of Actual Production	£98,205	

2.7 Using the budget data to calculate the standard data for one unit:

Direct Materials   40,000 kg ÷ 20,000   = 2 kg
                                   @ £300,000 ÷ 40,000   = £7.50 per kg.
                                                                              = £15.00 per unit

Direct Labour   10,000 hrs ÷ 20,000   = 0.5 hrs
                                   @ £60,000 ÷ 10,000   = £6.00 per hr
                                                                          = £ 3.00 per unit

Direct Material Price Variance: (37,000 kg x £7.50) – £278,000 = £ 500 A

Direct Material Usage Variance: £7.50 x ([2 kg x 19,000 units] – 37,000 kg) = £ 7,500 F

Direct Labour Rate Variance: (9,800 hrs x £6.00) – £58,600 = £ 200 F

Direct Labour Efficiency Variance: £6.00 x ([0.5 hr x 19,000 units] – 9,800 hrs) = £ 1,800 A

Reconciliation:

Standard Cost for Actual Production Level

19,000 x (£15.00 + £3.00)	£ 342,000	
Add: Direct Material Price Variance	£ 500	A
Less: Direct Material Usage Variance	(£7,500)	F
Direct Labour Rate Variance	(£200)	F
Add: Direct Labour Efficiency Variance	£1,800	A
Actual Cost of Actual Production	£336,600	

2.8 The following comments are valid: (b), (c), (e), (f), (g), (h), (i), (j).
The remaining comments are false.

2.9   Using the budget data to calculate the standard data for one unit:

Variable Materials 3,000 kg ÷ 30,000   = 0.1 kg,
                   @ £75,000 ÷ 3,000   = £25 per kg.
                                             = £2.50 per unit

Variable Labour   15,000 hrs ÷ 30,000   = 0.5 hrs
                   @ £75,000 ÷ 15,000   = £5.00 per hr
                                             = £ 2.50 per unit

Variable Material Price Variance: (3,100 kg x £25.00) – £81,000 = £ 3,500 A
Variable Material Usage Variance: £25 x ([0.1 kg x 32,000 units] – 3,100 kg) = £ 2,500 F
Variable Labour Rate Variance: (15,900 hrs x £5.00) – £77,900 = £ 1,600 F
Variable Labour Efficiency Variance: £5.00 x ([0.5 hr x 32,000 units] – 15,900 hrs) = £ 500 F

Reconciliation:

Standard Marginal Cost for Actual Production Level

32,000 x (£2.50 + £2.50)	£ 160,000	
Add: Variable Material Price Variance	£ 3,500	A
Less: Variable Material Usage Variance	(£2,500)	F
Variable Labour Rate Variance	(£1,600)	F
Variable Labour Efficiency Variance	(£500)	F
Actual Marginal Cost of Actual Production	£158,900	

2.10   Direct Material Price Variance: (71,500 kg x £9.45) – £678,700 = £ 3,025 A
Direct Material Usage Variance: £9.45 x ((96 kg x 700 units) – 71,500 kg) = £ 40,635 A
[Note: 5 hours 6 minutes = 5.1 hours.]
Direct Labour Rate Variance: (3,850 hrs x £6.30) – £24,220 = £ 35 F
Direct Labour Efficiency Variance: £6.30 x ([5.1 hr x 700 units] – 3,850 hrs) = £ 1,764 A

Reconciliation:
Standard Cost for Actual Production Level

700 x ((96 x £9.45) + (5.1 x £6.30))	£ 657,531	
Add: Direct Material Price Variance 32∩3	£3,025	A
Direct Material Usage Variance	£40,635	A
Less: Direct Labour Rate Variance	(£35)	F
Add: Direct Labour Efficiency Variance	£1,764	A
Actual Cost of Actual Production (£678,700 + £24,220)	£702,920	

CHAPTER 3: STANDARD COSTING – FIXED OVERHEADS

3.1 (a) Absorption rate = Budgeted overheads / budgeted output
= £500,000 / 25,000 units = £20 per unit

Fixed overhead volume variance:
Actual output x absorption rate - Budgeted output x absorption rate
= (30,000 x £20) - (25,000 x £20) = £100,000 F
The volume variance is favourable because actual volume is greater than budgeted.

(b) Fixed overhead expenditure variance:
Budgeted cost of fixed overheads - Actual cost of fixed overheads
= £500,000 - £480,000 = £20,000 F
The expenditure variance is favourable because actual costs are less than budgeted.

3.2 (a) Absorption rate = Budgeted overheads / budgeted output in standard hours
= £60,000 / 500 std labour hours = £120 per std labour hour

Standard labour hours per unit = Budgeted hours / budgeted units
= 500 hours / 5,000 units = 0.1 hours per unit

Standard hours for actual output
= 3,500 units x 0.1 = 350 standard hours

Fixed overhead efficiency variance:
(standard hours for actual output x absorption rate) – (actual hours x absorption rate)
= (350 x £120) - (430 x £120) = £9,600 A
The efficiency variance is adverse as it took longer than standard to produce the output.

(b) Fixed overhead capacity variance:
(actual hours x absorption rate) - (std hours for budgeted output x absorption rate)
= (430 x £120) - (500 x £120) = £8,400 A
The capacity variance is adverse because less resources (labour hours) were used than budgeted.

3.3 (a) Fixed Overhead Expenditure Variance
£440,000 - £428,000 = £12,000 F

Fixed Overhead Volume Variance
(2,150 x £200) – (2,200 x £200) = £10,000 A

(b) One disadvantage of absorbing overheads on a per-sofa basis is that each sofa will absorb an identical amount of overheads. This may not be appropriate if different types of sofa use different amounts of resource – for example, some sofas may take longer to manufacture.

3.4   (a)   £94,600 ÷ 2,200   = £43 per hour

(b)   Exp = £94,600 – £99,000   = £4,400 A
Vol = £43 x (2,500 – 2,200)   = £12,900 F
Eff = £43 x (2,500 – 2,600)   = £4,300 A
Cap = £43 x (2,600 – 2,200)   = £17,200 F
Total = (2,500 x £43) – £99,000   = £8,500 F

(c)   True: 3, 4, 8, 10.

3.5   (a)   £448,000 ÷ 14,000   = £32 per hour

(b)   14,000 ÷ 2,000   = 7 hours each

(c)   7 x 1800   = 12,600 hours

(d)   Exp = £448,000 – £455,000   = £7,000 A
Vol = £32 x (12,600 – 14,000)   = £44,800 A
Eff = £32 x (12,600 – 12,000)   = £19,200 F
Cap = £32 x (12,000 – 14,000)   = £64,000 A

(e)   Reconciliation:
Overhead Absorbed   £403,200
Expenditure Variance   £7,000 A
Volume Variance (£64,000 – £19,200)   £44,800 A
Actual Overhead   £455,000

3.6   (a)   (5,100 desks x 5 std hrs) + (7,000 chairs x 2 std hrs) = 39,500 std hrs for actual production

(b)   £600,000 / 40,000 standard direct labour hours = £15 per standard direct labour hour

(c)   Variances:
Fixed Overhead Expenditure Variance
        £600,000 - £603,500 = £3,500 A
Fixed Overhead Volume Variance
        (39,500 std hrs x £15) – (40,000 bud std hrs x £15) = £7,500 A
Fixed Overhead Efficiency Variance
        (39,500 std hrs x £15) – (38,700 actual hrs x £15) = £12,000 F
Fixed Overhead Capacity Variance
        (38,700 actual hrs x £15) – (40,000 bud std hrs x £15) = £19,500 A
Total Fixed Overhead Variance
        (39,500 std hrs x £15) - £603,500 = £11,000 A

CHAPTER 4: STANDARD COSTING – FURTHER ANALYSIS

4.1   The following statements are true: (b), (c), (d), (f). All the other statements are false.

4.2   (a)   (i)   Standard usage of steel is 20,000 sq mt / 5,000 radiators = 4 sq mt per radiator
Standard price of steel is £30,000 / 20,000 sq mt = £1.50 per sq mt
direct material (steel) usage variance:
(5,200 radiators x 4 sq mt x £1.50) – (21,320 sq mt x £1.50) = £780 A

        (ii)   Standard labour rate is £27,500 / 2,500 hours = £11.00 per hour

                direct labour rate variance:
(2,650 hours x £11) - £31,800 = £2,650 A

        (iii)   Standard labour hours per radiator is 2,500 hours / 5,000 radiators = 0.5 hours per radiator

                direct labour efficiency variance:
(5,200 radiators x 0.5 hours x £11.00) – (2,650 hours x £11.00) = £550 A

    (b)   'An adverse variance is **a debit to** the income statement (profit & loss account), and a favourable variance is **a credit to** the income statement.'

4.3   (a)   Labour Rate Variance:

                (3,200 hours x Std Rate) – Actual Cost
(3,200 hours x £7.25) – £23,744   = £ 544 Adverse

    (i)   Analysed into:
Part due to actual pay award:
3,200 hours x (Std Rate – Revised Std Rate)
3,200 hours x (£7.25 – (£7.00 + 4.5%))
3,200 hours x (£7.25 – £7.315)   = £ 208 Adverse

        Part due to other influences:
(3,200 hours x Revised Std Rate) – Actual Cost
(3,200 hours x £7.315) – £ 23,744   = £ 336 Adverse

    (ii)   Analysed into:
Part due to movement in index:
3,200 hours x (Std Rate – Revised Std Rate)
3,200 hours x (£7.25 – (£7.00 x 150÷140))
3,200 hours x (£7.25 – £7.50)   = £ 800 Adverse

        Part due to other influences:
(3,200 hours x Revised Std Rate) – Actual Cost
(3,200 hours x £7.50) – £ 23,744   = £ 256 Favourable

(b)   The first analysis is more useful because it uses the actual pay award implemented for the labour force to calculate a revised standard rate. This effectively amends the standard into what it would have been had the company accurately predicted the pay rise. The £208 adverse variance illustrates for week 12 the effect of the pay rise being greater than was originally expected, whereas the £336 adverse variance is due to other factors (for example bonus payments or overtime premium).

The second analysis is based on the increase of the wage rates in the region as a whole, and does not reflect the actual pay rise awarded in this organisation.

4.4

	Favourable	Adverse	
Standard cost for actual production*			£15,015
Variances	Favourable	Adverse	
Direct materials (liquid soap) price	£700		
Direct materials (bottles) price	£113		
Direct materials (liquid soap) usage		£150	
Direct materials (bottles) usage		£30	
Direct labour rate	£262		
Direct labour efficiency		£110	
Fixed overhead expenditure		£250	
Fixed overhead volume	£350		
Total variance			£885 F
Actual cost of actual production			£14,130

calculated as £13,650 x 5,500 units ÷ 5,000 units

CHAPTER 5: MEASURING QUALITY

5.1   'Quality' can be considered as the fitness of a product or service for the purpose for which it is to be used. In the case described, the opinions of the members indicate that the majority of members think that the paper and the printing on the cover are suitable for the journal and changes would not increase its fitness for the purpose for which it is used. More expensive printing and paper would not, in this case, add to the quality of the product.

'Enhancement of value' means increasing the value of a product or service, by adding desirable features for example. In the case described, most members do not want a crossword in the journal, because it would not enhance the value of the journal in terms of its purpose. However, a majority of members would like more pages, provided the cost of postage is not increased. Value for money would be obtained from the postal service and these members think that the journal's value would be enhanced by having more pages.

5.2   Prevention Cost: (b)
Appraisal Cost: (e)
Internal Failure Costs: (a) (d) (f)
External Failure Costs: (c) (g)

5.3   2,000,000 organisers are sold and 1 in 2,000 develop the fault. Therefore 1,000 are faulty, but only 750 of these are returned.

The external failure cost of repairs is 750 x £10 = £7,500.

The internal failure cost of advertising to replace lost customers is £50,000.

Other costs, which cannot be measured on the information available, are the internal failure costs which have been incurred in analysing the fault to find out what repair is necessary.

To improve the situation, the company must eliminate the fault. As repair is possible, it seems likely that the design could be altered to replace the part which develops the fault. Reviewing the specification would be an internal failure cost. Otherwise, stringent quality control or testing of the organisers must be carried out, which would increase prevention and appraisal costs.

5.4   (a)   'Explicit costs of quality' are those which are recorded in the accounting information and can be identified. You may have given as examples in this case:

- the cost of replacement decoders at £52 each, ie £52 x 3,860 = £200,720.

- the cost of the customer helpline £1,400,000.

- the proportion of the cost of delivery which is for replacement decoders, which may be calculated on the basis that total deliveries were 8,500 + 3,860 = 12,360.

        £250,000 x 3,860 ÷ 12,360 = £78,074.

    (b)   'Implicit costs of quality' are those which are not recorded or separately identifiable. Examples in this case include:

- the part of the subscriptions lost in this period due to customers' dissatisfaction with the speed of the delivery service (some customers may have cancelled for other reasons, but this is not known)

- the loss of future subscriptions due to poor quality service and resulting bad publicity, if any

- the part of the delivery cost which is due to disruption of schedules in order to ensure replacements reach customers quickly

5.5   'Cost reduction' refers to a positive programme of reducing costs throughout an organisation, without reducing the value of a product or service. In the case described, recruitment is an important function within the firm, although not its main business. If costs can be reduced for this function, without losing value, this would benefit the firm. It would be necessary to compare the cost of the service offered by Splash Ltd with the current costs. As senior staff time, storage costs and transport costs would be saved, using Splash Ltd may reduce costs. The value of the display stand at conventions would be maintained and possibly even enhanced when looked after by specialists in this field.

'Value analysis' means looking at every aspect of an existing product or service to see whether the same or a better result can be achieved in some other way. In the case of PQR and Partners, the firm offers an accountancy service to customers, but every aspect of the business could be looked at to see whether it contributes value. The value of the display stand and a presence at careers conventions seems to be assumed, but it could be investigated to see whether this assumption is justified. Is there an alternative way of recruiting the best trainees? If not, then Splash Ltd can be considered as a alternative way of carrying out this particular function.

5.6   (a)   Expected total sales revenue from Digisnap = £480 x 25,000 = £12,000,000

(b)   Target operating profit from Digisnap = 22% x £12,000,000 = £2,640,000

(c)   Total target cost for Digisnap = £12,000,000 - £2,640,000 = £9,360,000

(d)   Target operating profit per unit of Digisnap = £2,640,000/25,000 = £105.60

(e)   Target cost per unit of Digisnap = £480 - £105.60 = £374.40

5.7

Year	Details	Cash Savings £'000	Cash Outflow £'000	Discount Factor	Present Value £'000
0	Cost of machine and installation		375,000	1.000	(375,000)
1	Running costs		20,000		
	Labour savings	96,000			
	Year 1 net savings	76,000		0.952	72,352
2	Running costs		20,000		
	Labour savings	120,000			
	Year 2 net savings	100,000		0.907	90,700
3	Running costs		20,000		
	Labour savings	120,000			
	Year 3 net savings	100,000		0.864	86,400
4	Running costs		20,000		
	Labour savings	144,000			
	Year 4 net savings	124,000		0.823	102,052
				Net Present Value	(23,496)

The net present value is negative, so the savings are less than the costs. The machine should not be purchased based on these figures.

CHAPTER 6: MEASURING PERFORMANCE

6.1   **Consistency** means that performance measures being compared must be prepared using the same policies and methods, so that the comparison is of like with like.

Benchmarking means that performance is measured against standards, targets or industry averages, relating to what is important to the organisation. Benchmarks may be set either internally or externally.

Qualitative data is data which cannot be measured numerically, for example opinions and judgements of performance.

6.2 Answer (c) is correct, because the gross profit = £500,000 x 24% = £120,000

Therefore £500,000 – Cost of sales = £120,000

And cost of sales = £500,000 – £120,000 = £380,000

Gross profit – Expenses = Operating profit

Therefore £120,000 – expenses = £50,000

And hence expenses = £120,000 – £50,000 = £70,000

6.3

	31 May 20-3	31 May 20-2
Gross Profit % of Sales	28%	30%
Net Profit % of Sales	16%	18%
Administration expense as % of Sales	4.8%	5.3%
Selling expense as % of Sales	7.2%	6.7%

Comments: Looking at the original figures, it can be seen that Sales Revenue, Purchases and Expenses have all increased in the second year. Administration, which would probably be expected to be a fixed cost, has remained relatively stable. Inventory levels have built up in both years. Profits have also increased.

Looking at the ratios, the percentage Gross Profit has decreased slightly, which could be due to increased purchase costs or having to reduce selling prices, or both. The expenses together still represent 12% of Sales, and as would be expected for a fixed cost, the administration percentage has gone down slightly. The selling expense, however, has increased as a proportion of sales, possibly due to increased advertising to generate more sales. The reduction in Net Profit percentage results from the decreased Gross Profit margin.

Toni Jones should consider whether there is a problem with the build-up of inventory – are there goods which do not sell? Also the reasons for the decrease in Gross Profit margin and increase in selling expenses should be investigated.

6.4 (a)

Gross Profit margin	= (1,910 ÷ 2,500) x 100%	= 76.4%
Operating profit margin	= (625 ÷ 2,500) x 100%	= 25.0%
Return on Capital Employed	= (625 ÷ 2,840) x 100%	= 22.0%
Asset turnover	= 2,500 ÷ 2,840	= 0.88 times
The average age of receivables	= (160 ÷ 2,500) x 365	= 23 days
Average finished goods inventory	= 0.5 x (30 + 90)	= 60

The average age of finished goods inventory (using average inventory)

= (60 ÷ 590) x 365 = 37 days.

(b) Both ROCE and Asset turnover depend on the value of the net assets. During the year ended 30 June 20-3, Subsidiary Jack Ltd has considerable additions to the non-current assets, but it is not known at what time of the year these were acquired. It is possible that these new assets have not yet generated additional sales (for asset turnover) or profits (for ROCE). These two measures would be lower as a result.

(c) If Subsidiary Jack Ltd had achieved the target Asset turnover of 1.5 times, its turnover would have been 1.5 x £2,840,000 = £4,260,000.

(d) Assuming Subsidiary Jack Ltd had maintained its operating profit margin of 25% on turnover of £4,260,000, its operating profit would be:

25% x £4,260,000 = £1,065,000.

With this operating profit, its ROCE would be

$(1,065 \div 2,840) \times 100\% = 37.5\%$, assuming that the Capital Employed is unchanged.

6.5   (a)   Gross Profit = 35% of £200,000 = £70,000

Turnover – Cost of Sales = Gross Profit

£200,000 – Cost of Sales = £70,000

Therefore Cost of Sales = £130,000

(b) $\dfrac{\text{Current Assets – Inventory}}{\text{Current Liabilities}} = \dfrac{\text{Current Assets – Inventory}}{£7,000} = 0.9$

Therefore: Current Assets – Inventory = 0.9 x £7,000 = £6,300

Current Assets = £6,300 + Inventory = £6,300 + £4,200 = £10,500

Current Ratio = Current Assets ÷ Current Liabilities = £10,500 ÷ £7,000

Therefore Current Ratio = 1.5 : 1.

CHAPTER 7: MEASURING PERFORMANCE – FURTHER ASPECTS

7.1   You may have given examples including any of the following:
(a)   Amount of gross profit, net profit, turnover, prices, variances, value added
(b)   Ratios, number of machine hours used, number of units produced, number of rejected units, number of orders processed, number of customer complaints, etc
(c)   Results of customer opinion surveys, peer reviews or appraisals

7.2   The method is to divide each figure by the index for its own year and multiply by the index for the required year, for example year 1 income, put into year 3 terms, becomes:

£260,000 ÷ 115 x 130 = £293,913.

	Year1	Year 2	Year 3
Income (£ in year 3 terms)	293,913	322,358	400,000
Expenditure (£ in year 3 terms)	226,087	253,659	330,000
Surplus (£ in year 3 terms)	67,826	68,699	70,000

It can be seen that the income and the surplus are both increasing in real terms, but not as significantly as the original figures suggest. (Percentages are useful for comparison: for example the surplus figures increased by 16.7% from year 1 to year 3, but in real terms the increase is only 3.2%).

7.3   Exe Ltd, for the year 20-3,
(a)   Value Added = £972,000 – (£216,000 + £324,000)
       = £972,000 – £540,000 = £432,000
(b)   Value Added per employee = £432,000 ÷ 54 = £8,000
       Output = 67,500 product units.
       Therefore the Unit Cost is calculated as follows:
(c)   Materials used: £216,000 ÷ 67,500 = £3.20 per unit
(d)   Total cost of inputs: £540,000 ÷ 67,500 = £8.00 per unit

7.4 Wessit Housing Association

(a) The ratios for each of the two companies are:

	Staylite Ltd	Temeglass Ltd
gross profit margin	45.3%	47.6%
operating profit margin	5.3%	6.6%
return on capital employed	65.4%	65.9%
current ratio	1.09 : 1	1.97 : 1
quick ratio	0.64 : 1	1.20 : 1
asset turnover	12.44 times	9.99 times
sales per employee	£478,750	£527,778
operating profit per employee	£25,188	£34,833

(b) Indicators of the profitability of the two companies include the profit margins and ROCE. Temeglass Ltd appears to be more profitable using any of these indicators. The financial position of the two suppliers can be seen partly from the original figures, in that Temeglass Ltd has no long-term liabilities, whereas Staylite Ltd has significant long-term loans (debentures). Also Temeglass Ltd has a better liquidity position, as can be seen from the current and quick ratios.

(c) The main performance indicators which may be used to indicate efficiency are ROCE and operating profit margin. (Profit per employee may also be significant).

(d) The performance indicator which may be used to indicate the productivity of the companies is sales per employee, although this is not ideal because comparative selling prices and volumes of output are not known. Output per employee would be a better indicator. Profit per employee could also be used here.

(e) The limitations of the above analysis are:

When using the published accounts of companies, it is not possible to guarantee that we are comparing like with like, as different policies (including those regarding depreciation, inventory valuation and goodwill, for example) will affect the results. Also there is the possibility that the Statement of Financial Position does not show a typical position. In this case, only one year's results are available for each company, so it is not possible to see whether there are any significant trends.

(f) A further indicator which Wessit Housing Association should seek to obtain would be some measure of quality or value for money. Suggestions include selling prices, product specifications, or some indication of customer satisfaction. The companies may be able to show their previous work and it would be particularly useful to the housing association to obtain opinions or references from previous customers. Numbers of customer complaints would be another possible measure, if available.

7.5 Efficiency ratio = (Standard hours of actual output ÷ Actual hours) x 100%
Standard hours of actual output = 2,400 units x 6 hours = 14,400 hours
Actual hours = 15,000 hours
Therefore Efficiency ratio = (14,400 ÷ 15,000) x 100% = 96%
Capacity Ratio = (Actual hours ÷ Budgeted hours) x 100%
       = (15,000 ÷ 14,700) x 100% = 102%
Activity Ratio = (Standard hours of actual output ÷ Budgeted hours) x 100%
       = (14,400 ÷ 14,700) x 100% = 98%

7.6   The aspects of value for money which are used are:

- *Economy*: controlling expenditure on costs. Economy can be measured in the same way as costs in businesses, by comparing with budgets and calculating variances for example.

- *Efficiency*: relating 'outputs' to inputs, meaning that obtaining more from the money spent shows greater efficiency. A possible indicator for efficiency is the cost per unit, where units of output can be defined.

- *Effectiveness*: relating 'outputs' to the aims of the organisation, so that achieving more of what it sets out to do shows greater effectiveness. Effectiveness may be measured by comparison with targets or with other similar organisations.

Some aspects of non-profit-making activities can only be assessed by qualitative measures: opinions and judgements of experts, users or those who provide the funding.

7.7   Up-to-You Gym: (your suggested indicators may differ from the following and only one is required for each perspective) NB: 'W' references below refer to the working notes at the bottom of the page.

(a)   The financial perspective: possible appropriate measures from the available information are profit margin (W1) and sales per employee (W2)

(b)   The customer perspective: customer satisfaction and loyalty may be seen from the visits per member (W3) or the percentage of previous years' members who return (W4)

(c)   The internal perspective could be considered by looking at cost per member visit (W5) or the staff : members ratio (W6)

(d)   The innovation and learning perspective could be assessed by measuring the percentage increase in new members (W7) or alternatively the new members as a percentage of the total (W8). Also an indicator of developing new services is opening hours per day (W9).

Workings: the method is shown for 20-4, check that you can agree the answer for 20-3.

		30 Sept 20-4		30 Sept 20-3
W1	profit margin	(230 ÷ 750) x 100%	= 30.7%	28.3%
W2	sales per employee	£750,000 ÷ 22	= £34,091	£42,857
W3	visits per member	60,300 ÷ 1,200	= 50	43
W4	% returning (of prev.)	(470 ÷ 700) x 100%	= 67%	30% (of 580 in 20-2)
W5	cost per visit	£520,000 ÷ 60,300	= £8.62	£14.22
W6	staff:members	1:(1,200 ÷ 22)	= 1:55	1:50
W7	% inc.in new mem.	730 ÷ 525	= 1.39, so 39%	not known
W8	new members %	(730 ÷ 1,200) x 100%	= 61%	75%
W9	open hrs per day	4,368 ÷ 364	= 12 hrs	10.3 hrs

7.8

	Scinso Soft Ltd	Laurelle plc
Selling price per unit	£7.50	£10
Material cost per unit	£2.00	£1.50
Labour cost per unit	£1.25	£1.00
Fixed production overheads per unit	£1.00	£1.36
Gross profit margin	43.33%	61.36%
Net profit margin	18.33%	7.95%
Advertising costs as % of turnover	5.56%	45.45%
Return on net assets	16.50%	20.59%

CHAPTER 8: SCENARIO PLANNING

8.1 (a) Given that the asset turnover is 1.5 times, capital employed = Turnover/1.5
= £6,000,000/1.5 = £4,000,000

(b) Return on capital employed = (1,640,000/4,000,000) x 100% = 41%

(c) Operating profit margin = (1,640/6,000) x 100% = 27.3%

(d) The average delay in fulfilling orders compares unfulfilled orders with turnover to calculate the time period:
Unfulfilled orders = Total value of orders – Turnover
= £7,000,000 - £6,000,000 = £1,000,000
Average delay = (1,000,000/6,000,000) x 12 months = 2 months

(e) Other possible measures of customer satisfaction:
Turnover from regular customers as a percentage of the total
= (4,800/6,000) x 100% = 80%
or expenditure on customer support per £ of turnover
= £600,000/£6,000,000 = £0.10

(f) One way of manipulating the operating profit margin and the ROCE would be to improve profits in the short term by cutting costs. Decisions can be made about the level of spending on certain costs. These are called discretionary costs, for example: training, research and development, customer support and some selling costs such as advertising. Reducing these costs would increase the operating profit margin and ROCE, but the long term effects on Tay Ltd would be adverse.

(g) Indicators that may help to measure performance from an internal perspective include:

- Percentage of sales returns = (200/6,200) x 100% = 3.2%

- Percentage of production cost due to reworking = (45/1,360) x 100% = 3.3%

(h) An indicator that would help to measure the innovation and learning perspective could be:

Percentage of turnover from new products = (3,150/6,000) x 100% = 52.5%
or expenditure on research and development as a percentage of turnover

= (1,100/6,000) x 100% = 18.3%

or expenditure on research and development as a percentage of production cost

= (1,100/1,360) x 100% = 80.9%

8.2 (a) Average age of inventory using closing inventory = (30/360) x 12 = 1 month

Gross Profit percentage = (240/600) x 100% = 40%

Operating Profit percentage = (90/600) x 100% = 15%

Return on Capital Employed = (90/370) x 100% = 24.3%

(Note that the Capital Employed = Capital on Statement of Financial Position + Loan)

(b) **Lambert Ltd Revised Operating Statement for the year ended 31 December 20-3**

	£000s	£000s
Turnover		600
Less: Cost of Sales		
Opening Inventory	70	
Purchases (increased by 30)	350	
Less: closing inventory (increased by 30)	(60)	360
Gross Profit		240
Administration Costs (less 15%)	85	
Selling and Distribution expenses	50	135
Operating profit		105
Note: additional Profit = 105 – 90		15

Lambert Ltd Revised Statement of Financial Position as at 31 December 20-3

	£000s	£000s
Non-current Assets at cost		380
Less: accumulated depreciation		110
		270
Current Assets:		
Inventory (as above)	60	
Receivables (600/12)	50	
Cash at Bank (balancing figure)	15	
	125	
Current Liabilities:		
Payables	60	
Net current assets		65
		335
Long-term liability: loan		–
		335
Financed by:		
Ordinary shares issued and fully paid		200
Retained Profits (increased by 15)		135
		335

Notice that the Statement of Financial Position total is found by increasing the Retained Profits. The total is then entered in the top part of the Statement of Financial Position, the loan is assumed to have been paid off and the Cash at Bank is the last figure to be entered.

(c) Average age of inventory using closing inventory = (60/360) x 12 = 2 months
Gross Profit percentage = (240/600) x 100% = 40%
Operating Profit percentage = (105/600) x 100% = 17.5%
Return on Capital Employed = (105/335) x 100% = 31.3%

(d) The revised figures show the same level of Gross Profit, but an increase in Operating Profit of £15,000, which is due to the administration cost savings. The higher operating profit and lower capital employed have resulted in an increase in the ROCE.

The improved control of receivables would bring in cash more quickly and allow the long-term loan to be paid off, and the bank balance to be increased. (The cost savings have also contributed to this).

The liquidity position would remain satisfactory. The current ratio would change from 2.7:1 to 2.1:1, and the acid test ratio would change from 2.2:1 to 1.1:1, due to the revised levels for each of the current assets.

8.3   (a)

	£
Sales price per unit	50.00
Profit margin (40% of £50)	20.00
Total costs (£50 - £20)	30.00
Fixed cost per unit	16.00
Labour cost per unit	6.00
Maximum material cost per unit	8.00
Target cost per kilogram (£8 x 1,000/200)	40.00

(b)   The trade price per kilogram quoted on the supplier's price list is £50 per kilogram. The purchasing manager has negotiated a discount of 15%. The discount should be **rejected** because the £50 reduces to **£42.50** which is **above** the Target cost.

(c)   The minimum percentage discount needed to achieve the Target cost is **20%**.

8.4   (a)

Year	0	1	2	3	4	5
Cash flow	200,000	16,000	16,000	16,000	16,000	(64,000)
Discount factor	1.000	0.952	0.907	0.864	0.823	0.784
Present value	200,000	15,232	14,512	13,824	13,168	(50,176)
Net present cost	206,560					

(b)

Year	0	1	2	3	4
Cash flow	50,000	50,000	50,000	50,000	50,000
Discount factor	1.000	0.952	0.907	0.864	0.823
Present value	50,000	47,600	45,350	43,200	41,150
Net present cost	227,300				

(c)   Based on the calculations it is best to **purchase** the machine, which saves a present value of

£20,740

Index

for your notes

for your notes

for your notes

for your notes

for your notes

for your notes